# WHEN RELIGION BECOMES LETHAL

# WHEN RELIGION
# BECOMES LETHAL

*The Explosive Mix of Politics and Religion in
Judaism, Christianity, and Islam*

Charles Kimball

**JOSSEY-BASS**
A Wiley Imprint
www.josseybass.com

Published by Jossey-Bass
A Wiley Imprint
989 Market Street, San Francisco, CA 94103-1741—www.josseybass.com

Jossey-Bass books and products are available through most bookstores. To contact Jossey-Bass directly call our Customer Care Department within the U.S. at 800-956-7739, outside the U.S. at 317-572-3986, or fax 317-572-4002.

Jossey-Bass also publishes its books in a variety of electronic formats. Some content that appears in print may not be available in electronic books.

**Library of Congress Cataloging-in-Publication Data**

Kimball, Charles (Charles Anthony), date
    When Religion Becomes Lethal : The Explosive Mix of Politics and Religion in Judaism, Christianity, and Islam / Charles Kimball.
        p. cm
    Includes bibliographical references and index.
    ISBN 978-0-470-58190-2 (hardback); 978-1-118-03054-7 (ebk);
    978-1-118-03055-4 (ebk);  978-1-118-03056-1 (ebk)
    1. Religion and politics.   2. Religious fundamentalism.   3. Abrahamic religions.
    4. Christianity and politics.   5. Islam and politics.   6. Judaism and politics.   7. Title.
    BL65.P7K5695   2011
    201'.7209045—dc22

                                                                2010052515

Printed in the United States of America

FIRST EDITION

*HB Printing*   10  9  8  7  6  5  4  3  2

# CONTENTS

Acknowledgments     vii

1   Christmas with the Ayatollah: The Volatile Mix of
    Religion and Politics     1
2   God Gave Us This Land: The Roots of Religion and
    Politics in Judaism     15
3   Israel: Deadly Conflict in Zion     33
4   "Render unto Caesar": Religion and Politics in Christianity     58
5   America: One Nation Under God?     75
6   There Is No God But God: Religion and Politics in Islam     96
7   Muslim vs. Muslim: The Struggle for the Soul of Islam     120
8   Iran and Iraq: Axis of Evil or Harbinger of Hope?     137
9   A Road to Disaster: The Fallacy of Fundamentalism     157
10   Hope for the Perilous Journey Ahead     178

Notes     193
Selected Bibliography     229
The Author     233
Name Index     235
Subject index     241

# ACKNOWLEDGMENTS

Unless otherwise noted, citations from the Bible are from the New Revised Standard Version. Quotations from the Qur'an are based, with revisions by the author, on *The Meaning of the Glorious Koran*, text and explanatory translation by Muhammad M. Pickthall (Mecca: Muslim World League, 1977).

Various perspectives advanced in this book have been shaped and modified over more than three decades. As is always the case, we all stand on the shoulders of and benefit directly and indirectly from predecessors, colleagues, friends, and people who see and interpret events differently. My indebtedness to many people is reflected in the text and notes. What I owe to a great number of others—from religious and political leaders and colleagues in religious studies and political science to people I have met in Tulsa, Tel Aviv, Tehran, and many points in between—will not be immediately visible. All have helped sharpen and refine my thinking. Among those who have offered valuable assistance and suggestions in the process of preparing this book, I am especially grateful to Chris Chapman, Jay Ford, Lee Green, Scott Hudgins, Jeff Rogers, and Cole Stephenson.

In addition to individuals, several institutions have been enormously helpful. I have enjoyed and benefited greatly from the congenial and supportive environment at both Wake Forest University and the University of Oklahoma. Several other colleges and universities have provided opportunities to present and refine what have become portions of the book. I thank the following institutions for their invitations to deliver lectures and for the constructive feedback from faculty, students, and community members: Oklahoma State University for the Converse-Yates-Cate Lecture, Bates College for the Andrews Lecture, the University of Tulsa for the William and Rita Bell Lecture, Greensboro College for the Jean Fortner Ward Lecture, Franklin and Marshall College for the Peace Lecture, McNeese University for the Banners Lecture, Illinois College for the Khalaf al-Habtoor Lecture, Georgetown College for the Collier Lecture, Stetson University for the Pastors' Conference Lectures, Ottawa University for the Hostetter-DeFries Lectures, Oklahoma Christian

University for the McBride Lecture, Southern Nazarene University for the Ladd Lecture, and Arizona State University, Franklin College, Pacific Lutheran University, Elon University, Meredith College, Drury College, and Presbyterian College for convocation and campuswide lectures. I am also grateful to many church and other religious communities throughout the United States that also have generously invited me to present lectures or deliver sermons on themes woven into this book.

Steve Hanselman and Julia Serebrinksy of LevelFiveMedia offered wise counsel, invaluable assistance, and personal friendship before, during and after completing this book. Working with Alison Knowles, Joanne Clapp Fullagar, Jennifer Wenzel, Tom Finnegan, and the other professionals at Jossey-Bass has been delightful. Most notably, I am deeply grateful to Sheryl Fullerton, the executive editor who guided my work on this book from start to finish. She has helped both to frame larger issues and fine-tune points through incisive questions and editorial suggestions. No author could hope to work with a more insightful, constructive, or congenial editor than Sheryl.

Writing this kind of book is both a solitary and a family process. Our adult children, Sarah and Elliot, along with my brother, sisters, and other close family members, have been supportive in numerous ways. My spouse, Nancy, has lived through the academic, experiential, and vocational adventures that shaped our lives for four decades. Nancy has been and remains my best friend, confidante, and loving critic.

Finally, I offer a brief word about my Jewish grandfather and Presbyterian grandmother. My paternal grandfather, Julius George Skelskie Kimball, was one of the most wonderful people I knew as a child. Despite the enormous challenges posed by a religiously mixed marriage a century ago, my grandparents remained within the traditions of faith in which they were raised. My grandparents, parents, and extended family members—both Jewish and Christian—modeled for me how religious diversity and religious commitment can illuminate and enrich our experiences as human beings and as children of God who share life in our community as well as on an increasingly fragile planet. With love and appreciation, I dedicate this book to the memory of my grandfather, whose gentle manor, love of laughter, and warm embrace helped set me on the journey of a lifetime.

*In loving memory of my grandfather*
*Julius George Skelskie Kimball*

# WHEN RELIGION BECOMES LETHAL

# CHRISTMAS WITH THE AYATOLLAH

## THE VOLATILE MIX OF RELIGION AND POLITICS

SITTING LESS THAN FIVE FEET FROM THE AYATOLLAH KHOMEINI in his modest home in Qom on Christmas Day of 1979, I was riveted not only by his words but also by his facial expression. In contrast to the fiery, defiant media images of the Ayatollah, his demeanor was warm and welcoming, his words softly spoken, his eyes alert and engaging. I found him both grandfatherly and charismatic. On that memorable Christmas Day in Iran, we talked about Jesus, the Iranian revolution, the U.S. hostages, and Christian-Muslim relations. On the many times after that when I saw Khomeini in person and live on television, my initial impressions were confirmed. Both inside and outside Iran, this intriguing, enigmatic man in clerical garb was fast emerging as an extraordinarily influential religious/political leader during the final quarter of the 20th century. I was not at all surprised when *Time* magazine named the Ayatollah Khomeini "Man of the Year" for 1979.

How had I, an American baby boomer from a middle-class family in Tulsa, Oklahoma, come to be here in Iran, in the very center of international media attention, spending Christmas with the Ayatollah Khomeini? Although I could not have predicted this scenario, it was far from accidental. A long-standing interest in and engagement with the interplay between religion and politics combined with a decade studying Judaism, Christianity, and Islam—in college, seminary, at Harvard, and in Cairo—had led to this pivotal moment.

Seven weeks earlier, on November 4, 66 hostages had been seized when student militants stormed the U.S. embassy compound in Tehran.

Fourteen people were subsequently released, while 52 Americans remained in captivity for 444 days. The hostage crisis had been the dominant focus of the world's political and media attention since that fateful day. The Iranian government was unwilling to meet directly with U.S. officials, in part because the deposed shah was in the United States at the time. Vivid memories of the CIA-led coup that had toppled Iran's popularly elected government of Prime Minister Mohammed Mossadeq and reinstated the shah in 1953 still fueled widespread fear and distrust.

In an effort to open talks and help resolve the standoff, Ali Agah, the Iranian ambassador to the United States, invited an ecumenical group of six clergy and one former Peace Corps worker[1] to travel to Iran for 10 days of meetings with Khomeini, other top religious and political leaders, and the students who were holding the hostages. Three other American clergy—led by the late William Sloane Coffin Jr., of New York's Riverside Church—also traveled to Tehran to conduct Christmas services for the American captives.

The distinctive interplay between religion and politics in revolutionary Iran signaled that something new, powerful, and unpredictable was unfolding in one of the most volatile and strategically important regions of the world. Nestled in the soft underbelly of the Soviet Union, Iran had well-trained and well-equipped armed forces funded by abundant revenues derived from its massive oil reserves. Henry Kissinger, former national security advisor and U.S. secretary of state, had underscored the critical importance of Iran when he famously called Shah Muhammad Reza Pahlavi the "rarest of leaders, an unconditional ally."

Iran was not the only country where political seismic shifts were taking place in an already unstable region. Lebanon was descending into a multisided civil war and fast becoming a proxy battleground for Israelis, Palestinians, and other regional powers; Saddam Hussein, who had just seized power in a coup in Iraq, would soon launch what would become a devastating 10-year war with Iran. In a harbinger of the deep rancor that produced Osama bin Laden and 15 of the 19 hijackers who carried out the attacks on the World Trade Center on September 11, 2001, heavily armed, militant Muslims from within Saudi Arabia stormed and then occupied the Grand Mosque in Mecca for two weeks late in 1979. Events in the new Islamic Republic of Iran added a potent and distinctively religious dynamic to the turbulent upheavals in the Middle East.

For those who were paying attention to events beyond the locked gates of the U.S. embassy in Tehran, shock waves from the revolutionary tsunami were being felt not only throughout the Middle East but also in faraway lands such as the Philippines, South Africa, and Guatemala. Under

Khomeini's influential leadership, the Iranian revolution was a major watershed event in the final quarter of the 20th century, a tipping point with powerful regional and global ramifications. Three decades later, the impact and consequences of these tumultuous events are still being felt in various parts of the world.[2] My direct involvement with many of the key actors during the course of the hostage crisis in Iran was life-changing, in several ways. I went back to Iran twice more; with John Walsh, one of the chaplains at Princeton in our initial group, I spent two months in Iran during three trips. As "trusted" clergy who were not U.S. government officials, we were invited to bring mail for the hostages and facilitate communications with government and religious leaders as well as with the students occupying the American embassy. In this crucible, I saw and experienced the powerful new combinations brewing the volatile mix of religion and politics among the Abrahamic religions.

In the United States, this unique access to Iranian leaders under the white-hot spotlight of the hostage crisis led to scores of media interviews,[3] speaking engagements, and opportunities to write op-ed articles for major newspapers. Several Harvard professors—lawyers, Islamic scholars, Middle East and international affairs experts, and various others who specialized in conflict resolution—met regularly with me to help prepare for the next trip to Iran. My doctoral dissertation was put on hold. As George Rupp, the dean of Harvard Divinity School, said to me shortly after the hostages were released, "You have had about 20 years of experience crammed into the last 400 days."

Looking back, I would say George Rupp was probably correct, most strikingly so when it came to the popular perceptions or conventional wisdom that informed most people on all sides. As a student of comparative religion, I was keenly aware of the long and often troubled history among the Jewish, Christian, and Muslim descendants of Abraham. As I found in my trips to Iran between late 1979 and early 1981, that history was further complicated by contemporary media images and sound-bite analyses that often led to simplistic and therefore misleading perceptions. The images projected daily for those 444 days created and reinforced narratives about militant Islam that continue to dominate our current understanding. The stunning attack orchestrated by radical extremists on September 11, 2001, reinforced and deepened the most threatening aspects of this narrative.

There were—and still are—major differences between popular Western views of religion and politics in Iran and the more complex realities within the Islamic republic, as we discovered with the massive worldwide attention directed at the protests during the Iranian presidential election of June 2009. The protests, demonstrations, and declarations by various religious and political leaders illustrated clearly that Iran is far from monolithic. There are multiple levels of religious and political organization as well as several visible centers of power in this predominantly Shi'ite Muslim nation.

Despite all the attention focused on Iran since the 1979 revolution, very few Americans—not to mention members of Congress—had moved beyond stereotyped images and conventional wisdom before the surprising events following the 2009 presidential elections. As major news organizations and cable TV networks gleaned information from Iranians and Iranian Americans (often via social networking sites), a more nuanced and accurate view of religion and politics within the Islamic Republic emerged. For several weeks, Americans and others around the world had an exceptional opportunity to push beyond monolithic perceptions of Iranian Muslims and venture into a vibrant, richly layered, and clearly diverse society in Iran. The episode underscored just how misleading popular perceptions and conventional wisdom can be.

In recent years, best-selling authors Malcolm Gladwell, Steven Levitt, and Stephen Dubner have all pulled back the curtain on various types of conventional wisdom to reveal how reality isn't what we think. Gladwell's number-one best sellers changed the way many of us think about the big impact of small things (*The Tipping Point*, 2000), how we think about thinking (*Blink*, 2005), and our understanding of success (*Outliers*, 2008). In Levitt and Dubner's 2005 book *Freakonomics*, readers were dazzled by revelations of what was boldly called "the hidden side of everything." Investigating a more somber and grim phenomenon, Robert Pape's 2005 book *Dying to Win: The Strategic Logic of Suicide Terrorism* is a detailed study of every suicide attack since 1980. Pape demonstrates how suicidal terrorism is not primarily a product of Islamic fundamentalism; 95% of the attacks occur as part of coherent military campaigns with clear secular and political goals. Each of these books shows how a different way of looking at data can often dismantle conventional wisdom and raise many questions that cannot be answered accurately without a more reliable framework for understanding, one that transcends conventional wisdom.[4] An important distinction between Gladwell's books and Pape's research relates to the broader subject matter. Whether or not people are personally religious, it is more challenging for most of us to learn to think in new ways about religion and politics than to think anew about the types of economics presented by Gladwell.

At one level, this book fits the genre. At various critical points, our conventional wisdom is dangerously inadequate. My involvement with the Iranian hostage crisis opened numerous doors and facilitated opportunities to study and work amid settings where many Jews, Christians, and Muslims have been wrestling with issues of religion and politics for the past 30 years. In my experience and study, many popular perceptions of the relationships between religion and politics in the Middle East—and in the United States—often do not hold up under careful scrutiny. Far too few of us know or think about the rich history shaping the different religions. Far too few of us are considering the importance of on-the-ground realities that do not square with popular perceptions or media images. And far too few of us have come to terms with the world of the 21st century, a world where "other" religions are not simply "out there"; all religions are everywhere.

How can we hope to move forward constructively—locally, nationally, and internationally—in the exceedingly dangerous years ahead if decisions and actions are based on faulty assumptions and inaccurate perceptions? We need better ways to comprehend what is going on, and why. We need a new paradigm, a much more accurate framework for understanding and action.

## The Volatile Mix of Religion and Politics

Throughout history, religion and politics have always been intertwined and interdependent, but today the volatile mix of the two is more lethal than ever. The Iranian revolution proved to be a catalyst for several militant Muslim groups in the 1980s and beyond. Several examples illustrate the point.

In Afghanistan during the 1980s, Muslim militants (*mujahideen*), supported by Osama bin Laden of Saudi Arabia and others who shared his puritanical Wahhabi[5] view of Islam, vigorously fought the Soviet troops and laid the foundation for what would become the government of the Taliban. In Lebanon, the Party of God (*Hizbullah*) was born among Shi'ites in the aftermath of Israel's 1982 invasion of that war-torn land. Supported by Iran, Hizbullah quickly became Israel's most powerful enemy and a major force in Lebanese and regional politics. Among the Palestinians, the Islamic Resistance Movement (HAMAS) emerged in the occupied Gaza Strip even as the political strength of militant Jewish settlers grew dramatically under the Likud governments of Menachem Begin and Yitzhak Shamir. Begin's 1977 election as prime minister, which ended three decades of Labor Party rule, was widely considered a fluke. However, the next two national elections revealed how much the Jewish state had shifted to the right. Meanwhile, in the United States President

Ronald Reagan embraced the Rev. Jerry Falwell's Moral Majority, the most visible face of a potent new force in U.S. politics, "the religious right."[6]

In the 1990s, the volatility of the interactions between religion and politics continued and the pace quickened as the Taliban seized the reins of government in Afghanistan and al-Qaeda became a formidable international, nongovernmental movement willing to use violent extremism to achieve its goals. The growing strength of these holy warriors was shockingly evident as their numerous attacks were aimed ostensibly at toppling Muslim regimes they deemed illegitimate and at fighting Israel, the United States, and any other Western power whose support or physical military presence enabled Egyptian, Saudi, and other Islamic governments to remain in power.

In the decade following September 11, even more explosive new combinations of religion and politics have become the focus of concern throughout the Middle East and in the United States. In our interdependent and religiously diverse world of nation-states, the intersections of religion and politics played central roles in the Iraq war, which began in 2003; the 2006 war between Israel and Hizbullah in Lebanon; and the virtual civil war that erupted among Palestinians in 2007. In a given year, we learn of many other groups whose grievances are usually coupled with a plan—sometimes violent—to rectify the perceived problems. Though not as overtly violent, there were many heated discussions about religion and politics during the 2008 U.S. presidential election, including hateful religious-based rhetoric aimed at President Barack Obama. On Election Day, reports showed how approximately 15% of the populace believed Obama was really a Muslim who was hiding his true beliefs. Two years later, an August 19, 2010, Pew Research poll showed the proportion had risen to 18%.[7] Some religious zealots on the far right suggested he might be the ultimate wolf in sheep's clothing: the Antichrist.

In the decades since the Reagan presidency, various manifestations of the Christian religious right have been evident in the corridors of power. The depth of involvement and influence set off alarms during the presidency of George W. Bush as attention focused on several ill-prepared, fundamentalist Christians with high-level political appointments in the White House and the Justice Department. By the end of George W. Bush's second term, some probing journalists, authors, and former Bush administration officials were exposing the potential consequences of Christian zealots shaping U.S. policies. Michelle Goldberg's *Kingdom Coming: The Rise of Christian Nationalism* and Chris Hedges's *American Fascists: The Christian Right and the War on America* illuminate more visible manifestations of contemporary Christian leaders and movements determined to infuse American government with their radical vision of a Christian state. Kevin Phillips's 2006 best seller, *American Theocracy*,[8] goes further. Phillips identifies the perils looming where the politics of radical religion, oil, and borrowed money converge in the 21st century. His warnings about an impending economic debacle were validated shockingly in 2008. Phillips and others fear that empowered religious zealotry portends catastrophe. Articulating constructive ways to move forward, however, is more challenging.

Despite continuous media attention on developments in the United States, Israel, Iran, Iraq, and other nations during the first decade of the 21st century, many basic, unanswered questions still loom large: What drives religion into politics, and vice versa? Why are the turbulent religious forces seemingly more threatening than ever before? What do violent extremists operating in the name of Islam really want? Is (or should) America be a Christian nation? What is a *Christian* nation? How does unwillingness or inability to understand what is going on in different religions increase the perils on a global scale? Is peace among Israel, the Palestinians, and neighboring Arab and Muslim states really possible? Why do some leaders say Israel will be the setting for the conflagration that ends the world, while others insist peace between Israel and its neighbors is both possible and essential? Where do we find sources of hope and answers in an increasingly interdependent world where people with vastly different worldviews often clash violently? These questions perplex many of us as daily headlines remind us all how even a small number of religious zealots can wreak havoc on a massive scale.

This book identifies and addresses these and other pressing questions. It focuses on the most urgent contemporary challenges visible in particularly influential and explosive settings, most notably Israel/Palestine, Iran, Iraq, and the United States. Now, more than ever, these challenges require urgent attention and thoughtful action. If we hope to mitigate the highly charged and explosive dangers looming before us, we must understand events and their causes.

The stakes are now far too high for deferential silence or casual indifference. Ignorance is not bliss; indifference is proving deadly. Although the urgent need for informed analysis and widespread public discussion is clear, for most people the issues remain confused and confusing. Neither sound-bite media coverage nor simplistic declarations from podiums and pulpits and a growing number of partisan books can shed the light that is needed on these issues. For many, the dizzying swirl of events and proclamations produces what I call "detailed ignorance." The steady stream of images and proclamations presents many "details," but most people do not have a framework for understanding that puts the images and sound bites in a coherent context. Predictably, conventional wisdom often surfaces to fill in the gaps. I can't count the number of times I've heard reasonably intelligent people say things like "There will never be peace in the Middle East . . . Jews and Muslims have been fighting for thousands of years . . . it is part of their religion . . . it is the only thing they know," or "Muslims are taught to fight and kill infidels or anyone who disagrees with their religion," or "For Muslims, religion and politics are all one thing; Muslims won't be satisfied until the whole world is conquered and under Islamic rule."

Media reports and images are essential, of course. But the focus is all too often on the most dramatic and sensational events. What we need desperately today is a coherent frame of reference, a more accurate and useful way of thinking about and engaging issues of religion and politics. The challenges of the 21st century require that we draw from the best of our traditions for the wisdom and resources needed in a globally connected world community. Otherwise, detailed ignorance and religious zealotry will combine to increase exponentially the probability of ever more deadly sectarian conflict. In a world filled with weapons of mass destruction, it is frighteningly possible to imagine the end of the world as we know it. New, more constructive paradigms offer us hope for the perilous journey ahead.

## Why Is It All So Confusing?

In the three decades since the Iranian revolution, Israel's shift to the right as led by Begin, and the political rise of the religious right in America, new and often violent manifestations of religion and politics have become daily reality. The number of stories has grown sharply, and the pace of events has quickened markedly in the years following September 11. We have literally been inundated with "information" about religion and politics through two presidential elections; multiyear wars in Afghanistan and Iraq; clashes among Israel, the Palestinians, and Hizbullah in Lebanon; and ubiquitous stories related to the rubric of the "worldwide war against terrorism." The information overload comes from an exploding array of 24/7 television, radio, Internet, social networking, and newspaper sources. Despite the abundance of information, however, few of us consider the unstated assumptions shaping the headlines and stories: What presuppositions inform a particular television or newspaper story? What models of religion and politics are being employed? Why do so many people appear to speak with such cocksure certainty about the "ideal" provided by their religion and the fallacy of rival religions? How representative are the snapshot images of particular nations, groups, or religions? How can one speak meaningfully of "Christian," "Muslim," or "Jewish" approaches to political organization and goals?

The picture is confused further by oversimplified pronouncements regarding the separation of church and state. Many enlightened, secular progressives believe that religion ought to be privatized and kept out of public life. They want an insurmountably high wall to separate religion and politics. At the other end of the spectrum are those Muslims, Christians, Jews, and others so convinced that they know God's plan for society that they are prepared to use whatever means necessary to establish the theocracy envisioned in their particular interpretation of sacred texts and sacred history.

Many modern exponents of the separation of church and state interpret events today as a showdown between the progress of democracy with its humanizing benefits and the regression and damage of theocracy. In this view, excesses and misadventures of religious movements shaping political structures—particularly within Judaism, Christianity, and Islam—can be seen in the sordid history of triumphal conquest of one dominant interpretation of one tradition. This interpretation is further reinforced by the resurgence and overt political ambitions of various fundamentalist movements around the world. It is a convenient but terribly inadequate and inaccurate way to simplify a complex history.

Practical considerations are also important. Although some secularists might prefer to see religion as nothing more than an anachronistic way of viewing the world, this simple fact remains: the vast majority of people who have lived and who are alive today perceive themselves to be religious or spiritual. Put simply, religion permeates human society. Religion will continue to be a powerful and pervasive force that weaves through social, political, and economic structures for the foreseeable future. Realistic steps forward simply must include ways of understanding and appropriating elements of religion into viable political life and structures in the 21st century.

It gets more convoluted when it comes to democracy. Whose democracy? And which of the many forms of democracy are we talking about? Most Americans would be surprised to learn that more than half of the roughly 56 countries with Muslim majorities are substantially democratic. The variations present in non-Muslim-majority countries as diverse as Israel, the Islamic Republic of Iran, India, Sweden, Russia, Lebanon, and the United States illustrate the malleable nature of "democracy" in many national settings. The raging debate about globalization makes

clear that the issues cannot be distilled down to straightforward choices
between democracy and theocracy. More accurate and nuanced understanding of the interactions of religion and politics within cultures and
social settings is required if we are to fashion a more viable future in an
interdependent world of nation-states.

For some, the questions about religion and politics may seem overwhelming. It is far easier not to think deeply about these matters, or to
simply let preachers, politicians, pundits, journalists, and talk show
hosts do the thinking for them. It may be easier, but in my view it is a
recipe for disaster. If concerned people of faith and responsible citizens
hope to offer a better future to their children and grandchildren, we
must be willing to wrestle with a range of presuppositions and questions.
As we will discover, this task is challenging, though not as daunting as it
might seem.

## In Search of Understanding

The pages that follow are based on more than three decades of study
and experience working in and around many of the most highly charged
flashpoints in the Middle East and the United States. My academic, professional, and personal pilgrimage has included some 40 journeys to the
Middle East and hundreds of trips to Washington, DC, to colleges,
churches, and conferences throughout the United States, Canada, and
Europe. I have had extraordinary opportunities to study the major religious traditions and to engage firsthand many of the leaders, people, and
groups animating the compelling controversies that most Americans
know primarily through news stories and headlines. This extensive expo-
sure has made me sympathetic to the ambiguity surrounding the multiple, converging issues and the shifting religious-political landscape.
I believe we are at a point now, however, where we can take a step back
and see the bigger picture more clearly.

Constructing a coherent framework for understanding begins with
transcending the one-dimensional either-or thinking that too often
defines approaches to religion and politics. Theocrats who believe they
possess God's template for a contemporary Islamic, Christian, or Jewish
state are wrong. There is no fixed template for any of the Abrahamic
religions. On the other end of the spectrum, secularists who insist that
religion is nothing more than an anachronistic way of viewing the world
and who call for a complete separation of religion and politics simply
don't get it. The truth is found between these extremes. The path to a
hopeful and healthy future is found in a more nuanced understanding of

the multiple ways in which religion and politics interconnect and have been manifest historically within Judaism, Christianity, and Islam. A clearer framework is an invaluable tool for evaluating and critiquing ideologies as they evolve and compete for support in the 21st century.

## A Way Forward

We can and must learn from the wisdom of history and tradition, if we hope to live together respectfully. We are helped enormously in this task by the comparative study of how Jews, Christians, and Muslims have approached the interplay between religion and politics. By looking back across the religious traditions and through the centuries, we can identify fundamental principles that inform political structures connected to these major religions. In fact, Jews, Christians, and Muslims have much more in common than we might think.

Contrary to popular images, all three traditions embrace enough flexibility to allow their adherents to adjust to very different times and circumstances. Historically, the moderate and flexible center of every faith tradition has helped it to survive in the face of extremism. The religions that survive the test of time have been able both to dismantle unhealthy and violent extremes and to encourage the constructive role of religion in society.

Many Christians, Muslims, and Jews now endeavor to build on the foundation of their traditions as they fashion structures that affirm and protect religious and political freedom and diversity. They face many formidable challenges, including extremists who articulate and sometimes employ violence in pursuit of a particular religious or social vision within their respective traditions. Accordingly, four of the chapters that follow include case studies that explore how conflicting visions are being played out in Israel, Iraq, Iran, the United States, and elsewhere.

These contemporary struggles are not new. Sincere but often overly zealous adherents have clashed frequently with their fellow believers as well as followers of other religions. Lawrence Wright elucidates this dynamic in his best-selling book *The Looming Tower: Al-Qaeda and the Road to 9/11*. In a compelling account, Wright describes how Osama bin Laden's pursuit of a pure Islamic state led him from Afghanistan to the Sudan in 1990. Bin Laden's close associates believed Hasan al-Turabi, an influential religious and political leader in the Sudan at that time, was fashioning the kind of Islamic state bin Laden envisioned. But what began as perhaps the happiest period in bin Laden's life quickly changed as it became apparent that these leaders had a distinctly different understanding of the template for an Islamic state:

> Now that he was finally living in a radical Islamist state, bin Laden would ask practical questions, such as how the Islamists intended to apply Sharia in the Sudan and how they proposed to handle the Christians in the south. Often he did not like the answers. Turabi told him that Sharia would be applied gradually and only on Muslims, who would share power with Christians in a federal system. . . . "This man is a Machiavelli," bin Laden confided to his friends. "He doesn't care what methods he uses." Although they still needed one another, Turabi and bin Laden soon began to see themselves as rivals.[9]

In my previous book, *When Religion Becomes Evil,* I examined five major warning signs that signal the danger of religion being used for violent and destructive purposes. As I did there, in this book I will use a comparative approach to reveal destructive, pathological patterns of behavior present among believers in a number of religions. Understanding what is unhealthy helps elucidate the healthy, life-affirming dimensions of these religions. We can find within Judaism, Christianity, and Islam the resources for constructive political structures that go far beyond tolerance, to a respectful affirmation of diversity.

At another level, the world today is distinctly different—and far more dangerous—than at any other time in human history. Among the many lessons in the years since September 11, 2001, everyone can agree on three. The first lesson is that religion is an extremely powerful force in human society, sometimes a force used to inspire or justify violent extremism. Second, the world is full of weapons of mass destruction. In addition to the growing threats posed by nuclear, chemical, and biological weapons, we've learned that there are many ways people determined to harm or kill others can accomplish the goal. Commercial airplanes, trains and buses, and combinations of commonly available ingredients such as agricultural fertilizer can easily become weapons of mass destruction. And finally, we now know with certainty that it doesn't take very many people to wreak havoc on a global scale. Violent extremists claiming inspiration from their religion do not represent the vast majority of Christians, Muslims, and Jews. They may be very much on the fringe, but just a few can produce devastating results.

Jonathan Sachs, the chief rabbi of England, articulates the challenge we must face squarely:

> As one who deeply believes in the humanizing power of faith, and the stark urgency of coexistence at a time when weapons of mass destruction are accessible to extremist groups, I do not think we can afford

to fail again. Time and again in recent years we have been reminded
that religion is not what the European Enlightenment thought it
would become: mute, marginal and mild. It is fire—and like fire,
it warms but it also burns. And we are the guardians of the flame.[10]

Together, adherents within Christianity, Islam, and Judaism make up
roughly half the world's population. Jews, Christians, and Muslims—
all of whom trace their history and theology to a common ancestor,
Abraham—have traveled a long road together. Examining the intertwined
history of these communities reveals common patterns of behavior and
significant differences across religious lines. It also offers instructive
examples; some can serve as a framework for viable future models in
pluralist societies, and some show us approaches Jews, Christians, and
Muslims dare not repeat.

Many of the most dangerous global flashpoints today involve political
dynamics where dedicated believers from one, two, or all three of these
religious communities are visibly engaged. Many of these flashpoints are
potential catalysts for even wider conflagration. The 2006 war between
Israel and Lebanon illustrates the point because the U.S., Syrian, and Iranian connections to Israel and Hizbullah were readily apparent. The more
people in all communities can learn to demystify and understand what is
happening, the more likely we will be able to avert potential disasters.

In the chapters that follow, we examine both destructive and constructive ways in which Israel, the United States, and even Iran can help
facilitate inclusive pluralism in predominantly Jewish, Christian, and
Muslim lands.

Chapters 2, 4, and 6 begin by identifying foundational principles that
are found in the Hebrew Bible, the New Testament, the Qur'an, and the
*hadith* (the authoritative sayings of the Prophet Muhammad). A brief
historical overview follows in each of these chapters to illustrate multiple
ways in which devout believers have tried to apply these foundational
principles and teachings in varying settings over many centuries.[11] These
experiments neither define strictly nor limit substantially how descendants of Abraham have structured approaches to political rule. On the
contrary, what appear to be distinctive contributions in the Hebrew Bible,
the New Testament, the Qur'an, and the hadith inform various systems
that adherents in the other traditions embrace over the centuries.

The picture that emerges shows that a variety of political structures are
not only possible within each tradition but also necessary as circumstances change. Far from being limited to singular, reified, and rigid political structures commanded by God, the descendants of Abraham have
modeled flexible approaches that draw on religion even as they adapt to

real and changing circumstances. There is great hope woven into this unfinished tapestry, hope that is especially important for those who see the glass as half-full and the life of their religious community as a work in progress.

It is also quite possible, of course, to see the glass as half-empty. Many of the most ardent advocates of narrowly focused religious-political worldviews today interpret the historical diversity as the problem that must be rectified. This fundamentalist approach weaves through all religions today. Ardent believers in each tradition tend to be ahistorical. They neither know much about history nor feel it is important, except to illustrate what is wrong. They long to re-create the "ideal time" that once prevailed, or in many cases an "ideal" that exists only in theory. They have a carefully constructed model of God's perfect plan for society. Chapters 3, 5, 7, and 8 describe examples from all three religions as we examine contemporary challenges converging in Israel, the United States, Iran, and Iraq. The ninth chapter underscores how this type of narrow sectarian approach by Jews, Christians, or Muslims offers little more than a dead-end or a road to disaster in the 21st century.

Chapters 2 through 8 attempt to bring clarity in the midst of confusion about the multifaceted and often lethal interplay between religion and politics today. Religion and politics have always been linked, but none of the religions offers a clear template to guide faithful adherents every step of the way. Rather, flexible adaptation to contemporary circumstances is not only required at a practical level; the traditions also endorse it. Even though the road ahead will be circuitous and the short-term future in many lands will be volatile and deadly, the way forward toward a more peaceful future is not blocked.

The final chapter builds on and draws together insights and conclusions from throughout the book. It presents a hopeful path into our shared future, a way that is both feasible and consistent with the basic tenets of the three religions. Having spent most of my professional life studying and working directly with the problems and challenges at the heart of this study, I remain hopeful. My experiences that began during Christmas with the Ayatollah Khomeini include harbingers both of hope and of deadly conflict. The danger signs are all around us today. Disastrous developments—real and potential—are readily discernible. The mix of religion and politics in the 21st century has been lethal and can become ever more so. But the future for our shared life on this planet need not be played out in violent conflagration. For people of faith and good will, there are compelling and legitimate reasons for hope.

# GOD GAVE US THIS LAND

## THE ROOTS OF RELIGION AND POLITICS IN JUDAISM

---

*Now the Lord said to Abram, "Go from your country and your
kindred and your father's house to the land that I will show you.
I will make of you a great nation, and I will bless you and make
your name great, so that you will be a blessing. I will bless those
who bless you and the one who curses you I will curse; and in
you all the families of the earth shall be blessed."*

—Genesis 12:1–3, New Revised Standard Version (NRSV)

THE ISLAMIC MOSQUE OF ABRAHAM (Ibrahim in Arabic) sits adjacent to
the Cave of the Patriarchs in Hebron (the city called *al-Khalil* in Arabic),[1]
some 30 miles south of Jerusalem. The traditional burial site for Abraham
and Sarah, Isaac and Rebecca, and Jacob and Leah, the Cave of the
Patriarchs is hallowed ground for Jews, Christians, and Muslims. On
February 25, 1994, this sacred space became the venue for mass murder.
As hundreds of Palestinian Muslim men and boys were gathering for
morning prayer at the mosque, Baruch Goldstein, an American medical
doctor living in the nearby Jewish settlement of Kiryat Arba, entered the
mosque disguised as an Israeli soldier. He opened fire with an automatic
weapon, killing 29 and wounding many more before being subdued and
then killed by those he sought to murder.

The time and place of his premeditated massacre were carefully chosen
to occur on the Jewish holiday of Purim, an annual commemoration of
the deliverance of Jews from extinction. The vast majority of Jews in
Israel and worldwide reacted in horror to Goldstein's deranged actions,

but to some extremist Jewish settlers and activists he was a hero. His grave became a pilgrimage site, complete with streetlights, a sidewalk and paved area for people to gather, and a cupboard with prayer books and candles. The marble plaque on his grave reads, "To the holy Baruch Goldstein, who gave his life for the Jewish people, the Torah and the nation of Israel." On the six-year anniversary marking his attack in the mosque, the BBC reported on a celebration by extremists who gathered at his grave, "dressed up as the gunman, wearing army uniforms, doctor's coats and fake beards." The story concluded by noting that an estimated 10,000 people had visited his grave in six years.[2]

The Jewish settlement of Kiryat Arba sits adjacent to a large Palestinian population precisely because of the sacred space associated with Abraham and the Patriarchs. It has long been a place where tensions run high. With more than 200,000 residents, al-Khalil is the second-largest Palestinian city in the Occupied West Bank. To protect the Jewish settlers, a substantial military presence and various barriers separate the inhabitants. All Israelis and Palestinians recognize that the Jewish settlers at Kiryat Arba are among the most vocal and vehement in pressing their belief that God gave *all* of the land to the Jews (including the occupied Palestinian territories the settlers call Judea and Samaria).

Baruch Goldstein, a devoted follower of Rabbi Meir Kahane, moved from the United States to join others in this highly controversial settlement. Both men openly advocated forcing the Palestinians out of the lands Israel conquered in the 1967 war. It mattered not to Kahane, Goldstein, and their confreres that the Arab Christians and Muslims living there could trace their family history back hundreds of years, sometimes more than a thousand. Having met some of the settlers from Kiryat Arba, I can attest to their unwavering position: God gave this land to the Jewish descendants of Abraham. Contemporary proponents of this view often overlook the fact that even when the ancient Israelites ruled over the land, other inhabitants lived there as well. Dr. Goldstein willingly sacrificed his life even as he murdered 29 others in pursuit of his narrow vision of what God intended for the Jewish people in the Holy Land.[3]

In the next two chapters, we take up vital questions about the basis on which Kahane, Goldstein, and many others construct their worldview and advance their vision for the contemporary Jewish state. How representative are their extreme positions compared to those of most Israelis, most Jews outside of Israel, and many Christian supporters of modern Israel? And to what extent do they drive the volatile mix of religion and politics in this troubled region? We begin our exploration of the obstacles and opportunities for a 21st-century Jewish state where the people of Israel began: the Hebrew Bible.

## Abraham, Patriarch and Prophet in Three Religions

The biblical story of Abraham, which begins in the 12th chapter of Genesis, will be somewhat familiar to many of us, but some of its key components are often overlooked. We need to recapitulate the basic story line because it is the foundation on which many heartfelt claims—theological and political—ultimately rest.

In the biblical narrative, Abraham responds to God's call to move his household to the land that God promises to provide. God assures Abraham that his descendants will number like the stars in the heavens (Gen. 15:5). The plot thickens early on, however, as famine strikes the land God has given them, forcing Abraham and his wife, Sarah, to flee to Egypt. They later return to the Promised Land, but 10 years later they still have no children. According to Genesis, Sarah is now in her 70s and presumably too old to bear children. So Sarah devises a plan whereby Abraham will produce an heir through Hagar, Sarah's Egyptian slave. The plan is successful, and Hagar has a son named Ishmael (Isma'il in Arabic). Some 15 years later, Sarah miraculously conceives, and their son, Isaac, is born. Sarah is apparently threatened by Ishmael's existence and demands that Abraham send Hagar and Ishmael away. Despite Abraham's distress, God tells him to follow Sarah's wishes. Although Isaac is to be the heir of God's promise to Abraham (Gen. 21:12), Genesis records three assurances about Ishmael, saying that his descendants will multiply greatly (Gen. 16:10) and that he too will be the father of a great nation (Gen. 21:13 and 18). Ishmael later becomes the link through which Arabs and Muslims trace their connection to Abraham. For Muslims, Abraham, Ishmael, and Isaac are all revered as prophets. The descendants of both sons are thus embraced as following the true religion God has revealed through various prophets and messengers.

The biblical story of Ishmael doesn't end there. He and his mother are saved miraculously by a spring in the desert. The Islamic version of the story associates this spring with Zamzam, the well situated within the confines of the Great Mosque complex surrounding the Kaaba in Mecca. Genesis 21:20–21 reports that "God was with the boy (Ishmael), and he grew up . . . and his mother got a wife for him from the land of Egypt." The final mention of Ishmael suggests there was ongoing contact between Abraham and both his sons. When Abraham dies, both Isaac and Ishmael are there to bury him (Gen. 25:9).

Abraham is thus the spiritual patriarch and prophetic figure venerated by Jews, Christians (through the Jewish tradition), and Muslims. References and interpretations of stories and acts associated with Abraham appear throughout the Hebrew Bible, the New Testament, and the

Qur'an. Non-Muslims are often surprised to learn that the Qur'an includes many references to elements of the Abraham stories.[4] Much more can be found in popular traditions and noncanonical materials. Bruce Feiler's intriguing book *Abraham: A Journey to the Heart of Three Faiths* (2002), reveals the depth of connection each religion has with this seminal, though enigmatic, figure. Feiler's exploration includes tensions and conflicts among communities with a shared history but concludes with a hopeful call to interfaith dialogue based on the common appreciation for Abraham and the one true God that Jews, Christians, and Muslims all claim to know through this foundational figure. Feiler is also keenly aware of the long history of contentious conflict among those who have so much in common.[5]

The second half of Genesis records stories of the two generations of patriarchs and matriarchs who follow the deaths of Sarah and Abraham. It ends with the dramatic story of Joseph, one of the 12 sons of Jacob. Ten of the brothers conspire to get rid of Joseph, Jacob's most beloved son. But Joseph ends up in Egypt and rises to a top position under the pharaoh. When famine strikes the land, the brothers flee to Egypt for relief, only to be confronted by the brother they left for dead. This migration to Egypt begins several hundred years of enslavement for Israelites living outside the Promised Land. The second book of the Bible, Exodus, tells the story of Moses, who responds to God's call to lead the children of Israel out of Egypt and toward the same land promised to Abraham.

The foundation for Israelite religion and what became the biblical nation of Israel is contained in the stories connected to Moses. Most of the remainder of the first five books of the Hebrew Bible (the Pentateuch or Torah) set forth the precise and extensive legal framework that will guide the people of Israel. At the end of the 40-year sojourn in the wilderness of Sinai, Moses is allowed to see the Promised Land from the east side of the Jordan River, but he dies before he can cross. His successor, Joshua, leads the Hebrews back into the land promised to Abraham and his progeny. Since many tribes and people had come to inhabit this land during their time in Egypt, the Hebrews must fight to reconquer the territory. For the next 200 to 300 years, the Hebrew people settle in various places and are linked together as a loose confederation of tribes. The stage is set for the merging of religion and politics in the formation of the biblical state of Israel.

## Dynastic Rule in Israel

The first book of Samuel records the momentous events 3,000 years ago when the emerging nation of Israel transitioned from a loose confederation of mostly autonomous tribes to a more centralized, monarchical structure that was born, in part, from the imposing threat of the Philistines. As the book of Samuel tells us, a tribal council of elders approached Samuel, the revered prophet and judge, with this plea: "Give us a king to govern over us!" (I Sam. 8:6) The elders wanted to have a king "like other nations" (I Sam. 8:5). Although their urgent appeal displeased Samuel, the Bible reports that God told him both to heed the demand of the people and to issue a stern warning about life under a monarch:

> These will be the ways of the king who will reign over you: he will take your sons and appoint them to his chariots and to be his horse- men, and to run before his chariots. . . . He will take daughters to be perfumers and cooks and bakers. He will take the best of your fields and vineyards and olive orchards and give them to his courtiers. He will take one-tenth of your grain and your vineyards and give them to his officers and courtiers. . . . He will take one-tenth of your flocks and you will be his slaves [I Sam. 8:11–17].

Samuel anoints Saul, described as tall, handsome, and a formidable warrior, as the first king of Israel. During the course of his brief reign, he becomes an increasingly tragic figure. He's haunted by the popularity and success of David, the young shepherd boy who felled the mighty Philis- tine warrior Goliath. Saul ultimately loses God's favor completely when, in a gruesome episode, he fails to carry out God's command that he utterly destroy the Amalekites.[6] On the eve of a great battle, Saul is depicted as particularly desperate. God had stopped communicating with Saul through prophets, dreams, and the *Urim*, a device for casting lots used by the high priest as a means to determine God's will. The now- pathetic Saul seeks out a medium (after he had banned mediums and wizards from the land) to summon the spirit of the deceased Samuel. Samuel appears and delivers the bad news to Saul: "The Lord has torn the kingdom out of your hand, and given it to your neighbor, David. . . . Moreover, tomorrow you and your sons will be with me." (I Sam. 28:17–19)

Monarchy, which begins as a divinely sanctioned form of government under Saul, continues with establishment of dynastic succession under Israel's second and third kings, David and Solomon. Under the unified leadership of these two monarchs, the Bible depicts Israel at its zenith. David establishes Jerusalem as the capital for the nation. It becomes the focal point for religious life in Israel when Solomon completes the mag- nificent Temple as the permanent home for the Ark of the Covenant.[7] The Temple becomes the *axis mundi*, the connecting point between heaven and earth. As dynastic rule is enshrined, religion and politics are thus joined in Jerusalem. The story of Israel flows from this ideal with the added promise that the longed-for savior, the Messiah, would come from the royal line of King David. A small minority of contemporary Jews anticipate that this theocracy will be established when the Messiah arrives on earth. The traditional Christian view is that Jesus was the Messiah. Before Matthew's New Testament narrative about Jesus' miraculous conception and birth, he sets forth a genealogy placing Jesus in the line of King David.

In addition to being portrayed as highly successful political rulers, both David and Solomon are distinguished by their spiritual insights and leadership. Many of the Psalms are traditionally ascribed to David, while the wisdom of Proverbs and Ecclesiastes is associated with Solomon.

The images of God woven throughout these narratives are mixed. Through Samuel, God relays a dire warning about oppression that would flow from kingly rule. But there are also indications of God's delight with the new political organization, and especially the choice of Zion (Jerusalem) as the permanent home for Israel's religious and political life. The Psalmist conveys God's pleasure and a conditional promise to David:

> The Lord swore to David a sure oath from which he will not turn back:
> "One of the sons of your body I will set on your throne.
> If your sons keep my covenant and my decrees that I shall teach them, their sons also, forevermore, shall sit on your throne."
> For the Lord has chosen Zion; he has desired it for his habitation:
> "This is my resting place forever; here I will reside, for I have desired it.
> I will abundantly bless its provisions; I will satisfy its poor with bread.
> Its priests I will clothe with salvation, and its faithful will shout for joy.
> There I will cause a horn to sprout up for David; I have prepared a lamp for my anointed one.
> His enemies I will clothe with disgrace, but on him, his crown will gleam" [Psalm 132:11–18].

The story of Solomon's reign depicts an expanding and increasingly wealthy kingdom, but the unity of his rule gave way to rival factions. Two kingdoms were formed: Israel in the north and Judah (with Jerusalem as the capital) in the south. Biblical accounts of David's descendants paint a dismal picture of mostly self-serving, authoritarian, and oppressive rulers. The divided kingdoms often warred with one another even as they encountered a variety of external threats. In the year 722 BCE the northern kingdom of Israel was overwhelmed by Assyria and a large segment of the Hebrew people were dispersed. The southern kingdom of Judah continued to function for another 136 years, until it too was crushed by powerful Babylonian invaders.

The biblical story of the people of Israel moves from an era of patriarchs (Abraham, Isaac, Jacob, and the 12 sons of Jacob) through the rise of Moses, the one who leads the Hebrews out of Egypt and delivers God's laws to the time of the judges; and finally, the creation of a nation under the rule of a monarch. Each part of the story is punctuated with a familiar pattern: future hope for God's chosen people is reflected in God's covenants, the leaders and the people of Israel continually fail to follow God's moral precepts and laws, and God's response to repeated human failures includes the possibility of renewal and hope for the future. It is instructive that the primary voices offering religious guidance during these four centuries of theocratic rule by monarchs are found in the proclamations and writings of the prophets.

## Who Were the Prophets of Israel?

Like many American Christians, I grew up thinking of biblical prophets as people who predicted or foretold the future, most notably the first and second coming of Christ. The prophetic books of the Hebrew Bible were cited, in highly selective ways—a verse from Ezekiel here, something from Isaiah or Jeremiah there—to piece together a more or less coherent set of signs pointing toward the earthly appearance of the Messiah. In this framework, the prophets were regarded as agents of God foretelling events hundreds or thousands of years into the future. But such an approach is rife with problems. Many, if not most, evangelical Protestant churches and a large majority of television ministries employ this interpretive framework. In my experience of four decades of studying, teaching, and preaching, no issue related to the Bible has been more confused or misunderstood than that of biblical prophets. Even more surprising, of the many hundreds of people I've encountered who see the prophets through such a lens, many have not actually read or studied the prophetic literature in the Hebrew Bible. They appear to be taking someone else's word for what is found there, just as I did before I began to study the biblical texts closely.

As a college student, I was actively involved with Campus Crusade for Christ as well as a local Southern Baptist church. I'd read and half-memorized Hal Lindsey's wildly popular best seller *The Late Great Planet Earth*.[8] A deepening personal religious commitment and a desire to study religion led me to take university courses on the subject. Against the advice and despite the warnings of several friends and leaders in my religious communities, I enrolled in a course called "The Prophets" at Oklahoma State. On the first day of class, the professor, Kyle Yates Jr., announced that the prophets were first and foremost people who spoke directly to the circumstances of their day. Some of their utterances related to the future, but primarily in the context of what would happen if religious and political leaders as well as the people of Israel failed to respond to God's message. Professor Yates introduced the two primary texts for the course: the Bible, and a monumental work by Abraham Joshua Heschel, *The Prophets*.[9] I began a process of unlearning some of what I thought I knew, a process that will be recapitulated here because, working in the Middle East, among U.S. policy makers and Christians in various churches, I am keenly aware that this fast-forward predictive approach to biblical prophecy can have serious and sometimes deadly political consequences.

## The Religious and Political Role of the Prophets

The biblical prophets, who are set apart to receive and convey God's words to humankind, are one of several types of "sacred people" who play a pivotal role in the world's religions.[10] Even though prophets are found in many traditions, they are particularly prominent in the religions tracing common ancestry to Abraham. Major prophets are described as perceiving and shaping their messages somewhat differently. Moses meets God in a burning bush, on Mt. Sinai and in the Tent of Meeting "face to face as one would speak to a friend" (Exod. 33:11). In response to Jeremiah's protest that he wouldn't have the words since he was "only a boy," God put forth his hand, touched his mouth and declared, "Behold, I have put my words in your mouth" (Jer. 1:4). Islam affirms that God's revelation to Muhammad was mediated by the angel Gabriel. According to Islamic understanding, the magnificent poetic verses of the Qur'an are literally God's words mediated through the human instrument of the prophet Muhammad.

Amidst great diversity over time and traditions, two common elements link the Hebrew prophets with others in the Abrahamic traditions. First, the prophets address the circumstances of their particular time and place. Their words may be interpreted as having wider or even universal application, but they are linked directly to particular times, places, and events.

Second, the messages delivered by the prophets always challenge the status quo. Prophets don't arrive with words of affirmation that God is pleased with what is happening and everyone should "keep up the good work." Rather, their messages speak directly to excesses, infidelities, and injustices even as they identify the path to righteousness and redemption. Political and religious leaders are frequently the objects of the blunt and critical words from prophets. Let's take a look at three brief examples that both illustrate these two common features of prophets and clarify why it is crucial that Jews, Christians, and Muslims today grasp the significance of these two shared elements.

Nathan, who was a prophet in the time of King David, models a common pattern among Hebrew prophets with his willingness to confront the king and rebuke him for his behavior. Nathan upbraided King David for his horrific crime against Uriah. After falling in love with the beautiful Bathsheba, the wife of Uriah, David hatched a plan to send Uriah on a military mission certain to end in death. The plan worked, and he was then able to take Bathsheba for his wife. The prophet Nathan went to David and delivered his message by means of a parable:

> When the wife of Uriah heard that her husband was dead, she made lamentation for him. When the mourning was over, David sent and brought her to his house, and she became his wife, and bore him a son. But the thing that David had done displeased the Lord, and the Lord sent Nathan to David. He came to him, and said to him, "There were two men in a certain city, the one rich and the other poor. The rich man had very many flocks and herds; but the poor man had nothing but one little ewe lamb, which he had bought. He brought it up and it grew up with him and with his children; it used to eat of his meager fare, and drink from his cup, and lie in his bosom, and it was like a daughter to him. Now there came a traveler to the rich man, and he was loath to take one of his own flock or herd to prepare for the wayfarer who had come to him, but he took the poor man's lamb, and prepared that for the guest who had come to him." Then David's anger was greatly kindled against the man. He said to Nathan, "As the Lord lives, the man who has done this deserves to die; he shall restore the lamb fourfold, because he did this thing, and because he had no pity." Nathan said to David, "You are the man!" [II Sam. 11:26–12:7]

Later in the narrative, Nathan intervenes and stops David from building the Temple in Jerusalem. He also plays a key role in securing the mantle of king for Solomon, the son of David and Bathsheba.

The prophet Amos was a shepherd and dresser of sycamore trees[11] when he was called to be a prophet around 750 BCE. He was from Tekoa, a village not far from Bethlehem and Jerusalem in the southern kingdom of Judah. His prophetic words, however, were directed against the northern kingdom of Israel. Amos appears toward the end of the 40-year reign of Jereboam II. Israel had expanded its territory and grown in material prosperity under Jereboam II (786–746 BCE).[12] But Amos saw no justice in the land (Amos 3:10). The judges were corrupt (5:12), and poor people were afflicted and exploited or even sold into slavery (2:6–8; 5:11). God's chosen people had turned away from the dual responsibility to be loyal to God and to care for those in need. In a powerful passage, Amos condemns the ritual and sacrificial practices as abhorrent to God in the absence of justice and righteousness:

> I hate, I despise your festivals, and I take no delight in your solemn assemblies.
> Even though you offer me your burnt offerings and grain offerings,
>     I will not accept them; and the offerings of well-being of your fatted animals I will not look upon.
> Take away from me the noise of your songs; I will not listen to the melody of your harps.
> But let justice roll down like waters, and righteousness like an ever flowing stream [Amos 5:21–24].

The utterances of Amos include a public declaration that the king of Israel would be killed and the people led away into captivity. A priest named Amaziah tells him to go back to Judah and never again prophesy in Israel. But Amos persists with his words of warning. He reports on a vision in which the Lord told him that "the end has come upon my people, Israel" (Amos 8:2).

The prophetic words of Amos connect to a specific place and time, conveying God's displeasure with the people, most notably the political and religious leaders. The man from Tekoa brings both a message of exhortation and words of hope. Although God deplores injustice, the possibility for repentance remains open: "Hate evil and love good, and establish justice in the gate; it may be that the Lord, the God of hosts, will be gracious to the remnant of Joseph" (Amos 5:15).

During M.Div. studies at the Southern Baptist Theological Seminary in Louisville, I took a course on the book of Jeremiah. Jeremiah's ministry began in 625 BCE during the reign of Josiah, spanned some four decades across the reigns of four kings, and extended beyond the fall of the southern kingdom and the destruction of Jerusalem in 587 BCE. Jeremiah ranks today as one of the most important and beloved prophets, but he was not a popular figure in Jerusalem during much of his lengthy tenure. In fact, he epitomizes the meaning of Jesus' words: "Prophets are not without honor except in their hometown, and among their own kin, and in their own house" (Mark 6:4). In Jeremiah's words, "I have become a laughing-stock all the days; everyone mocks me. For as often as I speak I have to cry out, I must shout, 'Violence and destruction!'" (Jer. 20:7–8). A careful study of the book that bears his name makes clear why his diatribes were not appreciated by the religious and political leaders of his day. At the same time, Jeremiah's hope for a new day explains why he is frequently cited by later generations, including many people today.

In the fourth year of King Jehoiakim (605 BCE), the word of the Lord comes to Jeremiah telling him to write down all that he has been proclaiming "from the first day I (God) spoke to you . . . until today" (Jer. 36:1–2). This directive arrives approximately 22 years after he began his prophetic ministry. Jeremiah enlists Baruch, a scribe, to assist him in this monumental task. He later instructs Baruch to go to the Temple to read out these prophetic utterances because he was not welcome there. Why? His earlier "Temple sermon," which is found in Jeremiah 7, so incensed the religious leaders that they threatened to kill him if he ever preached in the Temple again.

At the heart of Israel's religious life, Jeremiah confronts its leaders on their abuses in worship. Rather than walk in the way of God, he says, the priests followed their own counsel and trod a path of evil. In various passages, Jeremiah delivers his dire message: the end of the nation is coming, and Judah's enemies will lay waste to Jerusalem. In a well-known and very graphic image, Jeremiah says that God told him to visit a potter and use the experience to communicate through metaphor:

> The vessel he was making of clay was spoiled in the potter's hand, and he reworked it into another vessel as it seemed good to him. Then the word of the Lord came to me: Can I not do with you, O house of Israel, just as this potter has done? says the Lord. . . . At one moment I may declare concerning a nation or a kingdom, that I will pluck up and break down and destroy it [Jer. 18:4–7].

All is not gloom and doom, however. Woven through the lengthy collection are messages of hope. Continuing the passage above, Jeremiah says God's impending wrath is conditional: "but if that nation, concerning which I have spoken, turns from its evil, I will change my mind about the disaster I am about to bring upon it" (Jer. 18:8). There is a dual message here. The time to act is now. If Israel's leaders turn from their wicked ways, God will respond; if the injustice and self-serving unrighteousness continue, harsh judgment will follow. Even though the Babylonians overwhelm Jerusalem, Jeremiah expresses his hope for the future. Jeremiah buys a field in Anatoth and seals up the deed for a future claim. Toward the end of his long and very difficult ministry, at the moment when the catastrophe he has predicted is at the door, the prophet invests in a future that he will not personally experience. His behavior reflects God's assurance of Israel's continuing existence (Jer. 32:9–15). God, like a potter with clay, will rework Israel.

Time and again Amos, Jeremiah, and the other Hebrew prophets interweave their challenging words with a clear message of hope. Despite repeated human failures, God will not abandon Israel. If and when the nation turns back to God, they say a new beginning is possible. Beneath the visible practices of religion—sacrifices, dietary laws, and so on—God desires justice and righteousness. The words in Micah sum up majestically God's requirements that are conveyed throughout the prophetic narratives:

> He has told you, O mortal, what is good;
>    and what does the Lord require of you
> but to do justice, and to love kindness,
>    and to walk humbly with your God? [Mic. 6:8]

Prophetic figures also play a central role in Islam, but their function is somewhat different.[13] Whereas the personalities, experiences, and emotions of the Hebrew prophets are woven into the processes of delivering words from God, prophets in Islam are the human instruments who receive and transmit God's words verbatim. A comparative study illuminates distinct differences in the functional role of prophets within Judaism and Islam, but it also reveals common patterns. In both traditions, the prophets convey God's message to people in the midst of real circumstances. At the heart of their message is an imperative to follow God's moral precepts for justice, righteousness, and compassion. In both traditions, the religious messages address existing political structures directly. Thus God is perceived as guiding the community at the point where religion and politics converge.

## Religion and Politics in Biblical Israel

The unfolding story of the people of Israel in the Bible is the story of an experiment in process. Throughout the five centuries between the anointing of King Saul and the fall of Jerusalem during the time of Jeremiah, there is flexible interplay between religion and politics. God is described as expressing both delight and displeasure as events occur over time. We are reminded here of the early images of God in the primordial narratives recorded in the first 11 chapters of Genesis. The experiment of creation God pronounced "very good" had gone so awry by chapter 6 that God wiped out almost everything with the great flood during Noah's time. By the end of that well-known story, God created a new covenant, promised not to flood the earth again, and established a rainbow as the sign of this pledge. These images of God use human attributes and emotions to describe God's behavior, but they remain directly relevant to the framework for understanding what follows.

The second message woven into these narratives is that God is actively involved in the history of the people of Israel. In addition to how God is depicted in the formation of the monarchy, the prophetic books continuously paint the picture of God as taking initiative, calling the Israelites to pursue justice and righteousness. Despite the dire warnings and even stories of God's hand in bringing judgment through foreign armies, God remains open to repentance and stands ready to forgive transgressions. God is directly involved, but human beings remain responsible and accountable.

Third, the various revelations and messages from God occur in particular situations. In the examples we have cited above—Samuel and Saul, David and Nathan, Amos and the leaders of the northern kingdom of Israel, Jeremiah and the leaders in Judah—God is actively and organically involved in an ongoing process involving real people, real events, and real circumstances. The approach to issues at the intersection of religion and political structures of the nation is not fixed on some grand template. They are being worked out in a dynamic process over time. Options change as circumstances change, but justice and righteousness are constant as the basis for Israel's religious and political life.

Although Judaism is historically the first of the three great monotheistic religions, these principles are not unique to this branch of the Abrahamic family. We will see below how the history of Christianity and Islam, though distinct from Judaism and from one another, incorporate similar worldviews. For Jews, the foundational principles we see in the biblical narratives continue to be important for understanding their unique history, especially in the dramatic developments during the 20th century.

## Jewish History and the Rise of the Modern Zionist Movement

The Babylonian conquest in 587 BCE destroyed Jerusalem. Many Israelites were removed to Babylon, in what is southern Iraq today.[14] The captivity was relatively short-lived; some 50 years after Babylonian conquest, Persian forces led by Cyrus II became the dominant power in the region. Cyrus II recaptured Jerusalem, encouraged the rebuilding of the Temple, and issued an edict allowing Jews in Babylon to return home. The large majority, however, stayed in Babylon and other nearby lands where their families had been exiled. This, together with the earlier fall of the northern kingdom of Israel, began what would later become the dominant reality for most Jews: living in communities outside the land of Israel. The Jewish community that remained and grew in the Tigris and Euphrates river valleys (contemporary Iraq) would emerge as a primary intellectual center for new forms of Judaism.

The relative stability under Persian rule gave way to domination, first by the Greeks between 334 and 322 BCE, under Alexander the Great; next by the Macedonian Ptolemy, whose regime was based in Egypt; and by the Seleucids in Syria. An effort to rededicate the Jerusalem Temple for the worship of Zeus, together with active suppression of Jewish practices such as Sabbath observances and circumcision, helped fuel a national Jewish uprising, the Maccabean Revolt (168–164 BCE), led by Judas the Maccabee. Two decades later, Judas's brother Simon formally established the Hasmonean dynasty (140–37 BCE).[15]

The surprising success of this Jewish uprising restored national independence. The Temple in Jerusalem was purified and rededicated (events celebrated annually at Hanukkah), and Jewish national rule prevailed for more than a century, though not without problems, until the armies of Rome arrived and seized control in 63 BCE. The Hasmoneans annexed a large portion of Palestine and even converted many Gentiles, some by force, living within their borders. They combined the offices of high priest and king, a move that produced a monarch without constraints. Acclaimed author and Middle East analyst Milton Viorst notes how their tyranny over the populace fueled "excesses, like those of a succession of David's heirs." The behavior of the Hasmoneans and many earlier monarchs effectively disenfranchised them from the populace.[16]

The Hasmonean dynasty was replaced by the Herodian rule when Herod the Great was installed as king in 37 BCE. Jews lived under Roman rule for more than 130 years, including the decades in which Jesus lived and the early Christian church took root. There were Jewish kings—Herod and Herod Antipas are named in the New Testament—but there was no doubt that ultimate political power and authority rested with Rome. Some Jewish zealots clamored for rebellion against the Romans, but their views did not prevail in Jesus' day. Four decades later, however, open revolt was met with a resounding defeat. Roman armies sacked Jerusalem and destroyed the Temple in 70 CE. The last of the Jews in rebellion took refuge at Masada, a hilltop garrison near the Dead Sea, where they held out for two more years. Most Jews who had not previously relocated were scattered from the Roman districts of Palestine in all directions during the great revolt.

For almost two millennia following the destruction of the second Temple, the Jews lived as minority communities in the Diaspora, a term that came to describe the locations of Jews living outside the historic lands of Israel. The religious structures of Judaism in exile from Israel underwent many major changes over the centuries. New forms of organization and institutional life for Jews emerged as synagogues and rabbis supplanted the Temple, priests, and ritual sacrifices. A national religion that had been connected physically to Jerusalem was in exile and thus had to be transformed into an idea, a city of the mind. Ritual sacrifices in and traditional scholarly discourse near the Temple in Jerusalem were no longer possible. By the fifth century, massive collections of scholarly debate and commentary on Jewish laws and practices emerged in written form in the Babylonian Talmud and the Jerusalem Talmud. The rabbinical scholars who shaped the authoritative Babylonian collection were part of the extensive Jewish community tracing its roots to the exile enforced by the Babylonians a thousand years earlier in 587 BCE.

Some Jewish scholars remained in Palestine—most notably in Caesarea and Tiberius—but the intellectual center of Judaism shifted from Jerusalem to Babylon and later to lands under Christian and Muslim rule. To survive and thrive in Diaspora—often under duress or persecution by adherents of the ever-growing proselytizing religions of Christianity and Islam—was nothing short of miraculous. Many Jews worldwide did assimilate into the dominant cultures and religions over the centuries.[17] But a substantial remnant of loyalists held fast to the covenant their ancestors had accepted under Moses at Mt. Sinai. Memory of their historic past in Jerusalem stayed with Jews no matter where they lived and despite the many efforts to eradicate them, the most horrific of which was the Holocaust of World War II. "Next year in Jerusalem" has always permeated ritual life and daily prayers reinforcing these deep ties to and hope for a return to the Promised Land.

Rabbi Arthur Hertzberg, a prolific author of Jewish history and prominent leader during the second half of the 20th century, posed the "big
question" that this and all generations have faced:

> Will the saving remnant complete its journey and, in theological
> terms, witness the end of days—the coming of the Messiah, who will
> return the Jews to the Promised Land and bring peace to the world—
> or will the Jews wither and die?[18]

The collective experiences of Jews as a subservient and frequently per-
secuted minority[19] clearly influenced the Zionist movement and the
founding of the modern state of Israel in 1948. The Zionist movement
gained momentum after Jews were blamed for the assassination of Czar
Alexander II in 1881. In the immediate aftermath of the assassination, a
wave of pogroms and widespread pillage spurred emigration of more
than two and a half million Jews to the West, especially to the United
States, over the next three decades. Many people are at least vaguely
familiar with this sad chapter because it furnishes the backdrop for the
award-winning musical *Fiddler on the Roof*. It is in fact the story of a
large portion of my family. With his family, my great-grandfather,
a devout, Orthodox cantor who lived near the Russian-Polish border,
was forced out during this time of horrific Christian pogrom. My paternal grandfather was one of his nine children. The family, like so many
other immigrants, made it to the United States and settled in Boston,
where a large percentage of my extended family still lives today.[20]

The ideological underpinning for political Zionism came first from
Leon Pinsker, a Russian Jew living in Germany. His *Autoemancipation*,
together with Theodor Hertzl's *Der Judenstaat*, argued that the essence
of the problem of Jewish persecution was not so much individual as
national. Assimilation was a dangerous dream; a Jewish state was
needed—both for the Jews and as an answer to those who didn't want
Jews in their midst. Hertzl organized the First Zionist Congress in 1897.
In the decades to follow there were many, often heated, debates about the
location of the hoped-for Jewish state—candidates were the historic land
of Israel (*eretz Israel*), Argentina, Uganda, and a portion of the United
States—as well as the structure and nature of the new nation.[21] Assuming
a Jewish state could be established, there were differing opinions on precisely how the religion of Judaism would relate to the state and government. Religious Zionists, secular Jews, and others in between weighed in
through writings, Zionist congresses, and their response to unfolding
events. World War I, which marked the end of the Ottoman Empire and
the ascent of Great Britain with the British Mandate in Palestine, was a

major catalyst. The era of colonialism was ending; nationalist movements around the world were the birth pangs of what would become the new nation-state system.

The decades between World War I and the end of World War II included a swirling mix of international intrigue, political maneuvering and duplicity by major powers, coexistence, conflict and violent clashes between Jews and Arabs in Palestine, and much more. In the aftermath of World War II and the Holocaust, however, the momentum solidified toward a Jewish homeland in historic Palestine. Debate about assimilation or the nature of a Jewish state paled in comparison to the overwhelming conviction that future security required a Jewish commonwealth in their historic homeland. It is sad to say that the behavior of other nations in response to this movement was often shameful. Slow to acknowledge the Holocaust, many nations—including the United States—placed strict limits on Jewish immigration after the war. The message was now clear: if Jews hoped to live with any security at all, they needed a Jewish state.

Under the authority of the League of Nations, Great Britain was given a mandate to rule over a substantial portion of the former Ottoman Empire for the 25 years between 1923 and 1948. The British Mandate included historic Palestine and Transjordan (the areas of Jordan, Israel, and the occupied territories). As the Mandate was winding down and various other nation-states were emerging in the postcolonial period, the United Nations put forth a partition plan for two states—a Jewish state of Israel and a Palestinian Arab state—with Jerusalem as a protected international city. Most Jews embraced the plan, while most Arabs in Palestine and neighboring lands flatly rejected it. The Arabs viewed creation of Israel as a colonial state being forced on them by Western powers. On the day before the Mandate expired, May 14, 1948, Israel declared its independence as a nation. The United States and the Soviet Union immediately recognized the new Jewish state. The Arab states did not, and war broke out the next day. Israel prevailed in the war of 1948, capturing more land than was included in the UN partition plan. For the first time in more than 2,000 years, the Jewish people had political control of an independent state, in the very place where Abraham had followed God's call to the Promised Land.

What kind of state should it be? A Jewish state necessarily yokes religion and politics; this much was clear. Jews who fought for and helped establish the modern state of Israel were not the least bit interested in returning to the biblical model of dynastic rule from the time of Saul, David and Solomon, or the Hasmonean and Herodian dynasties. They understood that the ongoing story of God's relationship to the Jewish people remained an experiment in process. The biblical model of kingly rule, like animal sacrifices at the Temple in Jerusalem, was not appropriate for what were now different times and circumstances. Many Jews at the forefront of the nationalist movement were, however, deeply committed to the prophetic call for justice and righteousness.

The new Jewish state evoked a host of critical questions. How exactly would legal traditions and religious practices of Judaism relate to the state? How would the deep desire for democratic rule be connected with a large portion of the populace who were Muslims or Christians? Would everyone have exactly the same rights? If so, what would ensure future security for Jewish inhabitants? If Jews from anywhere in the world could come to Israel and be granted citizenship on the spot, what rights of citizenship were to be given to non-Jews whose families had lived within the boundaries of the new state for hundreds of years? These and many other questions arose, and in many instances they have remained problematic for the one nation formally linked with Judaism.

For more than six decades, the modern state of Israel has been a focal point for passionate, and frequently turbulent, religious and political machinations not only in the Middle East region but also on the larger world stage. Many dramatic and often convoluted events have shaped the landscape at the eastern end of the Mediterranean since Israel was founded in 1948, including regional wars, terrorist attacks, and growing militancy within Christian, Muslim, and Jewish groups who claim to be God's agents in preparing for (or even facilitating) "end of the world" theological schemes. Israel today is a work in progress. In the next chapter, we examine how distinct visions and approaches to shaping its future raise deadly serious concerns at the intersection of religion and politics.

# 3

# ISRAEL

## DEADLY CONFLICT IN ZION

---

ON THE EVENING OF NOVEMBER 4, 1995, Israeli Prime Minister Yitzhak Rabin was shot and killed at the conclusion of a peace rally celebrating the Oslo Accords. Officially called the Declaration of Principles on Interim Self-Government Arrangements, Oslo marked a major break-through as the first face-to-face agreement between Israel and the Palestinians. The signing ceremony featured the unforgettable image of Rabin shaking hands with Yasser Arafat on the White House lawn in front of President Bill Clinton. With Rabin's assassination, this celebrated, hopeful picture was suddenly replaced by scenes of mass public grieving as hundreds of thousands of Israelis held vigils daily in the square where Rabin was shot.

The assassin, Yigal Amir, was an extremist, right-wing, Orthodox Jew who adamantly opposed peace with the Palestinians. He believed murdering Rabin was saving Israel from a disastrous fate that would result from a negotiated peace treaty. Leaders of *Gush Emunim* ("Block of the Faithful"),[1] the powerful umbrella organization on the religious right, suggested that no one should be surprised by the murder. In numerous television interviews, they showed no visible signs of distress over events that stunned most Israelis, much as the assassination of President John Kennedy had shocked most Americans three decades earlier. Instead, their disgust for the slain prime minister was unambiguous.

These religiously devout leaders, who spearheaded rapid expansion of the illegal settlement movement in the West Bank and Gaza (territories occupied militarily by Israel since 1967), flatly rejected the negotiated peace process set forth in Oslo. Their tacit support for Amir exposed to the rest of the world the deep and dangerous internal divide within Israel. It highlighted a sobering question. Who presented Israel's government with the largest obstacles to a negotiated peace settlement: the Palestinians, neighboring Arab states, or the extreme religious right within Israel? This internal division had been displayed on the international stage before, most notably in violent confrontations when former Prime Minister Menachem Begin led the forced evacuation of 2,500 Israeli settlers from the Sinai town of Yamit at the end of the Egyptian-Israeli peace process in 1982. The internal strife erupted again for several weeks in 2005 when then Prime Minister Ariel Sharon dismantled the Israeli settlements and evacuated some 8,200 from within the densely populated Gaza Strip. The primary threat to the 55,000 Israeli soldiers dispatched to Gaza came from angry settlers. In both 1982 and 2005, generous financial compensation for those being relocated did little to diminish the hostility of the settlers. For them, the issue was not defined by economics or political expediency. It was and *is* religious and ideological: God gave the Jews this land and no one—including the government of Israel—had any right to take it away.

When I traveled in Israel several months after Rabin's assassination, I could readily see the shock as well as the anger and acrimony of the country's internal divisions. In this 30th trip to the Middle East in 20 years, I was leading a small group of 20 for an intensive study in Jordan, Israel, and the Occupied Territories. In addition to seeing numerous biblical sites important for Jews, Christians, and Muslims, we met with a variety of people and groups: members of the Knesset (Israel's parliament), academics, business leaders, rabbis, peace and human rights activists, and settlers as well as Palestinian educators, journalists, international relief workers, leaders within the PLO (Palestine Liberation Organization) and HAMAS, Christian clergy, Muslim imams, and people living in refugee camps.

One morning, we visited the cemetery on Mt. Herzl where Rabin, former Prime Minister Golda Meir, and other national leaders are buried. Expressions of dismay and deep sadness defined the faces of the 25–30 Israelis also standing in silence at Rabin's gravesite. With tears welling in his eyes, one man I estimated to be about 70 years old broke the silence: "Jews don't do this." About a minute later, slowly shaking his head in disbelief, he again spoke to no one in particular, "Jews don't do this."

That same afternoon, we visited a large settlement in the West Bank for an hourlong tour and two hours of conversation. With enthusiasm and confident certainty, the settlers described their godly enterprise. When our conversation turned to relations with their Palestinian neighbors, a young settler who had been with us all afternoon spoke for the group. "We have very friendly relations with the Arabs. Every morning when

I walk through his field, I say 'Shalom' to him. He says 'Salam' back to me. We have very friendly relations. Of course, I am carrying this Uzi [machine gun]. If I didn't have it, he would probably kill me since he believes we stole his land."

When one from our group pointed out that saying "Salam" to someone carrying a deadly weapon across his land hardly constitutes friendly relations, the settler, who had moved his family from New York 18 months earlier, replied in a crisp Brooklyn accent: "We want to live peacefully with the Arabs. But they must understand and accept that this land is ours. God gave us this land." We pondered this as we thought of the Palestinian farmer we had met who told us how his family had farmed their land for more than four centuries.

Still, for the settlers the bottom line was clear. The claim to the land—including the territories occupied militarily in 1967 almost 20 years after the founding of the state of Israel—was rooted in a theological framework. It rests on a literal reading of passages beginning with Genesis 12:1–3, where God promises to give a land to Abraham. Most Jews see historic ties to this land as well, but they also stress centuries of persecution and mistreatment as fundamental components underscoring the need for a secure homeland. Others emphasize the numerous examples where Jewish immigrants in the 20th century bought land—often seemingly infertile land—and labored mightily to make the desert bloom. For most Jews, a more pragmatic and far less theologically rigid orientation prevails. This is true for observant and secular Jews, for many rabbis, and for a range of political leaders such as Rabin and Ezer Weizman.

Both Rabin and Weizman lived their entire lives in the land of Israel. Rabin was born in Jerusalem in 1922, Weizman in Tel Aviv in 1924. Both men had distinguished careers as military and government leaders. In addition to two terms as prime minister, Rabin was Israel's ambassador to the United States and held cabinet positions as minister of defense and minister of labor. Weizman, whose legendary career as a fighter pilot inspired the moniker "father of Israel's Air Force," was minister of defense for Begin during the Camp David peace process with Egypt in the late 1970s. He later served in the cabinet and for seven years (1993–2000) as Israel's president.

I spent many hours with Ezer Weizman during visits to Jerusalem in the 1980s and 1990s. His deep love for his country came through in every conversation, even when his blunt candor left no doubt about his views on the policies of the Israeli leadership at any given time.[2] Although Weizman and Rabin were always in different political parties, both leaders became convinced over time that a negotiated peace with the Palestinians and neighboring Arab states was not only possible but absolutely necessary. These well-known, highly decorated military leaders both argued that Israel's security could not rest on military dominance alone. Israel's long-term safety and stability required peaceful coexistence and economic cooperation. They embraced the principle of exchanging land for peace. This principle, which was a cornerstone of UN Resolution 242 following the Six-Day War of June 1967, was an essential component in the Camp David peace process with Egypt, the Oslo Accords, and the 2005 Israeli withdrawal from Gaza.

The orientation and commitment of native-born leaders such as Rabin and Weizman illustrate clearly the sharp contrast with most of the 500,000 settlers living in territories outside the internationally recognized borders of Israel.[3] Even though they—and the overwhelming majority of Jews worldwide—share an unflinching commitment to Israel as a secure Jewish state, their ideological differences are deadly serious.

The Israeli-Palestinian conflict is the most explosive issue in a highly volatile region.[4] The status quo is increasingly less tenable as the possibility grows that neighboring states and transnational groups will have nuclear weapons. Israel's airstrike against the Iraqi Osiris nuclear site in 1981, a Syrian nuclear facility in 2008, and stern warnings directed at Iran beginning in 2008 underscore the growing threat Israel perceives. Military leaders such as Rabin and Weizman understood well that this kind of military escalation will not bring long-term security for Israel; this outcome will require a negotiated, durable peace with the Palestinians and neighboring states.

## The Unstable Mix of Religion and Politics in Israel

The description of Israel as a democratic Jewish state belies the many tensions among those three ingredients. Vigorous debates before and after statehood still raise these questions: What is truly "Jewish"? How "Jewish" should the state be, and who decides what defines a Jewish state? And how can Israel be both Jewish and democratic when 25–30% of the citizens are not Jewish and therefore do not enjoy all the same benefits of citizenship?

On one extreme, many Orthodox Jews did not support or recognize Israel as a legitimate state prior to or even after 1948. Rather, they connected the longed-for reconstitution of Israel with the anticipated Messianic age that is yet to come. In this view, the faithful should pray fervently for the day when God will establish the new Jerusalem. The ancient historic memory of military uprisings being crushed and the experiences of two millennia living as minority communities in the Diaspora framed this worldview. God, not human beings, would act when the time was right at the "end of days." In the meantime, the traditional Orthodox rabbis advised their communities to hold fast to the three oaths that had sustained Jews as minority communities in exile for almost 2,000 years: not to return en masse to the Holy Land; not to rebel against the nations in which they lived; and, in return for not being rebellious, to entreat their hosts not to oppress them unduly.[5] This long-standing position has changed for most Jews in the decades since Israel became a state.

On the other end of the spectrum were nonreligious Jews who supported and still support Israel's statehood primarily as a defensive cultural and political act, an essential place of freedom and safety from persecution and pogroms. Between these two points of view are many others, including provocative attitudes among a disproportionately influential minority of activist, religious zealots—manifest most visibly with the settlers associated with Gush Emunim or Meir Kahane. As we have already seen, these true believers will not wait passively for God to act. Rather, they see themselves as God's agents acting in history.

The modern Jewish state was created in the context of post-Enlightenment European political thought. The vast majority of contemporary Jews never imagined returning to the model of a monarchy or dynastic rule as set forth in biblical times. Rather, a completely different world called for a completely different political structure. The new Israel would be a parliamentary democracy. Many of the Zionist leaders were strongly committed to the ideals of socialism, as were many Europeans during the first half of the 20th century. Their influence can be seen in government programs, pervasive labor unions, and the *kibbutz* movement.[6] For them, concern for justice and the collective good connected naturally with the clear sense of identity and community that has always been a hallmark of Jewish life.

Although there was no formal constitution accompanying statehood, a Declaration of Establishment in 1948, the Basic Laws of the parliament (Knesset), and the Israeli citizenship law provided the functions of a constitution. Israel has always had a multiparty system. Each party puts up a slate of candidates for the parliament. Citizens vote for a party, and depending on what percentage of the overall vote it receives the party's respective slates receive a proportionate number of seats in the 120-member parliament. For more than six decades, no party has ever won an outright majority of the popular vote. So the party with the highest percentage of the vote is invited to form a government by building coalitions with one or more smaller parties. If they are successful, the person who heads the slate for the majority party becomes the prime minister.[7] For much of its history, Israeli governments have included one or more religious parties in the ruling coalition. In a parliamentary system, a vote of no confidence can be called at any time. Should a critical number of people (sometimes only three or four people) break from the governing coalition, the government can be turned out and new elections must be called. The way this system works explains in part why small religious parties (with roots in the Orthodox rather than Conservative, Reform, or Reconstructionist streams of Judaism) have played a disproportionately influential role over many decades. The disproportionate power of these religious parties has fueled ongoing and serious ideological differences at the intersection of religion and politics in the Jewish state.

Most Americans are surprised to learn that a substantial majority of Israeli Jews have always been nonreligious. The questions of what it means to be Jewish and how Jewish Israel should be are even more intriguing in this context. And they raise other questions: What role should the Jewish religion play in the formal structures of the state? For Orthodox Jews, the issues include such matters as who one marries[8] and how the Sabbath must be observed. For most Israelis, whether or not one observes the Sabbath is a matter of personal conscience. For the Orthodox, it is essential that the Jewish state reflect Jewish law. Thus they insist, for example, that the state should stop public transportation and public services from sundown on Friday until sundown on Saturday.

## Not All Israelis Are Jewish

This matter of the Jewish state being run by some laws linked to Judaism becomes more complex when you recall that 25–30% of Israeli citizens are not Jews. Most are Arabs who were already living there. Groups within the Zionist movement recognized problems related to the indigenous Arab population living in a Jewish state. As Jews, they had been on the receiving end of discrimination and were committed to opposing injustice. This heartfelt concern animated their debate. But it has not prevented the inequalities that the 1.5 million non-Jewish citizens (primarily Arab Muslims, Arab Christians, and Druze) have experienced. I've been surprised time and again over many years, for instance, at the high percentage of well-educated Americans who have no idea that around one in four Israeli citizens is an Arab Christian or Muslim, not a Jew. Knowing more about Israeli Arabs unmasks the inherent tension between religiously defined states and democracy. It presents a question that must be engaged more forthrightly by Israel in the 21st century: If one religion is clearly privileged by the state, won't adherents of other religions inevitably be second- or third-class citizens? The same question applies, of course, to Islamic states or Christian nations.

**Israel's borders 1948–1967**

Large numbers of Arabs in Palestine fled from their homes at the time of the 1948 war. Some were forced out or fled in fear, some left in response to political or military machinations of Arab leaders who urged them to leave, and most Arabs assumed they would return home after a short time. The vast majority of those who left, however, have never been able to return. Hundreds of thousands of Palestinians and their descendants still live in UN-sponsored refugee camps, especially in neighboring Lebanon and Jordan and in Gaza and the West Bank, territories controlled by Egypt and Jordan at that time. Hundreds of thousands more Palestinians live or work in various Arab or European countries and the United States but still identify their family's pre-1948 home and town as their "home." The "right of return," or some form of compensation for these displaced Palestinian Arabs, is one of the most highly charged unresolved issues in the Israeli-Palestinian conflict.

In sharp contrast, the right of return is granted to any Jew anywhere in the world. One can make *aliyah* ("ascent") or travel to Israel and be granted citizenship immediately. More than half a million Jews immigrated to Israel in the first three years after statehood, coming from Europe and various predominantly Muslim countries such as Iraq, Iran, Morocco, and Yemen. As conflicts occurred or life became too dangerous—as it was for more than 20,000 Iranian Jews after the 1979 Islamic revolution—many Jews continued to come to Israel from Muslim lands, the Soviet Union, Ethiopia, and elsewhere. The right of return extends also to some eligible non-Jews such as a spouse or children. Given the historical plight of many Jews living as minority communities under Christian and Muslim rule, I have always affirmed the law granting the right of return. I have also been keenly aware of the deadly discrimination I might have experienced because of my Jewish heritage.[9] But I have experienced as well the frustration and sense of injustice among Arabs. The issue is particularly poignant when sitting in refugee camps with people whose families lived for centuries within what became the 1948 borders of Israel but today have no "right" to claim Israeli citizenship.

The Arabs who stayed within the new borders of Israel in 1948 were granted Israeli citizenship. They have full rights of citizenship, including the vote and equal protection under the law. Whereas Israeli Jews have compulsory military service, Israeli Arabs cannot be drafted. Druze[10] and a small percentage of Arabs are allowed to serve in the military voluntarily. The distinctions here are understandable in terms of state security. But there is widespread discrimination woven into the system, as the government subsidizes various benefits (such as housing and employment) to citizens who have served in the military. Arab citizens of Israel enjoy freedom of religion and have jurisdiction over many aspects of personal status law (among them marriage, divorce, alimony, inheritance). But systematic discrimination is also readily visible in dramatic differences in funding for Arab and Jewish municipalities, excessive red tape, fees, and delays for everyday matters such as building permits.

The story of Father Elias Chacour illustrates the point. I became friends with him in 1982 when he was serving a Greek Catholic church in Ibillin, a small town in northern Israel, not far from the Sea of Galilee. For Chacour, being a follower of Jesus required a ministry of reconciliation. Born in Galilee in 1939, he had lived through many conflicts, the creation of Israel, and several wars. His commitment to nonviolence and peaceful coexistence for Christians, Muslims, and Jews was well known. When I first met him in his modest apartment, we talked at length about interfaith relations, sports programs, and community projects that brought together people from the three religions. He was particularly focused on education as a key ingredient in developing a more hopeful and healthy future within Israel. As the representative of Church World Service, the relief and development arm of the National Council of Churches in the United States, I, and others, began working with him to raise funds for the school he hoped to build and run. For most of the next decade, however, government officials repeatedly blocked Chacour's efforts. Although money flowed freely for Jewish schools and public projects, his privately funded initiatives to improve educational opportunities and facilitate interfaith cooperation were thwarted at almost every point.

Chacour was committed and persistent. In addition to the financial and political support of many people and groups in the United States and Europe, he ventured boldly where few would dare to go. On one visit to the United States he looked up the home address of James Baker, who was then secretary of state. In a move that would no longer be possible for obvious reasons of security, he went to the Baker home and knocked on the front door. Susan Baker answered it. As Chacour tells the story, Mrs. Baker happened to be in the midst of a Bible study with a group of friends. He offered to join them and give his insights as a contemporary "man from Galilee," a Greek Catholic priest trying to live out Jesus' message of reconciliation in a broken and hurting world. He was invited in and joined the group. A friendship was born that day. Not long thereafter, the secretary of state called attention to Chacour's good efforts among Israeli officials. Suddenly, most of the red tape disappeared. Today, the Mar Elias school system he founded and built in Ibillin serves around 5,000 students. These and other initiatives have led to many international

awards and several nominations for the Nobel Peace Prize for this contemporary Israeli Arab Christian man from Galilee.[11]

Support for Father Chacour's work also came from many individual
Israeli Jews and groups within Israel. In fact, there are a large number
of Israeli individuals and groups committed to protecting human rights
or lending legal assistance to Israeli Arabs as well as Palestinians living
under occupation. Among those with whom I've worked, some are
overtly religious while others self-identify as secular Jews. They share an
abiding commitment to the prophetic insistence on justice and righteousness in society. Such outspoken advocates for equality are well known
within Israel, but they don't receive much media attention in the United
States, where the primary focus is on armed conflict.[12]

Policies discriminating against non-Jewish citizens in Israel are no
secret. In addition to annual reports by various nongovernmental human
rights groups such as Human Rights Watch and Amnesty International,
the U.S. State Department publishes annual country reports on human
rights practices. The reports on Israel and the Occupied Territories detail
how Israeli policies create institutional, legal, and societal discrimination
against the country's Arab citizens.[13] As discriminatory practices get
attention and are challenged formally, the legal system within Israel
responds. After encountering many obstacles blocking Father Chacour's
educational initiatives for 25 years, it was encouraging to learn of the
February 2006 Israeli Supreme Court decision striking down the government education plan because it discriminated against Israeli Arabs. The
court ordered the government to develop a new plan within one year.

There are important signs of hope woven into the challenges presented
by Arab citizens within the Jewish state of Israel. Israeli leaders insist that
the Arab citizens have full civil rights. Although the examples noted
above illustrate some of the multiple problems Israeli Arabs cite, it is also
true that Israel has been engaged in an ongoing experiment about how to
balance a commitment to its identity as a state where all Jews have
national rights with full civil rights for the non-Jewish citizens. As is true
with the ongoing experiment in religious pluralism in the United States,
Israel's efforts to negotiate this difficult convergence of religion and politics may yet produce elements of a model for future states that self-define
as Christian or Islamic.[14]

## Judea and Samaria, or Occupied Palestine?

Whereas the multiple problems with the mix of religion and politics
within Israel are substantial and serious, in the adjacent territories of

the West Bank and Gaza Strip the problems are substantial and *lethal*. Hope for peace and stability—for Israel, for the Palestinians, and for the Middle East—depends largely on what happens in the territories Israel captured in the June 1967 war.[15] The convergence of several powerful dynamics for more than four decades has complicated a confused and confusing situation—from Israeli concerns about security to Jewish extremists' actions and demands, to evangelical Christians' theological convictions about the end times, to the rhetoric and actions of Palestinian extremists and shifting U.S. government policies. The challenges are formidable, but not beyond resolution. People on all sides have long known what will foster peace and economic cooperation among Israel, the Palestinians, and neighboring Arab and Muslim states. The obstacles lie in inflexible religious-based worldviews, or even worse, in the actions of ardent believers that may precipitate a violent conflagration in the near future.

A brief recap of events begins with the Israeli Labor government's confiscation of Arab lands and construction of settlements in the Occupied West Bank in the aftermath of the 1967 war. The stated purpose of these efforts was to provide more security to the Jewish state. Without question, the history of conflict and the proximity of large population centers in Israel to potentially dangerous borders reinforced the rationale for such security measures. Over time, however, legitimate security concerns became increasingly intertwined with theologically motivated settlement of the occupied territories. The settlement process escalated dramatically beginning in 1977 after Begin's Likud Party assumed power in a coalition with the National Religious Party. Soon after he became prime minister, Begin traveled to the Gush Emunim settlement of Elon Moreh in the West Bank, held up a Torah scroll, and announced there would be many more Elon Morehs.[16] Begin's government made good on this pledge, pouring more than a billion dollars into settlements in the West Bank and Gaza Strip. Massive support for building settlements, and new roads and water projects together with significant economic incentives, enabled the dedicated settlers to rapidly develop an infrastructure that increased the likelihood of Israel having permanent control of Judea and Samaria—the pre-1967 areas that Arab Muslims and Christians call Occupied Palestine.

The major "fact on the ground" in the Occupied West Bank and Gaza at that time, however, was the more than two million indigenous Palestinians. For the growing minority of Jewish settlers and the Likud coalition government that supported their aims, the large Palestinian population posed a serious dilemma. The areas under military occupation could not simply be annexed without giving citizenship to the inhabitants. The demographics were unambiguous: if all Palestinians living under military occupation became citizens of Israel, Arab Christians and Muslims would soon outnumber the Jews and Israel would eventually lose its distinction as a Jewish state. Most Israelis and many American leaders understood the problem but chose to sit on the fence or just not talk about it, focusing instead on legitimate concerns about Israeli security and Israel's role as America's top ally in the Middle East. Meanwhile, the increasingly powerful and religiously driven settler movement had a plan, articulated concisely by one of its most prominent and flamboyant leaders, Rabbi Meir Kahane: buy off Palestinians or confiscate their land, develop the infrastructure for Jewish settlers, recruit new settlers, and encourage all settlers to have as many children as possible. Increasing the Jewish population while working to decrease the Palestinian Christian and Muslim populations could produce a demographic shift whereby Israel would ultimately be able to annex Judea and Samaria without diluting the Jewish character of the nation. Many settlers pursued these practices. These efforts, combined with repressive military occupation and various types of daily harassment, proved somewhat successful over time. Economic and social life as well as physical dangers made things so difficult for many indigenous Palestinian Arabs that they immigrated to Jordan, Lebanon, Europe, or the United States if they were able to do so. Although most Israelis publicly rejected Kahane's brash extremism, he won a seat in the Knesset in 1984. Even though his views were denounced and ridiculed publicly, and many Israelis often dismissed him as someone on the fanatical fringe, the policies of the Likud governments of Begin and his successor, Yitzhak Shamir, and the actions of Gush Emunim settlers helped implement Kahane's plan.

The political impact of this religious-based ideological movement has been seismic. In a compelling book published by the Council of Foreign Relations, Ian Lustick succinctly summarizes the nonnegotiable worldview of these Jewish fundamentalists:

> The men and women of Gush Emunim have made it their life's work to ensure that the occupied West Bank and Gaza Strip are permanently incorporated into the State of Israel. . . . Their operational objective is to accelerate the pace at which the Jewish people fulfills its destiny. This includes, for most of these activists, establishment of Jewish sovereignty over the entire, biblically described, Land of Israel, substitution of "authentically Jewish" forms of governance for Western-style liberal democracy, and rebuilding the Temple in Jerusalem,

thereby implementing the divinely ordained, albeit long-delayed, messianic redemption. They insist that direct political action is the means to accomplish the rapid transformation of Israeli society according to uncompromisable, authentically Jewish, cosmically ordained imperatives.[17]

These ideologues see themselves as God's agents in completing a cosmic plan for the land of Israel. Gush Emunim leaders have also implemented effective political strategies that substantially strengthened support for their position among Israelis who do not share their extremist views. The hard-core Gush Emunim settlers recognized that their numbers were too small to settle all the land they deemed necessary. So they worked with the Begin government to seize land and build huge housing developments in the suburbs surrounding Arab East Jerusalem, areas that are included in the occupied West Bank. Israeli citizens were granted significant economic incentives to move into extensive apartment complexes within easy commuting distance of Jerusalem or other cities in Israel. The strategy has been highly effective in two ways. The building projects effectively block Arabs in East Jerusalem from expanding their communities to accommodate population growth. And these several hundred thousand inhabitants of the complexes now have a strong, vested interest in opposing a land-for-peace approach that would return to the 1967 borders. Twenty years after this major push for urban settlements began, these residents accounted for more than 350,000 of the half-million Israelis living in the occupied territories.[18]

Rebuilding the Temple in Jerusalem is a key focus for some of the most rigidly fundamentalist Jews. Two cherished Muslim buildings—the Dome of the Rock and the al-Aqsa mosque—now stand on the 35 acres that Muslims call *Haram ash-sharif* ("the Noble Sanctuary") and Jews call the Temple Mount, the area on which the Temple stood until its destruction by the Romans in 70 CE. Traditionally, Orthodox Jews have prayed for the day when God will move in history and miraculously restore the Temple. Some contemporary Jewish fundamentalists go well beyond prayer and seek to give God a helping hand. On at least a dozen occasions, Israeli security forces thwarted well-organized Jewish activists who were attempting to blow up the Islamic buildings. In their view, removing these buildings is a first step in the divinely ordered sequence of events they believe are about to unfold. For more than three decades, Israeli journalist Gershom Gorenberg has studied and written extensively about the perilous intersection of religion and politics manifest in what is arguably the most contested real estate on earth. His book *The End of*

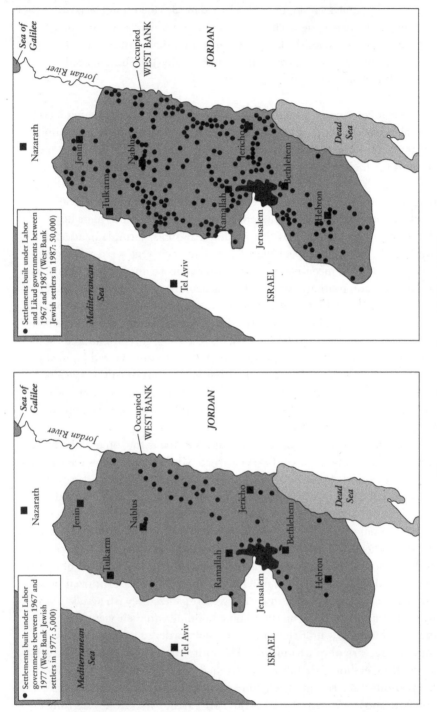

**Change in settlements from 1967 to 1987**

*Source: Adapted from Foundation for Middle East Peace/Jan de Jong*

*Days: Fundamentalism and the Struggle for the Temple Mount* documents the history and religious worldview of these activist Jewish fundamentalists. Gorenberg also details the powerful convergence between the Jewish extremists in Israel and an extensive network of tens of millions of evangelical and fundamentalist Christians who embrace a similar theological worldview. These Christians believe the rebuilding of the Temple is one of the final events preceding the second coming of Christ. We will take a closer look at the extensive and powerful political influence of these Western Christians later in this chapter and in Chapter 9.[19]

Along with the confiscation of land and massive expansion of settlements during the 1980s, Israeli government actions—whether motivated by legitimate security concerns or a desire to consolidate territory or facilitate a substantial demographic shift in percentages of Jews and non-Jews in the occupied territories—systematically demoralized and inflamed Palestinians by targeted deportation of leaders, administrative detention of thousands of people (for up to six months with no charges filed), demolition of homes, and repeated and unpredictable closure of schools, businesses, and even towns, along with other forms of collective punishment. These actions clearly contributed to the exodus of many Palestinians who had the means to depart. I have personally witnessed dozens of blatant forms of physical harassment and intimidation by soldiers, and more frequently by heavily armed settlers. Life under military occupation has been well chronicled by both Israelis and Palestinians.[20]

Palestinian resistance both within and outside the occupied territories often included violence directed at Israeli soldiers and settlers. When individual or organized groups of Palestinians lashed out at those they accused of oppressing and brutalizing them, Israel's usual response was to apply even tougher measures. The cycle of mistrust and violence continued to be fueled in this process. In my experience working both with Israelis and Palestinians over 30 years, there is a painfully clear pattern for the Arabs living under occupation: soldiers and settlers who deliberately intimidate, harass, and exploit indigenous Arabs have almost always acted with impunity, except for highly visible situations where violent extremists such as Baruch Goldstein and Ami Popper[21] intentionally committed mass murder.

This daily, on-the-ground dynamic is often overshadowed, of course, by the larger narrative of Israel's legitimate need for security in the face of harsh rhetoric and terrorist actions on the part of seemingly intransigent Palestinians. The unfolding realities have been far more complex—and even hopeful in various ways. A number of positive steps have been taken since the first Palestinian *intifada* or uprising, which began in 1987, and

Israeli negotiations with the PLO over the past two decades. Even so, refusal by some Palestinian leaders to recognize Israel, coupled with hundreds of rocket and suicide attacks on Israeli soldiers and civilians, reinforce understandable fears among Israeli Jews and their strongest advocates. In the past decade, most of the harshest language and deadly military actions have come from the Gaza-based, religiously inspired leaders of HAMAS. For Israeli Jews victimized by a suicide bombing or a rocket fired into a civilian population by members of HAMAS, the action is an all-too-real manifestation of religious-based rationales for lethal behavior.

## The Politics of Israel and the United States

Various leaders within Israel and successive U.S. presidents from Jimmy Carter to Barack Obama have protested the settlers' violent actions and their systematic effort to create irreversible "facts on the ground." The Oslo Accords of 1993, in particular, were a point where the United States was visibly requiring both Israelis and Palestinians to address their respective policies and tactics directly with the goal of a durable negotiated peace settlement. The image of Rabin and Arafat shaking hands in the presence of President Clinton on the White House lawn conveyed this powerfully. Rabin's assassination and the subsequent behavior of many in Gush Emunim exposed how a peace agreement directly threatens their vision for the Jewish state in all of Palestine.

On balance, U.S. policies have spoken louder than statements opposing settlements as a key to moving the peace process forward. These same administrations that protest settlements have continued to direct more than $3 billion a year in aid to Israel. Although there has been ongoing, vigorous debate within Israel about policies in the occupied territories, few American political leaders voiced public criticism of Israel for facilitating the extremist settlers. Why? Criticizing Israel has been political suicide in the United States. Senator Charles Percy of Illinois, Congressman Paul Findley of Illinois, and Congressman Paul McCloskey of California became the poster boys for what happens to incumbents who get too visible or vocal in ways that are not deemed "pro-Israel."[22] In 2002, two incumbent African American members of Congress—Cynthia McKinney of Georgia and Earl Hilliard of Alabama—were targeted as anti-Israel. Both were defeated in their reelection bids. Well-organized and well-financed pro-Israel political action committees, with support from Jewish and Christian constituencies in America, focused their national resources and influence on these Congressional races.

The smear campaign against former President Jimmy Carter following the release of his 2006 book *Palestine: Peace Not Apartheid*,[23] was widespread and unrelenting. Despite his deep ties to Israel and three decades of dedicated service in support of human rights, free and fair elections, and Middle East peacemaking, Carter was assailed relentlessly as anti-Israel or anti-Semitic. Even so, Carter's credibility on Middle East and human rights issues combined with numerous media interviews help open more public debate about U.S. and Israeli policies that may be inhibiting the search for peace.

Carter's book helped pave the way for a vigorous response to the pro-Israel lobby that John Mearsheimer and Stephen Walt precipitated with their 2007 book *The Israel Lobby and U.S. Foreign Policy*. Mearsheimer and Walt, distinguished chaired professors at the University of Chicago and Harvard University, respectively, detailed specific and multiple ways in which the pro-Israel lobby has influenced Congress and every president since Richard Nixon.[24] It is vital to understand that the pro-Israel advocates have constituted what may be *the* most powerful and successful lobbying group in Washington, DC, for three decades. These advocates know, as most experts agree, that the United States is the key actor, and perhaps the only one capable of facilitating a negotiated settlement between Israel and the Palestinians. The forcefully constructive role the United States played in the process leading to the 1993 Oslo Accords validates this view.[25] The pro-Israel lobby knows well what is at stake; it is devoted to fending off undesirable alternatives and making sure that U.S. involvement supports its aims. The national debate generated by books like the two just mentioned, however, has helped open a wider dialogue about the U.S. role in facilitating what is best for Israel, for the Palestinians, and for neighboring states.

In addition to AIPAC (the American Israel Public Affairs Committee), the well-known leader of pro-Israel groups, numerous other Jewish and evangelical Christian organizations are at the heart of this phenomenon. The Rev. Stephen Sizer's 2004 book *Christian Zionism: Road Map to Armageddon?* asserts that "Christian Zionism is at least ten times larger than Jewish Zionism."[26] Without question, the political influence of uncritical evangelical Christian support for Israel is formidable. During the 1984 presidential primary season, a bill was introduced in Congress that would have required the United States to move its embassy from Tel Aviv to Jerusalem. Although the Israelis were not asking for this, the issue became a litmus test of one's support for Israel in the U.S. Congress. The Reagan administration opposed the legislation since the status of Jerusalem was one of the key issues to be addressed in any negotiated settlement. U.S. officials also knew that any unilateral move such as this would be like lighting a match in a room full of explosives, given the deep religious ties to Jerusalem that Muslims worldwide share with Jews and Christians. As the Middle East director at the National Council of Churches, based in New York, I gave congressional testimony in support of the Reagan administration and in opposition to the proposed legislation. Father Bryan Hehir, representing the U.S. Catholic Conference of Bishops, also testified in the same vein. The others on the panel for the three-hour hearing included Thomas Dine, head of AIPAC; and Moral Majority leader Jerry Falwell. A host of evangelical Christian organizations strongly endorsed the effort to move the embassy to Jerusalem.

To present balanced information and a voice for all people caught in the conflict—one that was both pro-Israel and pro-Palestinian—a small group of Christian leaders established Churches for Middle East Peace (CMEP) in 1985. Today CMEP is a well-known and respected resource on Capitol Hill representing 23 Christian denominations and organizations, including Presbyterians, Methodists, Quakers, Greek Orthodox, and Unitarians.[27] Individual denominations have also studied the situation and made their positions clear, often putting them in conflict with pro-Israel lobbying groups. The Presbyterian Church (USA), for instance, has been sharply criticized for documenting many of the same points about settlements and treatment of Palestinians living under military occupation for more than 40 years. At the Presbyterian General Assembly in July 2010, their Middle East Study Committee released a comprehensive two-year study that focused on Israel/Palestine within the broader context of the Middle East. The study was strongly criticized by the Jewish Council for Public Affairs and various individuals as an egregious diatribe against Israel. The report is labeled as "one-sided," "distorted," "biased," and "insulting." Some of the sharp criticisms are arguments from silence. In other words, the Presbyterian study committee report was assailed for things it doesn't say, while the critic interprets what that means.[28]

Meanwhile, millions of U.S. Christians are guided by a theological orientation that equates contemporary Israel with biblical Israel and interprets virtually every event as a sign connected to God's unfolding plan for the consummation of human history. The theological scheme, called "premillennial dispensationalism," became a dominant interpretive framework for many evangelical and fundamentalist Protestant Christians during the past century.[29] Lindsey's The Late Great Planet Earth was a major catalyst in popularizing this theological perspective to millions of people in the years following the 1967 war between Israel and the neighboring Arab states. According to this view, history is divided into seven major time periods, or dispensations. We are now on the verge of entering the sixth dispensation, a seven-year period in which the world will suffer in the face of great turmoil, war, and famine. Lindsey and many other writers and TV ministers argue that a number of the prophetic signs in the Old Testament have been fulfilled; the last pieces of the puzzle—including the rebuilding of the Temple in Jerusalem—are now being put in place. At the end of the seven years, they believe Jesus will return to earth and lead the forces of good against the armies of Satan in a cataclysmic battle near Megiddo (Armageddon) in northern Israel.

The popularity of this theological frame of reference can be measured in the staggering sales of the "Left Behind" books by authors Tim LaHaye and Jerry Jenkins.[30] These fictional, but ostensibly biblically based, stories detail life during the seven-year tribulation leading up to Jesus' triumphal return in Israel to establish a thousand-year reign of peace on earth. One of the most visible and animated advocates of this theology is Pastor John Hagee of San Antonio. In Chapter 9, we examine Hagee's views and formidable efforts to shape political decisions in both the United States and Israel.

## The Jewish State in the 21st Century

What will be the status of the world's only Jewish state in the near future? Will the Jewish character of Israel be defined primarily by leaders of Gush Emunim and the "biblical position" articulated by Protestant fundamentalists such as Lindsey, LaHaye, and Hagee, or by others whose religious identity and priorities are shaped by another "biblical worldview," namely the prophetic call for justice, righteousness, compassion, and humility? Is peace among Israel, the Palestinians, and the neighboring Arab states possible? What are the most likely parameters for a negotiated peace settlement? These interconnected questions loom large.

The most widely held view centers on a two-state solution: the Jewish state of Israel alongside a Palestinian Arab state. The two-state model is rooted in the UN partition plan prior to Israeli statehood. The line defining the two states, the so-called Green Line, however, is based on the pre-1967 borders of Israel determined by armistice agreements in 1949–50. In various negotiations over recent decades, it is clear that there will have to be some modifications along the Green Line. The nature and extent of the modifications have been complicated by the settlements in the occupied West Bank. Few people envision dismantling of the suburban settlements around Jerusalem, but advocates of a two-state solution do see the need to dismantle many of the West Bank settlements. Given the hostility from Jewish fundamentalists when settlements in the Sinai were abandoned in 1982 and Gaza in 2005, the task of undoing the "facts on the ground" in the West Bank is daunting.

In addition to the settlements, another major obstacle now figures prominently in the mix: the security fence or separation wall that Israel constructed between 2002 and 2010. The highly controversial separation barrier project was implemented ostensibly to protect Israelis from suicide bombers and other attacks originating in the West Bank—and its supporters claim that it has done so. Most Palestinians and other opponents of the separation barrier call it the "Apartheid Wall." The whole enterprise is complicated further by the fact that the wall deviates from the Green Line by anywhere from 200 meters to as much as 20 kilometers. In many instances, these deviations have been made either to encircle Palestinian towns or to incorporate West Bank settlements on the Israeli side of the wall. Approximately 30,000 West Bank Palestinians have been fenced inside the wall and therefore cut off from their communities, and in many instances from their fields.

Israeli proponents of a peace process with Palestinians suggest that changes can be made to the route of the fence in the course of negotiating a settlement. Interestingly, many of the West Bank settlers have opposed the separation barrier on the grounds that it severely inhibits their goal of complete sovereignty over Judea and Samaria as part of Greater Israel. Consequently, for reasons differing with the faction, the massive separation barrier raises major questions about the economic viability of what might constitute a future Palestinian state. Even so, the two-state solution continues to be a widely supported option in the international community of nations. President George W. Bush repeatedly endorsed the two-state solution during his tenure in office. After assuming office in 2009, President Obama underscored the U.S. opposition to Israeli settlements, Palestinian "incitement against Israel," and commitment to a negotiated settlement leading to two independent states.[31]

The Obama administration pressed forward despite enormous pressures arising from ongoing wars in Iraq and Afghanistan, a severe global economic recession, and an ambitious domestic legislative agenda. On September 1–2, 2010, Obama and Secretary of State Hillary Clinton met with four key Middle East leaders—Israeli Prime Minister Netanyahu, Palestinian Authority President Mahmoud Abbas, King Abdullah II of

Jordan, and Egyptian President Hosni Mubarak—as the United States convened face-to-face negotiations for the first time in almost two years. The participants agreed to a one-year time frame to resolve the four key "final status" issues that have been in dispute since they were identified in the Camp David peace process of 1979: the status of Jerusalem in relation to the two states, borders for a Palestinian state, the right of return for Palestinians who fled their homes during times of conflict, and specific steps to ensure Israel's security.

Numerous knowledgeable individuals, groups, organizations, and countries have worked for three decades or more on the details necessary to hammer out a negotiated, two-state solution. One of the most comprehensive and well-publicized plans was unveiled in 2003 by two high-level participants in earlier official negotiations. Yossi Belin, a former minister in the Israeli government, and Yasser Abed Rabboo, a former minister of the Palestinian authority, presented the "Geneva Accord" in October. The unofficial negotiation process had been supported by then Palestinian Authority leader Arafat and by many world leaders. Although Israeli Prime Minister Sharon vehemently rejected the whole project, the initiative undermined the frequently repeated refrain among those Israelis who protest that "there is no one to talk to" on the other side. And it revealed that well-intentioned people could constructively address many of the contentious issues.[32]

In the past decade, some Israelis, Palestinians, and Middle East analysts have believed that the numerous changes in the West Bank since 1967 effectively eliminate the possibility of a viable Palestinian state.[33] Accordingly, a number of well-informed people on both sides now advocate either a one-state solution or other interim steps to defuse the conflict. As with the two-state solution, support for one state in Israel/Palestine also has a long history. Prior to statehood, some within the Zionist movement—including Judah Magnes, the president of Hebrew University; and the distinguished philosopher Martin Buber—favored this approach. But David Ben Gurion, Israel's first prime minister, and other leaders prevailed in pursuit of an exclusively Jewish, or almost exclusively Jewish, state. In the mid-1960s, the Palestine Liberation Organization supported a single, secular, democratic state in all of Palestine. The PLO position changed in the 1970s in favor of a separate Palestinian state. Continuing hostile rhetoric and military actions aimed at Israel led many Jewish Israelis to fear that a two-state solution would simply amount to a staging ground from which the Palestinians would seek to take over all the land and effectively accomplish the extremists' goal to push Israel into the Mediterranean Sea.

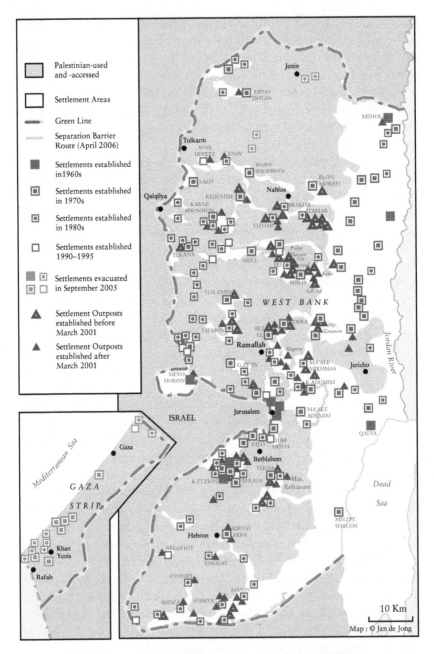

**Settlements established and evacuated, 1967–2008**
*Source: Foundation for Middle East Peace/Jan de Jong*

The Oslo Accords of 1993 have failed to produce a viable two-state outcome. With the growth of Jewish settlements, the rise of HAMAS, and the deep divisions revealed by several elections within the Palestinian community, many former supporters of a two-state approach now advocate for one state. Meron Benvenisti is one such voice. The former deputy mayor of Jerusalem and a prolific author and columnist on Israeli-Palestinian issues, he argues that both Israelis and Palestinians must give up the expectation of full sovereignty and work out a shared polity in the land where both communities have deep roots.[34] Similarly, Sari Nuseibeh, president of the Palestinian al-Quds (Jerusalem) University and a former PLO official, believes the prospect for an independent Palestinian state has diminished as the settlement process increases. If the settlers won't leave, he advocates a one-state solution.[35]

Rabbi Arthur Hertzberg, the celebrated religious leader, scholar, and community leader, spent much of his remarkable six-decades-long career engaging this challenge. Hertzberg understood well the multiple issues converging around the future of the Jewish state and the ongoing Israeli-Palestinian conflict. A leading scholar on Zionism,[36] he was an activist whose commitment to social justice led him to march with Martin Luther King Jr., in 1963, personally challenge the pope and Catholic leaders over Vatican positions on Jews during World War II, and to publicly debate Meir, Begin, and other leaders concerning Israeli policies toward the Palestinians. Hertzberg, who died at age 84 in 2006, served as the rabbi for a congregation in New Jersey for more than 30 years and as a university professor for some 20 years.[37]

Hertzberg was an early and passionate supporter of a two-state solution, first calling for it shortly after 1967 war. At the end of his life, however, he had come reluctantly to the conclusion that a two-state solution was no longer viable. Hertzberg puts forth his analysis and plea in the last of his 13 books, *The Fate of Zionism: A Secular Future for Israel & Palestine*. In this thoughtful book, he underscored conflicting truths that converge in Israel/Palestine, namely that both Jews and Palestinian Arabs have legitimate, though different, claims to the same land. Both communities are here to stay. Israel cannot and must not force Palestinian Arabs out of their homeland. And no one of any political persuasion wants to put an end to the Zionist state. He argued that the most viable way forward now requires direct intervention by the United States because it is "the only sheriff in the global village with the power to 'enforce the law.'" Hertzberg understood well the problems inherent in a one-state solution that could compromise the Jewish character of Israel. Although he acknowledged that a "grand settlement" was not in sight, he insisted that immediate steps must be taken in order to lead both sides away from confrontation and toward accommodation. He believed that it would be possible for both Israelis and Palestinians to deal positively with a better future once peace and stability were established.[38]

The urgency of Hertzberg's appeal is connected to two compelling truths: the central and powerful role of religious extremists on both the Israeli and Palestinian sides, and the daunting prospect of increased access to nuclear weapons. The clock is ticking, and the status quo is not tenable. What to do? With attention to multiple dimensions of the highly charged dynamics in Israel/Palestine and among Jews, Muslims, and Christians who have deep ties to this Holy Land, he pressed the case for a secular future. Hertzberg argued that this is consistent with the vision of the large majority of Zionists and contemporary Israelis as well as most Palestinians historically. The primary obstacle remaining is the dominant role of religious extremists, both Jewish and Muslim.

As a person of faith, Rabbi Hertzberg argued that the mix of religion and politics in contemporary Israel/Palestine is a recipe for certain disaster. In a world full of weapons of mass destruction, he saw that the politics of religious zealots such as the leaders of Gush Emunim, Muslims who believe suicide bombers are martyrs on the way to heaven, and influential premillennial Christian visionaries all offer a clear path toward Armageddon. Descendants of Abraham who are convinced they know precisely what God wants for them and for everyone else connected to Israel/Palestine are capable of lethal actions toward any and all whom they believe are thwarting God's will. Hertzberg reminds us all that religious zealots on a mission from God are quite prepared to put bombs on buses and in marketplaces, or assassinate a prime minister who dares to work for peace.

There are no easy answers or risk-free solutions, but the way forward is not blocked. We know what issues require careful attention and resolution through the many studies that have been done and extensive discussions of every grievance or concern. This much is clear: the shared future of Israel/Palestine will be shaped by whose vision of religion and what kind of politics prevail. Will politically powerful Jews, Christians, and Muslims who believe they possess God's template determine the future state in the Holy Land? Or will Israel/Palestine reflect the convictions of those who draw on their religion to fashion political structures that contemporary circumstances require?

Religion has often been and may yet be an increasingly lethal ingredient in the highly charged Israeli/Palestinian conflict as a countdown to an Armageddon-like conflagration is under way. People of faith and goodwill in all three Abrahamic religions have the resources to fashion a healthy, shared future in the Holy Land. Christians who are guided by Jesus' call to be peacemakers can and should contribute enormously as agents of reconciliation in a broken and hurting world. Today, more than ever, Muslims can and should live out the meaning of Islam as a "religion of peace." And Jews, in Israel and elsewhere, can and should embrace the powerful messages of justice, righteousness, and mercy proclaimed repeatedly by their prophets and take to heart the wisdom and pragmatic guidance of religious and political leaders such as Hertzberg, Rabin, and Weitzman. A viable future for the world's only Jewish state requires nothing less.

# "RENDER UNTO CAESAR"

## RELIGION AND POLITICS IN CHRISTIANITY

WHEN JOHN F. KENNEDY WAS RUNNING for president in 1960, I was 10 years old. Even at that young age, I can clearly remember the sharp questions Kennedy had to field—and the opinions I heard from those around me—about his Roman Catholic faith. Many wondered aloud whether Kennedy's faith would trump his duties as president. Would he defer to the pope on some matters and thus fail to maintain the separation of church and state? I heard some people voicing overt hostility toward Catholicism, speaking of "Catholics" and "Christians" as though they were two different categories. The idea of a Catholic as president was new; the first 34 men elected to the presidency were all Protestant, and three-fourths of them were Presbyterian (10), Episcopalian (9), or Methodist (4).

Growing up in Tulsa with a Jewish grandfather and several close family friends who were Catholic, I heard these "concerns" about Kennedy and now know they made a strong and lasting impression on me. By the time of the 1976 presidential election, I had made the interplay between religion and politics a focus of my academic study both in seminary and in my doctoral program. The spotlight focused on Jimmy Carter, a one-term governor and openly devout Southern Baptist peanut farmer from Plains, Georgia. The October 25 cover of *Newsweek* declared that 1976 was "The Year of the Evangelical." Carter's faith came squarely into view when he confessed in an interview with *Playboy* magazine that he had committed adultery in his heart many times because he had looked upon a lot of women with lust.[1]

As a Baptist minister, I was intrigued by the mocking and befuddled reactions to Carter's candor and his obvious comfort level in talking about Christ and the Bible. I wasn't aware that only three of the 38 presidents before Carter were affiliated with Baptists.[2] By 1980, the role of evangelical Christianity in presidential politics had moved to a new level as all three candidates were born-again, evangelical Christians. In the end, Ronald Reagan defeated both Jimmy Carter and independent candidate John Anderson decisively. Reagan energized the religious right—including what became the Rev. Jerry Falwell's Moral Majority and the Rev. Pat Robertson's Christian Coalition—in ways that transformed the political landscape for the next three decades.[3] (I explore that topic in more detail in the next chapter.)

In 1977, less than a year into Carter's presidency, Egyptian president Anwar Sadat abruptly traveled to Jerusalem and began a U.S.-facilitated peace process with Israel. In the months leading to what came to be known as the Camp David Accords, Carter's personal faith was often visible. His close attachment to the "Holy Land" and determination to facilitate peaceful conflict resolution among the descendants of Abraham were distinguishing features of his presidency.

As someone who was studying about and living in the rapidly changing religious and political landscape in the Middle East at that time, I could see various points of connection in the United States. I started asking Christians how they understood a "Christian" approach to religion and politics. I have continued to ask these kinds of questions for more than 30 years. My unscientific results show that the vast majority of clergy and laypeople reflexively answer by quoting Jesus' statement, "Render therefore unto Caesar the things which are Caesar's; and unto God the things which are God's." When asked to explain what this means, most of the people I talk with immediately tell me that church and state should be separate, and that is the "Christian" model. As we continue to talk, their clarity about what separation of church and state means usually becomes more ambiguous. Most people will illustrate where they think the line should or should not be drawn.[4]

Contemporary European and American approaches to judiciously separating religion and politics in various ways are, for the most part, expressions not inherent in the faith. Rather, they have been framed by a post-Enlightenment worldview. Throughout Christian history, many Christians have advocated clear distinctions between the temporal and spiritual realms, but many others have sought to merge the two. This chapter examines how self-proclaimed followers of Jesus have defined and tried to live out a proper relationship between religion and politics, beginning with the earliest forms of Christianity and on down through the centuries.

## New Testament Principles and the Early Church

Jesus' well-known statement about rendering to Caesar and to God, recorded in the gospels of Matthew, Mark, and Luke, is at once compelling and ambiguous. Although there are differences in the three accounts of Jesus' teaching, the version in Matthew includes the key elements:

> Then went the Pharisees, and took counsel how they might entangle him in his talk. And they sent out unto him their disciples with the Herodians, saying . . . What thinkest thou? Is it lawful to give tribute to Caesar, or not? But Jesus perceived the wickedness, and said, Why tempt ye me, ye hypocrites? Shew me the tribute money. And they brought unto him a penny. And he saith unto them, Whose is this image and superscription? They say unto him, Caesar's. Then he saith unto them, Render therefore unto Caesar the things which are Caesar's; and unto God the things which are God's. When they heard these things they marveled, and left him, and went their way [Matt. 22:15–22, King James Version].

Matthew 22 presents this as the first of three efforts to entrap Jesus. In addition to the question about paying taxes, Jesus was asked about the nature of the resurrection and about which was the greatest commandment. Matthew reports that Jesus' responses "amazed" and "astounded" the crowd. Instead of a "yes" or "no" to the questions about taxes, his response has been interpreted in several ways. It may mean that spiritual obligations are paramount over earthly ones but don't necessarily eliminate them. It can be understood to suggest that the demands of the governing authority are mandatory. It may mean that religious authority must be kept separate from earthly authority. Or, it can be interpreted to favor the view that it is appropriate to support the governing authorities when asked to do so.

Those Jewish Zealots who hoped Jesus would help lead a political uprising were surely disappointed with his response because it didn't support rebellion through nonpayment of taxes. The version of the story in the Gospel of Luke indicates that the purpose of the attempted entrapment was to have grounds for handing him over to the authority of the governor. The issue surfaces again when Luke reports one of the false charges presented to Pontius Pilate was that Jesus opposed payment of taxes.[5] The charge was quite serious; it suggested Jesus was aligned with a Jewish rebel movement against the Roman authorities.

A second important ingredient in the early Christian sense of the relationship between religion and politics is found in the Apostle Paul's

Epistle to the Romans. At the beginning of the 13th chapter, Paul pointedly insists on submission to government authorities:

> Let every person be subject to the governing authorities; for there are no authorities that exist except from God, and those that exist have been instituted by God. Therefore whoever resists authority resists what God has appointed, and those who resist will incur judgment . . . for the same reason you also pay taxes, for the authorities are God's servants, busy with this very thing [i.e., punishing bad conduct]. Pay to all what is due them—taxes to whom taxes are due, revenue to whom revenue is due [Rom. 13:1–2, 6–7].

In a similar vein, the pastoral letter of I Timothy, which purports to be written by Paul, urges followers of Jesus to pray for those in positions of authority:

> First of all, then, I urge that supplications, prayers, intercessions, and thanksgivings be made for everyone, for kings and all who are in high positions, so that we may lead a quiet and peaceable life in all godliness and dignity [I Tim. 2:1–2].

The gospels present Jesus' teachings as focused more on individual behavior than on an overt sociopolitical call to action. He does introduce a radical ethic by calling on followers to love their enemies, pray for those who persecute them, and embrace and help meet the needs of poor and marginalized people in society. Mennonite scholar John Howard Yoder argues persuasively that Jesus teaches and embodies a pacifist—not passive—approach to behavior in the world. Yoder illustrates how this social ethic develops in the early Christian community, most notably in the perspectives and guidance given by the Apostle Paul.[6]

The New Testament gospels do not suggest that Jesus left specific guidelines for institutional organization for his followers. Rather, we can see them working out various issues as they arise. The book of Acts and the letters of Paul offer a window through which we can see the developments shaping the earliest followers of Jesus. Under the leadership of Peter and other apostles, they organized a community designed to meet the needs of everyone. They gave up private ownership of their possessions to share everything in common, including daily distribution of food.[7] The growth of the church created logistical problems that led to new organizational structures. Acts 6, for instance, reports on conflict between the Jewish and non-Jewish believers over perceived uneven distribution of food. To better meet the needs and free up the apostles from administering this daily task, they decided to set aside (or ordain) others for this service. Ordination of the first deacons began a new organizational structure in the church.

The apostles disagreed initially about those for whom the Good News of Jesus' life, death, and resurrection was intended. Was it only for the Jews? Or was this a universal message of hope and salvation for all people?[8] Paul and Peter's conviction about the universality of the gospel prevailed. The first generation of Christians encountered many theological and practical challenges. Their circumstances were complicated further by the much-anticipated imminent return of Jesus. Various sayings of Jesus in the gospels seem to suggest the coming of the Kingdom of God would be experienced by "this generation." Paul's first letter to the Thessalonians, the oldest of Paul's letters, reassures the faithful that Jesus' second coming could occur at any time.[9] The second letter to the Thessalonians reflects the intense hope of Jesus' return but warns believers to keep working and not sit idly in anticipation. II Thessalonians also identifies another major problem for the first generation of Christians: persecution.

Continuing confrontations with Jewish leaders, and increasingly with the Roman governing authorities, are woven into the narrative of the first century. A major theme in the Epistle to the Hebrews addresses the problem of persecution directly and admonishes these second-generation Christians not to "fall away." Hebrews states that "it is impossible to restore again to repentance" those who have tasted of the heavenly gift of God and then become apostates.[10] Persecution of Christians is a continuing theme throughout the first three centuries. There may have been as many as 10 major waves of persecution, between the emperors Nero in 64 CE and Diocletian in 303 CE.

Paul's views about earthly authorities being in place by God's hand is particularly curious. Why would he tell early Christians to obey a government that was persecuting them and that required them to worship the emperor as a god? Several factors appear to be at work simultaneously. Many Roman provincial leaders had little interest in what was usually perceived to be a Jewish sect so long as their beliefs and practices did not create problems for the state. On some occasions, Jewish leaders initiated the persecution of Christians either directly or through complaints to the Roman rulers. In this context, and in view of the early Christian community's focus on a kingdom not of this world, Paul's views are more understandable. He was a Roman citizen. Although he endured many hardships,[11] the relative peace of the Roman Empire made it possible for him and others to travel and start churches in many lands bordering the northern and eastern shores of the Mediterranean.

Paul's insistence that earthly authority is in place through God's actions also addresses a larger theological issue that arises in all religions, namely theodicy. *Theodicy* refers to the "justice of God" in the face of human suffering. The problem is particularly acute for Jews, Christians, Muslims, and other monotheists. If God is Omniscient, Omnipotent, and Omnipresent, what is God's relationship to evil and injustice? If God knows everything and is all-powerful, is God responsible for all that happens? Does God knowingly allow or even cause birth defects, tragic illness, untimely death, and "natural" disasters? For Paul, God is the God of all creation and of all that happens, so it makes sense for him to declare that earthly leaders are in place because of divine intent and action. He is not the last in Christian history to see the world and life in this way.

After the apostles and the first generation of Christians passed away without experiencing the physical return of Jesus, Christian communities continued to spread and grow. But these emerging churches could no longer seek guidance from those who had walked with Jesus. The disputes and differing views reflected in Acts and in many New Testament letters were a harbinger of things to come. We know that there were many types of Christianity in the first three centuries. These early Christians expended a great deal of energy determining which doctrines and practices would be deemed "orthodox" and which would be considered "heretical."[12] Many Christian communities experienced sporadic persecution at the hands of the state, but the structures of the state also enabled the nascent communities to grow in the service of a kingdom not of this world. Even so, these early Christians were wary of close association or entanglements with governing political rulers, including a predominantly pacifist stance on military service and warfare. All that changed in the fourth century with the emperor Constantine.

## Constantine and the Holy Roman Empire

With several edicts beginning in 303 CE, the Roman Emperor Diocletian, who insisted on absolute power as a semidivine ruler, promulgated the final, systematic, and widespread wave of persecution of Christians. Clergy were targeted, churches and books were burned, and all subjects under his rule were required to sacrifice to the Roman gods. Everything changed with the emergence of Constantine. Inspired by a dream in which he saw a white cross and the words "in this sign you will conquer," he fought under the sign of the cross and defeated his rival Maxentius in 312. Constantine, whose mother, Helena,[13] was a Christian, embraced the God of Christianity. He supported the Edict of Milan in 313, a directive in which freedom of worship was guaranteed to all, including Christians, and possessions lost by churches during Diocletian's rule were to be restored.

Constantine consolidated power and became sole emperor of the Roman Empire in 324, established Byzantium (later renamed Constantinople and now Istanbul) as his capitol in 330, and sought to unite political and military rule with the Christian churches. As he was drawn into contentious doctrinal debates within the churches, Constantine played a major role in what became the first of the great ecumenical councils, that at Nicaea in 325, where orthodox doctrines were codified. (One result was the Nicene Creed, which is a statement of faith still used by many Christians today.) Only 22 years after the start of Diocletian's persecution, Christianity was becoming the official religion of the empire. Rather than paying a high price for being a follower of Jesus, citizens henceforth might be in danger if they were *not* believers, or if they promoted doctrines deemed heretical by those in power.

As pressures from tribes in Germany intensified in the fourth and fifth centuries, the Western provinces of the Roman Empire grew vulnerable, culminating in the sack of Rome by Visigoths in 410 and Vandals in 455. The remnant of the empire in Rome's Eastern provinces remained strong for several centuries as the Byzantine Empire.

Around what had been the Roman Empire, particularly in the East, new forms of Christianity multiplied and thrived. Early in the fourth century, for example, the Armenian people collectively embraced Christianity. The Armenians remained a remarkably cohesive community throughout Christian history, joined together by language, culture, and religion despite rarely enjoying political independence. Armenian Christians have functioned under the political rule of Persians, Arabs, Turks, and Russians for most of the last 17 centuries.

Alexandria, on Egypt's Mediterranean coast, was one of the four preeminent centers or sees in early Christianity. The Coptic Orthodox Church in Egypt traces its origin to St. Mark, who visited Egypt and spread the gospel to the Egyptians in the first century. Two centuries later, Egyptian Christians were profoundly affected by the persecutions of Diocletian. This ancient Christian community was then among those declared heretical at the Council of Chalcedon in 451 because of its strong emphasis on the divinity of Christ.[14] But the Coptic, Armenian, Syrian, and Ethiopian Orthodox churches continued to grow and later became known as the Oriental Orthodox. Because of their separation from both the Roman Catholic and other major Orthodox churches (such as the

Greek, Serbian, and Russian Orthodox churches, which are often called "Eastern Orthodox"), many Western Christians know very little about the history, polity, and theology of these ancient communities of faith.

The Coptic, Armenian, and Syrian Orthodox have always made up the majority among Christian communities in the Middle East. As director of the Middle East Office for the National Council of Churches during the 1980s, I worked closely with the leadership of these churches—the Coptic pope (in Cairo), the Armenian catholicos (in Beirut), and the Syrian Orthodox patriarch (in Damascus)—along with many bishops, pastors, and congregations. As with other long-standing communions in the Middle East such as the Greek Catholics (Melkites) and Assyrians, these self-standing churches have highly developed organizational structures. But they remain largely independent of their respective political systems. The reason is simple: the Oriental Orthodox churches have functioned in settings where others exercised political power over their communities of faith.

These Middle Eastern Christian communities parallel somewhat the experiences of Jewish communities living in the Diaspora. They have maintained and perpetuated strong communities of faith while continually negotiating space for their churches while others held political power over them. For several centuries, they were ruled by the Byzantine Empire; from the mid-seventh century until today, these churches have been minority communities in predominantly Muslim countries. The specific dynamics with the different churches varied significantly over time. There have been many periods when tensions were high and the minority Christian communities functioned under some duress, along with periods of peaceful coexistence. The continuing vitality of these Christian communities today speaks to their historical flexibility in negotiating the challenges of religion and politics in an ever-changing landscape. The Maronite Church is the one major exception among Middle Eastern Christian communities. Until the mid-20th century, the Maronites constituted the largest religious community in the Lebanon region for many centuries.[15]

## The Rise of the Papacy

During the three centuries before the emergence of Islam, the centralization of the Eastern churches that began with Constantine increased. Constantinople was growing in importance as the locus of imperial control, but the bishops of Rome continued to gain prominence and power. The primacy of Rome was due in large part to its close association with both Peter and Paul and its history during the formative centuries of Christianity.

Constantine's rule was also critical for the development of the papacy. As the Western provinces and Rome itself were in turmoil, papal elections became connected with the emperor in Byzantium. Popes were not considered valid unless and until the emperor formally approved them. The Catholic theologian and historian Richard McBrien identifies actions by three influential popes that helped set the stage for a new wedding of religion and politics in what came to be known as the Holy Roman Empire of Western Europe:

> Leo I (440–461), "the Great". . . was the first pope to claim to be Peter's heir. . . . Leo is also celebrated for his courageous personal confrontation with Attila the Hun near Mantua in 452, when the warrior was laying waste to northern Italy and preparing to move south toward Rome. Heading a delegation from the Roman Senate, Leo persuaded Attila to withdraw beyond the Danube. . . . Gelasius I (492–496) . . . was the first to assume the title "Vicar of Christ" . . . [and] advance the theory of the "two powers" or the "two swords" (referring to the authority of the pope in both the sacred and temporal spheres)—a theory that would be so influential in the Middle Ages. . . . Gregory I (590–604), "the Great" . . . took the lead and fashioned a truce . . . when the imperial exarch (viceroy) in Ravenna proved incapable of doing anything about the Lombard threat. Gregory became virtually the civil as well as the spiritual ruler of Rome. He negotiated treaties, paid the troops, and appointed generals and governors.[16]

Another manifestation of the intertwining of religion and politics is seen around the beginning of the sixth century, when Clovis (d. 511 CE), king of the Franks, converted to Christianity. Clovis and most of his followers were then baptized. Although he was known to be ruthless and cruel, his military success was linked to religion, and he benefited from the assistance of bishops in governing his lands. The next step in an emerging paradigm for religion and politics came during the eighth and ninth centuries. On Christmas day in 800 CE, Pope Leo III crowned Charlemagne, king of the Franks, as emperor. Charlemagne's coronation ended papal dependence on the Byzantine emperors and established a new power in support of the Church. Charlemagne, whose realm included most of today's France, Germany, Belgium, Holland, and Switzerland, thought of himself as a new version of the Israelite kings such as David and Josiah, the Jewish king who rejected idolatry and sought to reform worship in Israel. His successors further conflated their religious and political power, likening themselves to Solomon, who ruled with divine wisdom; and Moses, who promulgated God's laws.[17]

McBrien laments that the period from 800 to 1073 was "marred by papal corruption (including simony, i.e., the buying and selling of church offices, nepotism, lavish lifestyles, concubinage, brutality, even murder) and the domination of the papacy by German kings and by powerful Roman aristocratic families."[18] There were, happily, exceptions to the rule, with popes and emperors making positive contributions in various ways. Far more often than not, however, these centuries present case studies of confused and lethal combinations of politics and religion.

In an effort to halt abuses and cleanse the Church, Pope Gregory VII (1073–1085) launched a major reform movement. In the process, he claimed papal power in all matters and essentially turned the papacy into a monarchial office with more focus on enforcing the laws of the Church. Building on this model of an absolute monarch, popes Innocent III (1198–1216) and Boniface VIII (1295–1303) claimed authority not only over the Church but also over their realm of Christendom covering Western Europe.[19] Some of the most influential (and some of the most notorious) popes in history lived between the 11th and 15th centuries. The combination of religion and politics was especially deadly and enduring in this era, particularly in two multicentury movements that evoke images of religiously inspired violence: crusade and inquisition.

The first crusade was launched in 1095 after an impassioned sermon in which Pope Urban II called on the Franks of Germany and France to march to the East, ostensibly to expel the Islamic Turks from Jerusalem. For three years, crusaders terrorized and massacred Jews, Muslims, and many Orthodox Christians along the way. Once the fanatical warriors made it all the way to Jerusalem, they breached the walls of the city, set fire to the Great Synagogue where the Jews had gathered for safety, and slaughtered Muslims in the al-Aqsa mosque and throughout the city. One eyewitness, Raymond of Agiles, described the gory scene in which "piles of heads, hands, and feet were to be seen in the streets of the city . . . [and] men rode in blood up to their knees."[20] These shocking events set in motion a series of Muslim countercrusades and new crusades that continued for centuries. In addition to the Holy Land, some crusades were mounted to confront Muslims in Spain and parts of Europe. These wars initiated by the leadership of the Catholic Church reflect a striking reversal from the teachings of Jesus and the pacifist tradition of the first three centuries. Rather than doing penance for participating in war, crusaders were motivated by the Church with the promise of an indulgence (remission of a temporal penalty due for a forgiven sin) for their "service." There were few lines separating religion from politics in these massive military ventures.

A little more than a century after the first crusade, the Church established guidelines that were put in place for the Office of the Inquisition. Ostensibly employed to protect the doctrines of the Church from error and potentially to save people from hell, tribunals were commissioned to discover and prosecute heretics. The accused were normally not informed of the charges against them or allowed to call witnesses in their defense. Inquisitors in various settings worked in conjunction with secular authorities charged to carry out their sentence—including slow burning at the stake. If an accused person was deemed obdurate, inquisitors were allowed to use torture to extract a confession. Records indicate the confession rate was somewhere around 90%. The most notorious and widespread implementation of such inquisitions occurred in Spain during the 15th and 16th centuries. King Ferdinand and Queen Isabella (the same rulers who supported Christopher Columbus and his explorations) orchestrated a systematic assault on Jews and Muslims. For example, in 1492, the same year Columbus sailed West, Ferdinand and Isabella decreed that all Jews had four months to convert or flee Spain. More than a century later, religious and political leaders continued to collaborate in their prosecution of *conversos* and *moriscos*, the terms for Jews and Muslims who had embraced Christianity under duress. Salvation for lost souls was not the only consideration driving these cruel processes. The assets of the accused and their families were often subject to confiscation.[21]

By the 19th century, most of the horrific practices associated with the Office of Inquisition were no longer employed. Even so, the office remained an official part of the Vatican structure until 1965, when Pope Paul VI changed it to the Office of the Congregation for the Doctrine of the Faith. Three decades later, Pope John Paul II opened up some of the archival records detailing the almost-800-year history of the Inquisition. The deadly use of church-state powers directed at all kinds of "heretics" was one of many types of abuse that fueled the Protestant Reformation.

## The Protestant Reformation and John Calvin's Geneva

The Protestant Reformation was not one event. It occurred over many decades, taking various forms in multiple settings and with numerous differences among leaders who were breaking with the Roman Catholic Church.[22] The two most prominent names and widely influential reform movements of the 16th century were those of Martin Luther in Germany and the French theologian John Calvin in Switzerland. Calvin was only eight years old when Luther nailed his famous 95 theses on the Witten-berg door in 1517. Luther's challenge to the pope and the Catholic Church on the abuses of selling indulgences (rather than penance) for remission of sins is widely seen as the tipping point for the Reformation. Twenty-four years later, in 1541, Calvin implemented his distinctive vision for church and state in Geneva.

John Calvin was one of six children in a French Catholic family. At age 13, he began training for the priesthood. After a few years he shifted his study to law but later came back to theology. His break with being "obsti-nately addicted to the superstitions of the papacy" most probably occurred in 1533.[23] By 1536, Calvin had produced the first edition of his *Institutes of the Christian Religion,* a comprehensive theological treatise that would undergo many changes and expansions during his life.[24] Passing through Geneva in 1536, he became convinced of God's providential hand at work and stayed to lend leadership in Geneva's nascent reform movement. Calvin argued, like other Protestant reformers, that the New Testament and early Christian communities offered principles and models for reform. Not everyone agreed with his vision. He left in 1538 for a three-year pas-torate in Strasbourg but in 1541 returned to Geneva. At this juncture, he was able to persuade the city council to embrace his Ecclesiastical Ordi-nances, which were regulations to govern the community. Calvin assumed he would remain in Geneva for a few months, or possibly a couple of years; it turned out to be his home for the final 24 years of his life.

Because human depravity was a principal tenet of Calvin's theology, an essential key to serving God required that human will be subordinated to God's will. The Ecclesiastical Ordinances were the structure to discipline individuals in the reformed church of Geneva's city-state. Pastors and elders (selected by pastors and confirmed by the civil government) formed a disciplinary institution called a Consistory. Extensive records from Geneva offer vivid details of the scope of its weekly meetings. In addition to sharp rebuke or severe punishment for anyone expressing opinions con-trary to the doctrines of the church as articulated by Calvin, for not attend-ing church, or for failing to master the catechism, according to Church historian Owen Chadwick, there were other elements of their mandate:

> The consistory was indefatigable in its maintenance of the moral order. Its members tried to suppress fortune-telling and sorcery, were pitiless toward merchants who defrauded their clients, denounced short measures, excessive rates of interest, a doctor who extracted large fees, a tailor who overcharged, a traveling Englishman . . . gave opinions on the bank rate, on the level of interest for war loan, on

exports and imports, on speeding the law courts, on the cost of living and shortage of candles.[25]

Petitions for divorce and cases involving charges of adultery were often graphic. Men and women declared guilty of adultery could be put to death.[26] Imposing a death sentence or weighing in on the bank rates and all types of "moral" issues served to blur the lines between church and state. Calvin understood the civil and religious authorities as having differing roles, but they were clearly intertwined. Religious truth and doctrinal purity, however, constituted the final authority.

The church was responsible for combating sin, assisting believers in the process of becoming sanctified, and protecting the integrity of the church. Secular magistrates were to secure peace and tranquility in Geneva. But the magistrates were also obliged to carry out punishments for idolatry, sacrilege, and blasphemy as determined by the ecclesiastical authorities.[27]

The case of Michael Servetus was one of the most celebrated during Calvin's tenure. Servetus challenged the reformers concerning the nature of the divine Word and Jesus the man, the nature of the Trinity, and the legitimacy of persecuting perceived heretics. Calvin refuted Servetus in the process of revising *Institutes* in 1546, and Servetus replied by sending Calvin a copy of the *Institutes* covered with corrective annotations. Calvin was not amused. A few years later, in 1553, on his way to seek asylum in Naples, Servetus unwisely traveled through Geneva. At Calvin's insistence, he was arrested. Servetus was subsequently convicted of heresy and put to death by fire. Although Calvin has been strongly criticized for centuries for this act, such events were more common than most today imagine:

> Servetus suffered the fate that hundreds of heretics and Anabaptists suffered at the hands of Protestant authorities. . . . Calvin was convinced, and all the reformers shared this conviction, that it was the duty of a Christian magistrate to put to death blasphemers who kill the soul, just as they punished murderers who kill the body.[28]

John Calvin's theology famously included double predestination. He was certain that God had ordained some for salvation and some for eternal damnation. Those who were the beneficiaries of God's unmerited favor would persevere in the process of sanctification. Heretics such as Servetus who denied "true doctrine" as defined by Calvin could not be allowed to confuse people by introducing doubts about the Trinity or the divinity of Christ. This was also the rationale behind the brutal Spanish Inquisition, which began a half-century earlier, and the Salem witch trials of 1692–1693 in America. Bolstered by the cocksure certainty of what God's truth demands, Protestants and Catholics alike have often enthusiastically embraced lethal forms of religious conviction.

Whatever one's assessment of Calvin's theology, vision, and institutional practices, the Geneva experiment and numerous subsequent Calvinist derivations are notable on several levels. First, his approach presumes that the Bible and the practices of the early church are indispensable resources for developing institutional structures to manifest God's will in society. Second, one can easily see how his efforts are shaped by the context of his era. The iterations of his *Institutes* reflect his engagement with various issues being addressed by Protestant reformers and their critics. He is clearly in dialogue and often in disagreement with leaders of other reform movements. They share a commitment to challenge perceived superstitions and abuses by the Roman Catholic Church but are far from united on many critical issues, such as how to understand the Eucharist and whether or not church leaders can or should excommunicate delinquent members. Finally, Calvin works with new, though already existing, civil authorities to fashion an innovative approach to religion and politics. Prior to his first sojourn in Geneva, a localized civil government authority had recently replaced the long-standing medieval government of the prince and bishop. Calvin's efforts were often in tension with the civil authorities, but he worked within the context of the city-state in the mid-16th century. He created a template he believed was rooted in scripture and early Christian practices to meet the needs and theological understandings of his time and place.

The religious fragmentation manifest during the Protestant Reformation contributed mightily to social, political, and economic upheaval throughout Europe. In some settings, erosion of the Catholic Church's power increased the strength of monarchs. In other contexts, popular uprisings challenged political, social, and economic authorities. Multiple conflicts erupted during the 150 years following Calvin, including the horrific and convoluted Thirty Years' War between 1618 and 1648. Religious and politically fueled conflicts permanently dismantled the unity of the Holy Roman Empire. The 1648 Treaty of Westphalia ended the anarchy; the balance of power in France, Germany, and other parts of Europe had shifted, and equal political rights for Calvinists, Lutherans, and Catholics were ostensibly affirmed. But tensions and conflicts were far from over. Religious zealotry continued to intertwine with political and economic exploitation in multiple ways. The stage was set for a dramatic shift where sources of knowledge and authority as well as abuses of power and religious tradition would be subject to rational scrutiny. An entirely new framework for religion and politics in Western Christian lands was emerging. This was the era of the Enlightenment.

## The Enlightenment: Bridge to the Modern World

The beginning phase of the Enlightenment can be dated to the 1680s, the decade in which French King Louis XIV took up residence at Versailles and such influential thinkers as Sir Isaac Newton and John Locke were publishing books. Throughout the next century, scientific inquiry and religious debates converged with oppressive political excesses and increasing dissent to undermine traditional assumptions about both religion and politics in Europe. Rather than religious dogma promulgated by Catholic or Protestant leaders or acquiescence to the divine right of kings, Enlightenment thinkers promoted reason as the reliable source of knowledge. This worldview was made possible, in part, in the two centuries after the printing press made the Bible and other publications widely available and the reformers' emphasis on individual responsibility before God had taken root. Thinking for oneself and engaging in rational discourse on all subjects were more than ideals. These thinkers and activists prized justice and labored for the material and moral betterment of humanity. The Enlightenment fueled social and political changes in which individual human rights were elevated and revolutionary movements produced new forms of governance in Britain, France, the United States, and elsewhere.

Enlightenment thinkers were highly skeptical of organized religion and of the superstition, abuses of power, and misery to which it had contributed in previous centuries. Although some rejected religion altogether and others were sympathetic to atheism but less vehement, many more pursued various forms of "enlightened" religion in which reason and faith were compatible. David Sorkin, a scholar of the Enlightenment, summarized the challenge and the vision this way:

> To religious enlighteners, unreasonable meant an exclusive embrace of either reason or faith. Faith untempered by knowledge, or combined with excessively partisan forms, produced intolerant, dogmatic, or enthusiastic religion. . . . Reasonable, by contrast, signified a balance between reason and faith. . . . The idea of natural religion epitomized this coordination of reason and faith. . . . Natural religion emphasized not dogma or precise formulations of belief as represented in creeds or symbolic books but practice and morality.[29]

Many leaders of the Enlightenment (including many of founders of the United States of America) were deists.[30] Their deep commitment to reason led to affirmation of "natural religion" and wariness about claims based on "revelation" and stories of miracles that defy natural laws. This theological perspective put distance between God and the stories of miraculous or supernatural events that contradict rational understanding. Deism also helps with the age-old problem of theodicy. Deists did not need to explain why or how God is actively engaged or responsible for the brutality and religiously motivated destruction that characterized much of Europe's 17th century. In this worldview, God created and ordered the universe but is not now intervening daily in the affairs of the world.

In the context of the still-recent sordid and destructive religious wars of the 17th century and before, Enlightenment thinkers in France, Germany, England, and America sought to encourage respectful toleration of religious differences, identify a common morality, and fashion political systems that would encourage allegiance from a diverse citizenry. Many books have been written detailing their revolt against or significant attempts to modify traditional monarchies and aristocratic elites in the process of fashioning representative forms of government. The French Revolution was such an attempt—a violent one—whereas the political changes in England in the 18th and 19th centuries reflected a slower, more gradual process. For many Enlightenment thinkers, the clearest manifestation of their vision occurred in the revolutionary experiment of creating the United States of America. We will return to look closely at the vision of the founders and the ongoing interplay of religion and politics in the United States in the next chapter.

One of the most powerful symbols of the Enlightenment vision of religious toleration can be seen in Gotthold Lessing's 1779 play *Nathan the Wise*, which offered a highly favorable portrayal of a Jew. Lessing, son of a German Protestant clergyman, studied theology and medicine before turning to writing for the theater. As a deeply committed Enlightenment thinker, he rejected miracles and exalted human reason. Lessing was a good friend of the German Jewish philosopher Moses Mendelssohn, who was the inspiration for the play's central character, Nathan.[31] Lessing and Mendelssohn captured the spirit and hope of the Enlightenment. The vision of tolerance, cooperation, and friendship among Christian sects and across religious lines, though highly controversial at the time, inspired many for more than a century. The vision was destroyed in the 20th century when political power combined with religious hatred to produce the unspeakable horror of the Holocaust.

## Religion and Politics in Christian History

This brief overview of Christian history yields several lessons. The first is that religion and politics are always linked, but there is no "Christian" template or model for how to structure the dynamic relationship between them. Of the many models through the centuries, the most dominant has been some form of monarchy or dynastic rule in which a divine mandate or blessing has presumably been bestowed on a ruler.

The second lesson of church history is that some "Christian" approaches to religion and politics have been highly lethal. Some who promoted such approaches to religion and politics were undoubtedly motivated by a desire for power, prestige, or wealth. Many others, however, were likely sincere believers who were convinced they knew precisely what God desired and required. There is a sobering message here for our interdependent world of the 21st century, where small numbers of people are capable of fomenting chaos on a regional or even global scale.

A third lesson is that context is vitally important in the development and implementation of models for how religion and politics interact. Biblical and theological justifications for specific approaches to the relationship of religious and temporal authority are intimately bound up with particular times, places, and events. We have seen how the context repeatedly shaped the ways Christians interpreted and applied Jesus' advice to render unto Caesar the things which are Caesar's and unto God the things that are God's, and Paul's view that all earthy authorities "that exist have been instituted by God." The meaning of these New Testament teachings varies a great deal if you are a Coptic Orthodox Christian living under Islamic rule in Cairo, a subject under the dominion of the Holy Roman Emperor, a citizen in John Calvin's Geneva, or a king who is also the head of the Church in 17th-century England.

The interplay of Christianity in particular and religion in general in the United States represents a significant departure from the historic patterns and contexts we have highlighted in this chapter. From the beginning, the United States was distinctly different, an experiment that continues today with ongoing conflict about the appropriate relationships between religion and politics. The nature of the contentious debate and the serious consequences that are at stake in the world's most powerful nation is the subject of the next chapter.

# 5

# AMERICA

## ONE NATION UNDER GOD?

---

THE LATE REV. DR. JAMES KENNEDY, former senior minister at the Coral Ridge Presbyterian Church in Fort Lauderdale, Florida, articulated the presuppositions, fears, frustrations, and hopes shared by millions of 21st-century American Christians:

> If we know our history, we know that America was a nation founded upon Christ and His Word. But that foundation is crumbling in our time. Today some in our country are busily tearing apart that foundation. They would gnash their teeth at the idea that this is a Christian nation and will not be satisfied until they have removed every vestige of our Christian heritage. . . . May God grant that America become a truly Christian nation once again.[1]

Kennedy was well known for his nationally televised Coral Ridge Ministries broadcast and "Reclaiming America for Christ" conferences. Several versions of these convictions and prescriptions for how to restore America as a Christian nation can be heard daily (if not hourly) on Christian television and radio networks and talk radio programs, and among politicians who appeal to the religious right. In 2008, in response to a question based on a poll showing 55% of Americans believing that the Constitution establishes a Christian nation, then Republican presidential candidate Sen. John McCain said he agreed that it was true.[2]

One of the most frequently repeated of these lamentations has become a mantra summarizing a decisive turning point that must be corrected: "In 1963, the Supreme Court kicked God out of the public schools." This refrain refers to the June 17, 1963, U.S. Supreme Court decision in the case of *Abington Township School District* v. *Schempp*. The Supreme Court prohibited school officials from organizing or leading devotional Bible readings or prayers in public schools. The details of the ruling, which often are lost in the image evoked by the mantra, lay out thoughtful and constructive clarifications for public schools. No one is banned from bringing a Bible to school, or praying in school, or forming religious groups as long as the religious activities don't interfere with the rights of others or the educational mission of the schools. Nor does the ruling ban the study of religion as an integral component of human history and experience. To protect the religious freedom of students whatever their faith or beliefs might be, it does prohibit public school teachers and administrators from either promoting or denigrating religion.

Quite apart from the dubious theological position that assumes the U.S. government can dictate where the omnipotent and omnipresent God of all creation can and cannot be present,[3] the foundation for one of the dominant approaches to religion and politics in America is clear. Many people believe the United States was founded as a Christian nation, and actions such as the 1963 Supreme Court ruling as well as *Roe* v. *Wade* (the January 22, 1973, Supreme Court ruling that legalized abortion in America) illustrate how the country turned away from God. All types of calamities—from natural disasters to indicators of social disintegration (the divorce rate, teen pregnancy, drug abuse, rampant crime)—are routinely cited as proof of having lost God's favor.

At the other end of the spectrum we find people who insist that the founders intended a complete separation of religion and politics, church and state. Advocates for this view cite various quotations from founding figures who took a dim view of sectarian religious language conjoined with the newly formed government. They refer, for instance, to debate about whether or how to incorporate God into the language of the Constitution. Contrary to what John McCain asserted and a large percentage of Americans imagine, the Constitution of the United States does not mention "God," "Creator," " Jesus," or "Lord"—except in the writing of the date ("Seventeenth Day of September in the Year of our Lord one thousand seven hundred and eighty seven").

Neither of these positions is correct. The truth about the relationship between religion and politics in the United States is found in a distinctive, experimental approach that both recognizes the interplay and judiciously seeks to delineate appropriate boundaries. There is, in Thomas Jefferson's words, a "wall of separation" between the religious and political spheres. However, from the founding of the nation up to this very moment, how Americans have understood and appropriated the nature of this separation can best be described as "a work in progress."

In this chapter we consider the context out of which this unique and remarkably successful approach to religion and politics was forged. We also examine how some of the most difficult challenges and obstacles have provoked and continue to trigger vigorous debate. The exploration reveals yet again how changing times and circumstances require new frameworks and models. The story of the United States clarifies principles by which richly diverse religious communities can coexist, live out their faith, and thrive. These principles include strong support for freedom of religion and freedom from government-imposed religion, careful attention to the best ways to separate religion and politics, while allowing both expression of generic public religion and modifications as specific times and circumstances may require.

The powerful lessons of history are woven into this narrative. Jon Meacham, the former managing editor of *Newsweek* and author of *American Gospel: God, the Founding Fathers and the Making of a Nation,* draws a direct connection between the heated contemporary arguments and religion and nationalism in America and the thoughtful way the founders engaged similar challenges:

> A grasp of history is essential for Americans of the center who struggle to decide how much weight to assign a religious consideration in a public matter. To fail to consult the past consigns us to what might be called the tyranny of the present—the mistaken idea that the crises of our own time are unprecedented and that we have to solve them without experience to guide us. Subject to such a tyranny, we are more likely to take a narrow or simplistic view, or to let our passions get the better of our reason. If we know, however, how those who came before us found the ways and means to surmount the difficulties of their age, we stand a far better chance of acting in the moment with perspective and measured judgment.[4]

Meacham's point speaks directly to the ongoing struggle to maintain a healthy balance where the sacred and the secular converge. These issues could not be more relevant today, as powerfully influential voices seek to rewrite history and implement a sectarian approach to guiding the world's most powerful nation. Meacham's point goes well beyond heated debate within the United States. The compelling lessons from history will also be manifest in the forthcoming chapters on Islam. Learning from past successes, mistakes, and abuses of religion through the respective histories of the Abrahamic religions is essential if we hope to minimize the deadly dynamics clearly evident in our religiously diverse and increasingly interdependent world of the 21st century.

## Pilgrims and Founding Fathers

Shortly after moving to Cambridge, Massachusetts, in the summer of 1975, my spouse and I attended numerous events celebrating the Bicentennial. The United States of America was 200 years old. We joined with several million fellow citizens at events commemorating the Boston Tea Party, Paul Revere's legendary Midnight Ride, important early battles in Lexington and Concord, and so forth. The organizers of many events presented detailed histories and background information that went well beyond the versions of the stories most of us learned in elementary school. The issues swirling at the time of the Revolutionary War were many, often complex, and deadly serious.[5]

The events of 1776 didn't occur in a vacuum. Massachusetts had been settled for 150 years by the time of the revolution. I was particularly interested in the religious history of the first wave of settlers. We traveled south to Plymouth to visit the Pilgrim Memorial Park and see where the Pilgrims first settled in 1620, barely endured the first year, and celebrated the first Thanksgiving. We also made a short trip to the north shore that first year to visit "Salem Village," the site of the infamous Salem witch trials of 1692–1693. The witchcraft hysteria that had swept through Europe for more than three centuries took root in this part of the Massachusetts Bay Colony, where more than 200 were accused of being witches and at least 20 were executed.

Religion and politics are central components of the story of America. The pilgrims on the *Mayflower* fled the oppression of state-established religion, where there was little or no freedom of choice and at times overt persecution in England. The fledgling colony was reinforced with new waves of Puritans a decade later. When they established the Massachusetts Bay Colony in 1630, however, they did not advocate the principles of freedom *of* religion and freedom *from* religion that later became hallmarks of the new country. Rooted in the Calvinist tradition, the Puritans wanted to be free to practice their religion but showed little interest in extending the same rights to others whose views differed. The first governor, John Winthrop, envisioned a colony that would be a "city upon a hill," a shining example for other colonies to emulate. As thousands more arrived from England, numerous villages were established in the Boston area. Laws and codes of conduct were put in place with punishments for infractions that were based on biblical mandates, although some democratic principles for selecting leaders were put in place within this Protestant theocracy. Twelve "crimes"—including murder, idolatry, and witchcraft—warranted the death penalty. Those deemed heretical were to be removed from the colony if they did not repent.

Education was particularly important because people needed to be able to read the Bible for themselves. Parents were required by law to teach their children to read, and each village had a school. Banned from colleges in England, the Puritans supported John Harvard's initiative to establish a college for the education of clergy. In 1636, he donated 400 books and America's first college, Harvard, was created.

More than a decade before the *Mayflower* arrived, emissaries of King James landed in Virginia to establish a colony at Jamestown. This venture had religious trappings but was primarily a mission aimed at seizing possession of land and water resources, as well as relentlessly mining for gold, silver, and copper. As the potentially lucrative initiative foundered, more emissaries were dispatched, and stringent "divine, moral, and martial laws" were imposed. Failing to attend twice-daily worship services was penalized by loss of food rations. The second such offense was punished by a public whipping; the third within a span of six months was punishable by death. Missing church services or breaking rules on the Sabbath also brought harsh punishment, including death for the third transgression.[6] The colonizers in Virginia, certain of their rectitude, brought in slaves and began a horrific assault on the Native American population. Thus began what would become a long and painful saga of displacement, war, and massacres.[7]

Prior to the Revolutionary War, nine of the thirteen original colonies had some form of established religion. In distinct ways, Virginia and Massachusetts represented one end of the spectrum; the stories of Rhode Island and Pennsylvania reflect an intentionally different history.

Roger Williams, a clergyman in Massachusetts, broke ranks with Winthrop and was exiled in 1636. He spent the next four decades securing Rhode Island as a place honoring religious freedom. Williams was particularly concerned about the dangers posed by mingling church and state. He understood well the corrupting effect of power. In Williams's view, "render unto Caesar" meant keeping the affairs of church and state separated. He traced the corruption of the church to Constantine's making Christianity the official religion of the state. The numerous lethal combinations of religion and governance throughout Christian history—in evidence most recently with the devastating religious wars in Europe—furnished ample evidence for Williams.

By the middle of the 17th century, the Quakers, another influential Christian group, added to the religiously diverse mix. Begun by George Fox in England, the Quakers rejected Anglicanism and Puritanism in favor of a simple faith devoid of sacraments and authoritative clergy. The Quakers focused on direct experience with God and the "inner light" within each person. William Penn, who wrote compellingly on freedom of conscience, was granted a royal charter in 1681. He led the Quakers to a land, Pennsylvania, where they and others could live peaceably. It was no accident that other dissenting groups who embraced Christian pacifism and wished to live peaceably with all—the Mennonites, Amish, and Brethren—would find safe haven in Pennsylvania.

By the time of the revolution, America was already an experiment in religious pluralism, with distinct models for church-state relationships. Although the founders included deeply committed Anglicans, Puritans, Presbyterians, and Congregationalists, advocates for a sectarian base for the new country gained little traction. America's most influential founders were unapologetically shaped by the Enlightenment. They believed in God—often referred to as Nature's God or Providence—and the central-ity of reason. George Washington, Thomas Jefferson, and many others were deists, people who affirmed God as Creator and periodic actor in human affairs. They more easily saw the Creator's handiwork in nature than in the biblical materials. They believed in life beyond death but were far less interested in theology or dogma than in the manifestations of moral and ethical behavior. The founders' keen awareness of the history—both before and after the Protestant Reformation in Europe—of state-sponsored as well as religiously inspired abuses of religion were obviously part of the early history of colonization in America. They sought a new approach to the age-old challenge of religion and politics.

The founding documents (the Declaration of Independence and the Constitution) clearly reflect a consensus not to tie the new nation explic-itly to Christianity or any sect within it. The Declaration of Independence appeals to the Laws of Nature, Nature's God, the Supreme judge of the world, and most famously the Creator: "We hold these truths to be self-evident, that all men are created equal, that they are endowed by their Creator with certain unalienable Rights, that among these are Life, Liberty and the pursuit of Happiness." These generic theological affirmations are inclusive and not unique to Christianity. As noted above, focused debate on the Constitution a dozen years later resulted in a text that doesn't men-tion God. But the Constitution doesn't simply dodge issues about the rela-tionship between religion and the state. Article VI requires all office holders to take an oath to support the Constitution but immediately declares, "No religious test shall ever be required as a qualification for any office or public trust under the United States." The first of the 10 amendments known as the Bill of Rights specifically prohibits anything like a Christian nation:

> Congress shall make no law respecting an establishment of religion, or prohibiting the free exercise thereof or abridging the freedom of speech, or of the press; or the right of the people peaceably to assemble, and to petition the Government for a redress of grievances.

Many books have detailed the major debates and nuances as issues of religion and politics unfolded around the birth of the United States.[8] The first four presidents—George Washington, John Adams, Thomas Jefferson, and James Madison—had much to say on the matter. So too did Benjamin Franklin, Patrick Henry, John Jay, and many others.[9] Jefferson was arguably the single most influential figure, for three reasons. His perspectives on religion and the state reflect the consensus of the founders, and he also embodies flaws and contradictions that must be rectified by this "work in progress." Finally, Jefferson has recently come under attack by some advocates of a "Christian America" for what they believe was his nefarious, non-Christian role in misguiding the new country.

A central actor in the American Revolution and third president of the United States, Jefferson was an Anglican/Episcopalian and, later in life, a Unitarian. Like many other founders, Jefferson was biblically literate, well versed in theological issues; he regularly attended worship services. He believed in God and the centrality of human reason, concentrating on the moral teachings and exemplary behavior of Jesus while downplaying stories of miraculous events. Jefferson famously "created" his own version of the Bible. In an 1813 letter to John Adams, Jefferson acknowledged taking a razor to the text of the gospels and rearranging the materials to produce the essence of Jesus' teachings, "the most sublime and benevolent code of morals which has ever been offered to man."[10] He kept working on this project and produced in his later years *The Life and Morals of Jesus of Nazareth, Extracted Textually from the Gospels*, a text popularly labeled "the Jefferson Bible."[11]

Jefferson was passionately committed to liberty, learning, and freedom of faith. For all of his remarkable contributions, he wished to be remembered for three achievements. These are engraved on his tombstone: the founding of the University of Virginia, his authorship of the Declaration of Independence (in 1776), and the Virginia statute for religious freedom (in 1777). Emphasizing these accomplishments—and notably omitting two terms of service as president of the United States—underscores his lifelong commitment to liberty, education, and freedom of conscience.

For Jefferson, a child of the Enlightenment who knew well the abusive coercion so frequently perpetrated in the name of religion, judicious separation of church and state was essential. Liberty was a God-given birthright. The Statute Establishing Religious Freedom in Virginia was the foundation in what became a lifelong mission the success of which Jefferson viewed as central to his legacy. Given the history and deep roots of Anglicanism in Virginia, adopting this statute was an arduous process. It took a decade, with the able leadership of James Madison and strong support from Virginia Baptists, to accomplish the goal. The first section includes strong language to identify the history of abuses. It speaks of "coercion" and "impious presumptions" by civil and ecclesiological rulers who impose their "own opinions as true and infallible," and the practice of compelling "a man to furnish contributions of money for the propagation of opinions he disbelieves." The second section contains the resolution:

> Be it enacted by the General Assembly, That no man shall be compelled to frequent or support any religious worship, place, or ministry whatsoever, nor shall be enforced, restrained, molested, or burdened in his body or goods, nor shall otherwise suffer on account of his religious opinions or belief; but that all men shall be free to profess, and by argument to maintain, their opinion in matters of religion, and that the same shall in no wise diminish, enlarge, or affect their civil capacities.

Jefferson and Madison's tenacious efforts shaped the approach of the framers of the Constitution, as the First Amendment clearly indicates. This well-conceived experiment began a new era in the tortured history of religion and politics within predominantly Christian lands. Unlike the ferocious religious wars that engulfed post-Reformation Europe, religious differences in the colonies were characterized by a more tolerant and respectful ecumenism. To be sure, there were many perspectives and forces at work at the intersection of church and state during the 18th and 19th centuries. Jefferson continually addressed these issues right up to his death on July 4, 1826 (the 50th anniversary of the signing of the Declaration of Independence). For him and for us today, negotiating the dynamic relationship between church and state is always a work in progress. The principles were established, but then as now the devil is in the details.

The complications and confusions stem in part from the fact that religion and politics are never completely separated. Jefferson and other founders with varying ties to Christianity believed in Nature's God. George Washington's frequent refrain about the hand of Providence at work to secure and stabilize the fledgling nation has always been widely embraced. Benjamin Franklin, arguably the least overtly religious of the founders, nonetheless affirmed the hand of God at work in the American experience. At the 1787 Constitutional Convention, he said:

> God governs in the affairs of man. And if a sparrow cannot fall to the ground without his notice, is it probable that an empire can rise without His aid? We have been assured in the Sacred Writings that except the Lord build the house, they labor in vain that build it. I firmly believe this. I also believe that, without His concurring aid, we shall succeed in this political building no better than the builders of Babel.[12]

This perspective, that America has been the object of God's special favor, is a theme running throughout American history. A version of what Franklin called "public religion," or sociologist Robert Bellah termed "civil religion," is thus woven into the fabric of the country. America was not founded as a Christian nation, but the vast majority of the nation's citizens were Christians. God, broadly understood, was affirmed, but reason, not particular interpretations of revelation, constituted the source for collective wisdom and guidance. Religion is not eliminated from the political sphere; even so, sectarian interpretations were not to dominate or be imposed by the state. Thus the documents from the early decades—including Washington's strong written reassurance to Jewish congregations—went well beyond toleration to express respect.[13] And on many occasions, Washington, Adams, and Jefferson included Muslims in their list of upright people who can both revere God and live out their faith morally.[14]

We can see how the distinctive American formula for negotiating the interplay of religion and politics was made possible by the particular history and circumstances converging in the late 18th century. The prevailing ecumenical spirit and principled openness to people in non-Christian traditions embody an approach that is exceedingly relevant today. These values were not universally affirmed, of course. One can find fervent evangelical Christians, self-serving political opportunists, atheists, and an assortment of others in the midst of the fray. Even those who espoused and fought for the ecumenical and balanced approach were far from consistent in application of their stated values. The legal practice of slavery and the treatment of the Native American population are the most obvious points at which the contradictions can be seen.

## Slavery and Manifest Destiny

Donald Shriver, former president of Union Theological Seminary in New York City, articulated a moral and theological imperative in his award-winning book *Honest Patriots: Loving a Country Enough to Remember Its Misdeeds*.[15] Acknowledging and seeking to understand where we have failed as a nation is not only honest but also facilitates constructive change and decreases the likelihood of repeating the same behaviors. Religious justification for the deplorable treatment of African Americans and Native Americans requires such soul-searching honesty.

Most of the founders owned slaves. Although Jefferson understood the contradiction and expressed ambivalence at times, he nonetheless owned slaves. Alongside his enduring commitment to virtue, morality, and ethical principles, it is highly likely that Jefferson fathered at least one child, and as many as six, with his slave Sally Hemings. Viewed from a contemporary perspective, it is difficult to understand how Jefferson and most others could justify such a contradiction to their perception of the God-given rights of life, liberty, and the pursuit of happiness, as those very rights were denied to the slaves they owned.

The multifaceted story of slavery in America is familiar, perhaps too familiar. Far too many Americans can recite the narrative in general terms, without thinking deeply about or feeling strongly the horror of slavery and the continuing legacy of racial hatred and injustice that it has engendered in the land of the free and the home of the brave. It is significant how religious components helped justify, shape, and perpetuate this obnoxious indignity as official policy for almost a century.

Support for the institutions of slavery is rooted in the Bible. There are numerous references to slavery, and nowhere does the Bible explicitly reject the practice, although it does indicate some regulations.[16] There is no record of Jesus condemning or forbidding slavery. The Apostle Paul proffered these words:

> Slaves, obey your earthly masters with fear and trembling, in single-ness of heart, as you obey Christ. . . . Render service with enthusiasm, as to the Lord and not to men and women, knowing that whatever good we do, we will receive the same again from the Lord, whether we are slaves or free. And masters, do the same to them. Stop threatening them, for you know both of you have the same Master in heaven, and with him there is no partiality [Eph. 6:5–9].

The justification for enslaving Africans and not light-skinned Europeans was normally based on the "curse of Ham." After the great flood in

Genesis, Noah planted a vineyard and then partook a little too freely of the wine he'd produced. He became drunk and passed out naked in his tent. One of his sons, Ham, saw his father's nakedness and immediately went to tell his two brothers. The brothers did not want to see their father, so they backed into the tent and put a garment over him. When Noah learned what had happened, he cursed Canaan, the son of Ham, saying, "Cursed be Canaan; lowest of slaves shall he be to his brothers" (Gen. 9:25). Various 18th- and 19th-century American Christians cited this passage and labeled darker-skinned people of Africa as the descendants of Ham.

Heated debate raged in the early decades of American history. Massachusetts, New York, Pennsylvania, and other states took clear steps to end slavery, while states in the South tenaciously supported it. The Southern Baptist Convention, now the largest Protestant denomination in the United States, was formed in 1843 largely as a split with Baptists in the North over the issue of slavery. As ministerial students at the Southern Baptist Theological Seminary during the early 1970s, my classmates and I were shocked to read dozens of sermons preached from prominent pulpits in North and South Carolina, Georgia, and elsewhere that vehemently defended slavery as an institution ordained by God. We could see how passionate disagreement over slavery ripped apart the fabric of the nation.

The despicable practice formally ended following the Civil War. But racism, systematic discrimination, and physical violence did not end. We need not rehearse here a catalogue of horrific violence against black people. Despite federal laws, many state and local officials ignored the civil rights of African Americans or actively cooperated with avowedly "Christian" groups such as the Ku Klux Klan in perpetrating violence. The Civil Rights movement, led by the Rev. Dr. Martin Luther King Jr., was a full century removed from President Lincoln's Emancipation Proclamation.

How did this painfully slow process to abolish slavery occur? No one occupying a prominent pulpit in North or South Carolina today would proclaim enslavement of dark-skinned people as a God-ordained institution. The Bible did not change. But the interpretation of the Bible has changed, in light of experience and emphasis on foundational teachings. King and many other civil rights leaders appealed to the Bible compellingly. They spoke often of Jesus' teachings about love of God and love of neighbor, treating other people as you would like to be treated, resisting evil without violence, and loving those who persecute you.[17] They employed the language of the Exodus story to evoke images of people set free from bondage and full of hope for a new beginning in the Promised Land. King's final speech before his assassination in 1968 prophetically echoed Moses' experience. At that point in the long journey, King could see the Promised Land, though he acknowledged he might not get there.

Change is possible. The story of slavery in America illustrates how both the government and religious communities and ideology can be transformed. A similar pattern in the United States can be seen in institutional patterns of second-class citizenship and discrimination against women. Although the consequences for women were far less lethal on a massive scale than was true for slaves and African Americans, oppressive and discriminatory government policies have changed over time. So too have biblical interpretations in many quarters.[18]

Another deadly form of religiously inspired U.S. government action was found under the rubric of Manifest Destiny, a 19th-century view that the United States was destined by God to expand across the continent of North America in order to rule over the land from the Atlantic to the Pacific oceans. Manifest Destiny undergirded the efforts to secure the land that is now California, New Mexico, Arizona, Texas, and Oregon. Late in the century, the ideology was employed to support acquisition of Puerto Rico, Guam, Hawaii, and the Philippines. By the early 20th century, presidents Theodore Roosevelt and Woodrow Wilson spoke of "America's mission," a version of Manifest Destiny, in support of American expansionism and the need to make the world safe for democracy.

The theological roots for this worldview can be found in and traced from John Winthrop's biblical image of "a city set on a hill" and vision for America as a new Israel, a light unto the nations. It enjoyed the strong support of Washington, Franklin, and other founders' affirmations about the hand of Providence guiding and securing the success of the nation. One has only to listen to the rhetoric of more recent presidents such as Ronald Reagan and George W. Bush to hear the contemporary versions of these themes about God's special blessing on the mission and successes of the United States in the world.

The language may be moving, even inspirational, to many Americans, but to those on the receiving end of this "destiny"—most notably Native Americans—the reality was extraordinarily harsh and often deadly. Pick almost any part of the continental United States and study the history of conflict, displacement, and decimation of the native population. Genocidal policies developed on the confident belief that God's will for

America must be manifest in control of the land "from sea to shining sea." Growing up in a state whose history is deeply connected to this saga, I began to understand the other side of Manifest Destiny at an early age. My eighth grade Oklahoma history teacher pulled no punches. She had us read and discuss in great detail the tragic story of the "Trail of Tears," in which many Native American tribes (Cherokee, Chickasaw, Choctaw, Muskogee-Creek, and Seminole) were force-marched from the Southeastern United States to Indian Territory for resettlement. The process began when President Andrew Jackson passed the Indian Removal Act of 1830. Large numbers died along the way to what the U.S. government must have deemed the least desirable land—present-day Oklahoma—available for these people. Then, in 1889, the Indian territories were opened up in the famous "land rush" celebrated in the musical play and movie *Oklahoma!* Forty acres of land were available to any person who got there first to stake a claim. The behavior of the U.S. government toward the indigenous Americans may have been guided by the ideology of Manifest Destiny, but it certainly had nothing to do with Jesus' teaching of the Golden Rule.

## In God We Trust

The relationship between church and state continued to play out in various ways throughout the 20th century and beyond. There are continuing and recurring battles over the teaching of evolution in the schools[19]; on posting the Ten Commandments in courthouses, schools, or other public buildings[20]; about prayers in schools or before high school football games; on placing the Nativity Scene on public property; and the like. Such issues pull back the curtain to expose substantial differences in understanding the relationships between church and state. Even though these issues evoke strong responses, they rarely produce deadly violence. The same cannot be said of religiously based views about abortion and the civil rights of homosexuals. Contemporary examples of Christian extremists who have bombed clinics and sometimes murdered doctors and others working at abortion clinics illustrate the dangers as well. The legal rights of homosexuals to serve openly in the military or to marry (and enjoy the legal rights and responsibilities afforded by that institution) engender strong reactions and considerable concern about the views of potential nominees for the Supreme Court.

Some of the confusion and vigorous disagreement can be attributed to the inherent ambiguities in the U.S. system. Religion and politics are always linked, but they are to be judiciously separated. Where those lines are drawn opens the door for disagreement. And as we have noted, some of the confusion is also related to the affirmation of public religion throughout U.S. history. It is rooted deeply in the soil of America and continues to be manifest in various ways.

Ask a friend or acquaintance if she or he knows the official motto of the United States. Some think it is *e pluribus unum* ("out of many, one"). This was affirmed in 1782 along with the bald eagle as part of the Seal of the United States. The phrase continues to appear on U.S. coinage and some currency notes. It turns out, however, Congress never officially adopted *e pluribus unum* as the nation's motto. Another phrase was proposed and officially made the motto of the United States—during the Cold War era. In 1956, Congress approved "in God we trust" as the national motto. Two years earlier, also during the Cold War and shaped by fervent hostility toward godless communism, the Pledge of Allegiance was altered for the fourth and final time. In 1954, "one nation indivisible, with liberty and justice for all," was amended to read "one nation *under God,* indivisible, with liberty and justice for all." Such public forms of religious affirmation are generic and, when challenged, have not been seen by the U.S. courts as infringements on the First Amendment. For some American Christians, however, statements by founders, the motto, and the Pledge of Allegiance help validate America's foundation as a Christian nation.

For more than three decades, James Kennedy and a host of other such advocates have been hard at work to eliminate any wall of separation between church and state and constitute (or in their view reconstitute) the United States as a Christian nation. The well-organized and relentless advocacy for a Christian America now threatens the measured balance Americans have maintained for more than two centuries. The absolute certainty that emboldens some contemporary Christians is a clear warning sign: the potential for religion becoming lethal is all too real.

## A Christian America in the 21st Century

The United States has always been religiously diverse. Harvard professor Diana Eck presents compelling evidence that the nation is now the most religiously diverse country in the world.[21] At the same time, during the past 30 years conservative and fundamentalist Christians have emerged as dynamic, powerful, and well-organized forces in American politics. Given the U.S. role as the world's superpower—the most powerful nation in terms of political influence, economic clout, and military capabilities—many analysts are openly alarmed about the dangers posed by the "religious right" in America. A host of recent books and articles present the convergence of the religious right and zealous Christian nationalism as an imminent threat to the nation and the world communities. The titles of three recent books underscore the point: *Kingdom Coming: The Rise of Christian Nationalism,* by Michelle Goldberg; *American Fascists: The Christian Right and War on America,* by Chris Hedges; and *American Theocracy: The Peril and Politics of Radical Religion, Oil, and Borrowed Money in the 21st Century,* by Kevin Phillips.[22]

The religious right emerged as a potent political force in the late 1970s and throughout the 1980s. Many strands of 20th-century evangelical Christianity converged at that time, including the rapidly growing Pentecostal communities, the fundamentalist movements of the 1920s and 1930s, and Billy Graham's popular evangelical revivalism of the 1950s and 1960s. The two most important catalysts were Falwell's Moral Majority and Robertson's Christian Coalition. Jerry Falwell, who had long eschewed political involvement saying he was called by God to be a preacher, reversed his position in the wake of the *Roe* v. *Wade* U.S. Supreme Court decision. He plunged into the political arena and became a leading opponent of abortion and homosexuality while supporting dictators in El Salvador, the Philippines, and the Apartheid government of South Africa.[23] Although Falwell presented his positions as based on his Christian faith and biblical mandates, he was almost always in step with the policy positions of the Republican Party platform and the Reagan administration. He was ubiquitous until his death in 2007.

Pat Robertson's Christian Coalition gained a large following when he ran for president in 1988. Robertson surprised most pundits with a second-place finish in the Iowa caucuses, the first primary test, and second place in three of the first four primaries. He remained in the race almost to the end with consistent third-place finishes behind the future nominee, George H. W. Bush, and Kansas Senator Bob Dole. Robertson later determined that his idea of a top-down approach to changing America should be reversed. His Christian Coalition then implemented a highly successful strategy aimed at a bottom-up approach in which their candidates would begin to take over the reins of government by being elected to school boards, local offices, and seats in the House of Representatives. By the early 1990s, those loyal to the Christian Coalition functionally controlled the Republican Party in at least 20 states.

Robertson's efforts were guided by a form of dominion theology known as *reconstructionism.* He advocated reshaping America on the basis of biblical principles. The agenda included rewriting the Constitution on the basis of the Bible and stacking the Supreme Court with like-minded, Bible-believing Christians. On the one hand, Robertson's views were openly presented on his daily television program *The 700 Club*, and in his books. On the other hand, the Christian Coalition employed a tactic using "stealth candidates." Ralph Reed, the head of the Christian Coalition, famously referred to this practice by which the radical agenda of candidates would be hidden from the voters while the visible focus was on hot-button issues such as abortion and homosexuality. By the time the electorate knew what the victorious candidate really advocated, the voters would already be in "body bags," as Reed laughingly said to indicate how people would never know what hit them.

Robertson reflects two approaches to religion and politics, both of which threaten the principles of the American experiment and alarm many analysts. To conclude this chapter, we explore both the overt effort to establish a Christian America and the more secretive, disguised, and under-the-radar endeavors that have already established a firm foothold within the corridors of power.

Dominionism is based on Genesis 1:26–31. In this first creation story of Genesis, God gives human beings "dominion" over all creation. Followers of God should exercise their dominion in all spheres, including the political. The ideological foundation for this movement is found in R. J. Rushdoony's 1973 book *The Institutes of Biblical Law*. As the title intimates, Rushdoony was heavily influenced by John Calvin's *Institutes of the Christian Religion* and the model for a theocratic state reflected in Calvin's Geneva. Rushdoony explicitly argues for a Christian state with harsh penalties—including death for murder, adultery, blasphemy, homosexuality, and astrology. Yes, astrology would be a capital offense! In short, his version of biblical law should replace the current secular legal codes. Ultimately, if a Christian America is established, it could subdue and rule over the rest of the world.[24] Followers of Jesus who did not share this worldview would be in very serious trouble, not to mention the non-Christian and nonreligious citizens in the land.

While Rushdoony's work remains largely unnoticed, Robertson and others who advocate reconstructionism are transparent for all who pay attention. One of the leading thinkers and writers for the movement, Gary North, puts it simply: "[Reconstructionists seek] to remove the political and institutional barriers to God's law in order to impose the rule of God's law."[25] As the Christian Coalition was gaining momentum in the early 1990s, Robertson articulated his belief that successful implementation of God's rule was within reach. In his book *The Turning Tide*, he laid out what was happening and what was at stake where religion and the state converge in America:

> Satan has established certain strongholds. He goes after areas of our society which are crucial. He has gone after the education system and has been very successful at capturing it. He has gone after our legal profession and has been successful, through the ACLU and others, in capturing large portions of the legal system. He's gone after the government and moved it away from the more free enterprise system we've known and turned it into a socialist welfare state. . . . These places control society . . . I don't know if Satan has been able to capture the military yet, but he's tried. . . . We need to do spiritual warfare.[26]

Sociologist Nancy Ammerman has studied and written extensively on Protestants in America. Her assessment of Christian reconstructionism meshes with the ideological underpinnings expressed by Robertson, Rushdoony, and North:

> For reconstructionists there is no neutral ground, no sphere of activity outside of God's rule. One is either following God in all aspects of life or not following God at all. One is either engaged in godly politics or is participating in the anti-God structures that now threaten the home, the school, and the church . . . reconstructionists wait for a dramatic change in history. But they are not merely waiting.[27]

Robertson's theological views are well documented. So too are his "Bible-based" positions on foreign policy. Three and a half years into the debilitating war in Iraq, Robertson proposed a bold plan to President Bush on *The 700 Club*: merge Syria with Iraq. As long as Syria would agree to make peace with Israel, they could have Iraq and "its huge oil fields in the north and south." He added that "Syria is a more secular regime, which is what they need over there [in Iraq], they don't need these religious strifes." He suggested this "win-win" plan could also isolate Iran. Robertson concluded by asserting that if Bush would follow his plan, "he'd be in accordance with what the Bible says and God would bless it." "Iraq," he announced, "is not a prize we want to hold on to."[28] Here is dominion theology at work. The United States presumably has the authority to move pieces around on the chessboard of nation-states, create new countries, give the oil under the land occupied by Iraqi Kurds and Shi'ites to Syria, and so forth. Somehow this plan for a more secular government would help end religious strife. Apparently Robertson's Bible-based policy overlooked the fact that Iraq had a more secular government under Saddam Hussein and his Baathist Socialist Party. Syria is still governed by a different branch of the same secular Baath Party.

The catalogue of Robertson's Bible-based foreign policy positions and analyses is extensive. In 2005, he created a firestorm by publicly recommending that the U.S. government assassinate Venezuelan president Hugo Chavez. Former Liberian President Charles Taylor identified Robertson as his "man in Washington" during his February 2010 trial at the Hague on 11 counts of war crimes and crimes against humanity. In exchange for a 1999 gold mining concession, Taylor said Robertson lobbied the U.S. government on behalf of his regime in Liberia. The day after Haiti's devastating earthquake left more than 200,000 dead and millions homeless (in January 2010), Robertson identified the cause: Haitians had made a pact with the devil. When Haiti was under the heel of the French, Robertson said, "they got together and said 'We will serve you if you get us free from the French' . . . True story . . . and the devil said 'OK. It's a deal.' Ever since, they have been cursed by one thing after another."[29]

Religions—especially the monotheistic religions—create moral binaries of good and evil. When the understanding of church and state is presented in the context of a battle between God and Satan with America as the prize, there is hardly room for compromise or accommodation. The passion and urgency with which Robertson, James Kennedy, and others have pressed their agenda for a Christian America is consistent with their theological worldview. Framing the views of the founders as visionaries dedicated to a Christian America becomes an invaluable asset in the struggle to implement their understanding of God's will.

Although the visibility of the Christian Coalition faded significantly after the mid-1990s, followers of Robertson's vision for America didn't go quietly into the night. On the contrary, more than 150 graduates from Robertson's Regent University Law School were hired by the Justice Department during the first six years of President George W. Bush's administration. The stunning figures came to light in 2007 when Congress investigated the scandalous political firing of numerous U.S. attorneys. Monica Goodling, a top aide to then Attorney General Alberto Gonzales, was at the center of the storm. A 1999 graduate of Regent Law School with very little prosecutorial experience, Goodling had evaluated the performance of many seasoned U.S. attorneys who were relieved of their duties.[30]

Patrick Henry College was another school with highly disproportionate representation in Bush's executive branch. The fundamentalist Christian college concentrates on preparing home-schooled students to change the world. In 2004, the college's webpage revealed that seven of the 100 White House interns had come from the school, which had a total of 250 students. Several more of its students worked for top officials in the White House.[31] As Nancy Ammerman points out, reconstructionists are not merely waiting for a dramatic change. American Christians convinced that the world's most powerful nation should be guided by biblical imperatives are actively at work—sometimes visibly and sometimes quietly—within the governmental bureaucracy.

A particularly powerful and highly influential group known as "The Fellowship" or "The Family" emerged from the shadows in 2008 with publication of Jeff Sharlet's best-selling book *The Family: The Secret Fundamentalism at the Heart of American Power*. The Family comprises a group of men committed to following Jesus and changing the world through cultivating friendships and influence with powerful political and other leaders that the Fellowship believes have been chosen by God to direct the affairs of the world. Sharlet cites Chuck Colson, the Watergate felon who became a major actor in this network after being "born again" through his experiences with the Family:

> In his memoir, *Born Again*, [Colson speaks of] "a veritable underground of Christ's men all through government." This so-called underground is not a conspiracy. Rather, it's a seventy-year-old movement of elite fundamentalism, bent not on salvation for all but on the cultivation of powerful, "key men" chosen by God to direct the affairs of the nation.[32]

Doug Coe has led the group since the 1960s. The Fellowship is best known for organizing and hosting the annual Presidential Prayer Breakfast at the Washington Hilton. The event began in 1953 during the Eisenhower administration; I became personally involved with the Fellowship, as it was primarily known at that time, in 1971. I was one of 40 college student leaders from around the country invited to spend four days in Washington and attend the Prayer Breakfast. We spent many hours learning at the feet of prominent leaders such as Oregon Senator Mark Hatfield, Iowa Senator Harold Hughes, and Secretary of Defense Melvin Laird. These events, along with meetings with Doug Coe and others in the Fellowship, made a huge impact on the student leaders. The Prayer Breakfast included all nine Supreme Court justices, the entire Cabinet, the Joint Chiefs of Staff, more than half the members of Congress, more than 20 governors, official representatives from more than 100 countries, some 40 college and university presidents, and the 40 students. Billy Graham and President Nixon were the keynote speakers.

My enthusiasm for the experience led my close friend, B. J. Steinbrook, and me to organize a student prayer breakfast movement at Oklahoma State. The next year, we launched and hosted a national student prayer breakfast gathering for the following year. Leaders from the Fellowship flew in on a corporate jet from Washington to attend our event. Senator Hughes and then Oklahoma Governor David Hall spoke. Impressed by the initiative, I was asked back to Washington the next year prior to the Prayer Breakfast[33] and invited to intern with and consider becoming part of the Fellowship. Even though I was committed to pursue a vocation in Christian ministry, I was bothered by the seemingly undefined and amorphous nature of this group. I decided the best next step for me should be a master of divinity program in seminary.

Members of the Fellowship are far less outwardly rigid than most fundamentalist Christians. They make clear that they simply seek to follow Jesus. They embrace the Pauline view that all earthly authority comes from God and therefore seek to nurture relationships with leaders—including some notorious dictators and strong men—to shape decisions and events. They are less interested in democratic rule than in how God uses men in powerful positions. Although their theology is not easy to classify, Jeff Sharlet sees it as a form of dominionism. Their internal documents indicate that Jesus does not relate to all souls equally; some people are "chosen" by God for leadership. And among even the followers of Jesus, there are levels of relationships rippling out in concentric circles. Coe is thought by those who make up the Family to be as close to Jesus as the disciple John. This explains, in their view, why he can gain access to virtually any political leader anywhere. Sharlet articulates the veneration for Coe succinctly: "Jesus held the doors to power open."[34]

Sharlet's 2008 book and several highly visible political scandals in 2009 (notably the extramarital affairs of South Carolina Governor Mark Sanford and Nevada Senator John Ensign) combined to bring this extensive, influential network out of the shadows.[35] A number of prominent politicians have lived at a Fellowship-owned house on C Street. The names of current and former political leaders closely associated with the Family is a veritable Who's Who in Washington, including many senators and congressional representatives, several former attorneys general and secretaries of state and defense. Other stories began to appear involving close ties between past and present dictatorial rulers and leaders of the Fellowship and various members of Congress. James Inhofe, a senator from my state of Oklahoma, for instance, reportedly had taken some 20 "missionary trips" (using taxpayer funds and military transport planes), including many to Uganda. Inhofe took several Ugandan leaders under his wing and invited them to join the Family. One of these men, David Bahati, became part of a core prayer cell, where brothers seek to discern what God wants them to do in their powerful positions. In 2009, Bahati authored and introduced an extraordinarily harsh antihomosexual bill in Uganda in which offenders would automatically receive life imprisonment or the death penalty. Knowing someone is gay and not reporting it, having HIV/AIDS, or use of drugs or alcohol that leads to homosexual acts are among the offenses. Despite extraordinarily strong international criticism of this legislation, Bahati was invited to the U.S. Presidential Prayer Breakfast in 2010.

As this story broke and connections to the Family were exposed, numerous questions arose about other ways in which such close ties had been shaping policies with potentially lethal consequences in the United States and around the world. Given the long history and deep ties within the U.S. government, many more stories are likely to be discovered in coming years. The highly influential activity of the Fellowship is a sobering reminder that the relationship between religion and politics continues to play out in a variety of visible and not-so-visible ways. The work of the Family may well be heartening to advocates of a Christian America with a vision of Manifest Destiny. The founders who signed the Declaration of Independence and shaped the Constitution would surely not be pleased.

In Chapter 9, we return to consider more overtly militaristic approaches being advocated and pursued by fundamentalist Christians and their Jewish and Islamic counterparts. First, however, we will examine the theological foundations, the history, and contemporary manifestations of religion and politics in Islam, the world's second-largest religion.

# THERE IS NO GOD BUT GOD

## RELIGION AND POLITICS IN ISLAM

THE DRAMATIC TIME MAGAZINE COVER STORY on August 19, 2010, put the question bluntly: "Is America Islamophobic?" The lengthy article addressed major strands in a highly charged, monthlong controversy over proposed plans to build an Islamic community center (including a place for daily prayers) at 51 Park Place, two and one-half blocks from the site of the World Trade Center Towers. The ostensible focus for the debate centered not on the right of Muslims to build such a facility on privately owned land, but on the specific location of the Islamic center (dubbed erroneously by many as the "Ground Zero Mosque"[1]). The *Time* story highlighted anti-Muslim and anti-mosque activities in various parts of the United States. It posed the deeper question of widespread Islamophobia that was woven into the torrent of news stories, opinions articles, public statements by innumerable politicians, contentious debates, and commentaries on talk radio, cable news programs, and other media.

Shortly after the story appeared, the Rev. Terry Jones, a fundamentalist Pentecostal Christian minister whose Gainesville, Florida, church included fewer than 50 members, attracted massive national and international attention when he announced on Facebook that his church would hold a three-hour "Burn the Qur'an" event to mark the ninth anniversary of September 11, 2001. President Obama, Pope Benedict XVI, Secretary of State Clinton, and General David Petraeus, the U.S. military leader of the wars in Iraq and Afghanistan, headed the list of high-profile political and religious leaders who swiftly and strongly spoke out against this deliberately provocative action. Jones eventually canceled the Qur'an burning, but the episode was deeply disturbing on several levels. Jones's inflammatory rhetoric was magnified by signs posted outside his church declaring "Islam is of the Devil." These events provoked anti-Christian and anti-American demonstrations in Pakistan, India, Indonesia, and Afghanistan. At least one person was killed in Afghanistan, a Christian church was set afire, and other churches were damaged while threats of violence terrified the 800,000 indigenous Christian citizens of Pakistan. One extremist minister thus managed to demand global attention and ignite a firestorm by planning an event that was legally protected in the United States.

These dramatic stories underscored both the explosive mix of religion and politics in our increasingly interconnected world and how many people in the two largest religions view the other through the lens of a simplistic stereotype. Even though numerous thoughtful and measured voices tried to deescalate the contentious confrontations, many others in the United States who would not be readily identified with the extreme views of Terry Jones nonetheless spoke of Islam as a monolithic movement whose ultimate goal was world domination. Nine years after September 11, coherent understanding about the mix of religion and politics in Islam appeared lacking for most Americans.

Islam is not monolithic. The often convoluted and sometimes violent upheavals within Islam today cannot be dismissed simply by declaring that Islam is a religion of peace any more than they can be explained adequately by the words and actions of violent extremists like Osama bin Laden. As we have seen with both Judaism and Christianity, this Abrahamic religion includes people and movements ranging all the way across the religious and political spectrum. One striking difference with Islam, however, is evident at the starting point. Virtually all observant Muslims declare in unison that there is no distinction between religion and politics in Islam. They readily affirm Islam as a comprehensive way of life that joins religious, political, economic, legal, and social components into a seamless whole.

In actual practice, however, this theoretical framework proves far more elusive as varying, complex realities on the ground have shaped diverse approaches for more than 1,400 years. The great diversity evident within the "Islamic world" in the second decade of the 21st century illustrates the point. A cursory survey of the more than 50 countries with Muslim majorities today reveals anything but a seamless approach to religious, political, economic, legal, and social structures, in nations such as Afghanistan, Algeria, Iran, Indonesia, Turkey, and Tunisia.

These next three chapters develop a framework for understanding what is happening today within the world's second-largest religion. As we have done with Judaism and Christianity, we begin by identifying the definitive sources from which Muslims have fashioned approaches to religion and politics. We focus on the time of the prophet Muhammad (570–632 CE), the first four caliphs, and the early centuries dominated by the Umayyad and Abbasid dynasties. Clearly, Muslims have adapted and modified approaches to religion and politics over time, including the treatment of non-Muslims living under Islamic rule. This backdrop frames the subject of the next chapter: the contemporary struggle for the soul of Islam. Chapter 8 examines two countries that have been and will continue to be at the center of regional and international attention: Iraq and Iran.

## The Origins of Islam

Islam as we know it today is rooted in the life and messages conveyed through the Prophet Muhammad. Born in 570 CE in the Arabian city of Mecca, Muhammad was raised by his uncle, Abu Talib. His father died prior to his birth, and his mother passed away when he was six. Learning the caravan business from his uncle, Muhammad proved adept in business. His reputation for honesty is reflected in the honorific name by which he was known: *al-amin* (the "honest" or "trustworthy one"). At age 25, he married Khadija, a wealthy caravan owner. Though she was his elder by 15 years, theirs was a happy and mutually rewarding marriage lasting until her death 25 years later.

Muhammad periodically retreated to a cave in the mountains near Mecca for meditation and reflection. It was on such a sojourn during the month of Ramadan in 610 CE that he had a profound experience that would change his life—and the course of history. He saw a radiant figure on the horizon coming toward him. The figure, the Angel Gabriel, drew near and conveyed the first revelation: "Recite! In the name of your Lord, who created humankind from a blood clot" (Qur'an 96:1–2).

The earliest proclamations uttered by Muhammad, beginning in 610 CE, centered on the sublime majesty of the one, true God, Allah (the Arabic word for God),[2] the Creator, the Sustainer, and the Judge of all creation. Islam is defined by an uncompromising affirmation of monotheism: there is no god but God. Muhammad is the messenger from God. Muslims affirm that Muhammad received the words that constitute the Qur'an as direct revelation and repeated them faithfully. Therefore the Qur'an is the literal Word of God to Muslims, a merciful message providing guidance for humankind.

The Qur'an also validates Muhammad's role as prophet. Numerous prophetic figures in the Bible performed miracles as confirmation of their close connection with God. Moses struck a rock, and water flowed for the parched people; Elijah called down fire from heaven in a contest with the worshippers of Baal; Jesus healed people and cast out demons. Muhammad, by contrast, is not associated with such supernatural manifestations of divine power.[3] Rather, Muslims point to the Qur'an itself as the "miracle" that validates Muhammad's role, especially because he could neither read nor write. Muslims have always maintained that no human being could compose such magnificent poetry, especially not someone who was illiterate.[4]

The Qur'an identifies Muhammad as the last or "seal of the prophets" (Qur'an 33:40) God has appointed for the mission of revelation. The Torah, the revelation sent through Moses (Musa), and the Gospel, the revelation sent through Jesus ('Isa), is thought to be the same revelation as the Qur'an, sent through Muhammad. For Muslims Judaism, Christianity, and Islam are really the same religion. Thus Jews and Christians are frequently identified in the Qur'an as "People of the Book." Muslims contend that the main differences can be traced to how the followers of Moses, Jesus, and others distorted the revelation sent down by God. The Qur'an is affirmed as containing the truth of God's revelation in its pristine purity, while the Bible contains God's revelation mixed in with human distortions.

The Qur'an portrays Jesus as a great prophet and messenger, one who was born of a virgin and lived a sinless life. Jesus is mentioned by name 93 times in the Qur'an and is frequently cited with affection and reverence. In hundreds of meetings with various Muslim leaders throughout the Middle East, Europe, and North America, I have seen that their deep love and reverence for Jesus always comes through. But the Qur'an emphatically rejects that Jesus was divine or the son of God. Islam is unambiguous: there is no god but God. Thus Muslims maintain that the followers of Jesus who claimed he was the incarnation of God erred grievously and distorted Jesus' true revelation. Unlike the traditional Christian view that Jesus was the "Word of God" who became flesh and dwelt among us (John 1:8), Muslims affirm the Qur'an as the Word of God that was collected and preserved in its pristine purity.

Although the revelation in the Qur'an is considered eternal, Muslims also speak about the "occasions of revelation" as a necessary component for interpreting the meaning of a given passage. In other words, many of the verses in the Qur'an speak directly to particular circumstances. A good illustration of an "occasion of revelation" is found at the beginning of *surah* (chapter) 80, entitled "He Frowned." The first verses of the chapter read:

In the name of Allah, most benevolent, ever-merciful.
He frowned and turned away

Because a blind man came to him.
What made you think that he will not grow in virtue,
Or be admonished, and the admonition profit him?
As for the one who is not in want of any thing,
You pay full attention,
Though it is not your concern if he should not grow (in fullness)
As for him who comes to you striving (after goodness),
And is also fearful (of God),
You neglect.
Assuredly this is a reminder
For any one who desires to bear it in mind [Qur'an 80:1–12].[5]

According to Muslim commentators, the specific occasion for this revelation helps one to understand it in context as well as draw the larger principles being communicated. One day, during the early Meccan period, Muhammad was engaged in conversation with one of the prominent leaders of the Quraysh (the ruling tribe in Mecca). As Muhammad was seeking to persuade the man of the truth of Islam, a blind man came and asked him a question concerning the faith. The prophet was annoyed at the interruption. He frowned and turned away from the blind man. The revelation then comes that makes clear one should not judge the importance of another person on the basis of the person's appearance or status. Further, one should never turn away from another sincerely seeking to know about Islam. It is important to understand this approach to interpretation of the Qur'an because it helps prevent people from reading verses out of context to fortify an already established position. By establishing deeper principles, Muslims could be more flexible in applying those principles in very different times and circumstances.

The Qur'an identifies Muhammad as "a beautiful model" (Qur'an 33:21) and the authoritative leader: "O you who believe, obey God, and obey the Messenger, and those in authority over you" (Qur'an 4:62). Even though glimpses of Muhammad are woven into the Qur'an, a remarkably full picture of the man can be better discerned from the detailed records of his sayings and actions. From the beginning, Muslims endeavored to accurately preserve Muhammad's sayings (known as the hadith) and his practices and the actions that gained his approval (known collectively as the *sunnah*.)[6] Muslims look first to the Qur'an as the highest authority. Next in importance are Muhammad's words and guidance concerning the temporal religious, political, and military matters (preserved in collections of hadith), most notably in the development of Islamic law (*shariah*).[7] The extraordinary details about Muhammad's sayings and actions, coupled with his role as the model or exemplar of the faith, reinforces the strong and personal connection Muslims feel for the prophet. This deep love and respect for God's messenger helps explain why so many Muslims worldwide reacted angrily to the perceived denigration of Muhammad in Salman Rushdie's 1988 book *The Satanic Verses,* as well as to the 2005 publication in a Danish newspaper of 12 cartoons depicting Muhammad.[8]

The authoritative collections of hadith require approximately 2,000 printed pages published in multiple volumes. The hadith cover a range of topics, from details about the obligations related to the ritual-devotional duties known as the Five Pillars of Islam (the declaration of faith in one God and Muhammad as God's messenger, the five daily prayers, fasting during the month of Ramadan, giving alms, and pilgrimage to Mecca) to teachings elaborating on qur'anic revelations about the Day of Judgment, heaven, and hell. The hadith include all types of information, such as details about seemingly minor daily events. For example, one hadith recalls the story of a man who rushed up to the prophet to ask if spitting on the wall of the mosque near the time of prayer would subject the offender to hell fire. The prophet replied to the clearly distressed man that such an act would not result in eternal condemnation. But, he noted, it was not a good thing to do.

Throughout Islamic history, the hadith have furnished extensive resources for organizing individual and communal life in the religious, political, and economic realms. But Muslims have often not agreed with one another's interpretations and have appropriated the sayings and traditions of the prophet in ways that produce different approaches to important issues at the intersection of religion and politics. The sayings and actions of the prophet help us to construct a detailed picture of daily life in Mecca and Medina, including the interplay between religion and politics and the relationships between Muslims and non-Muslims in the emerging Islamic state.

## The Message of Muhammad

From the beginning of his prophetic utterances, the messages of Muhammad represented a direct threat to the religious, political, economic, and social structure of the tribal society in seventh-century Mecca. As an oasis and connecting point for caravan routes, Mecca was both a vibrant commercial center and a focal point for religious life in the Arabian peninsula. The leaders of Mecca embraced and promoted a diverse, polytheistic religious atmosphere. The oligarchy benefited enormously from religious practices and festivals, most notably an annual event connected to the Kaaba, an ancient cube-shaped stone building that then housed numerous gods. The radical monotheism preached by Muhammad challenged both the power of the Meccan leaders and a major source of their economic prosperity.

Muhammad's revelations were also an affront to the rigid, male-dominated, tribal social structure. Muhammad declared that all people are equal before God. When a slave of a prominent Meccan leader embraced Islam and was threatened with death, Abu Bakr, an early convert and one of Muhammad's closest friends, paid a high price for the slave and set him free. The former slave, Bilal, became prominent in early Islam as the first Muslim to sing out the lyrical public call to prayer.

In another bold rejection of established social norms, an early revelation forbade the practice of female infanticide. Whereas male children were highly prized in pre-Islamic Arabia, females were often unwanted, a source of shame, and a burden to parents. Baby girls were frequently buried alive in the desert sand shortly after birth. The Qur'an warned that those who killed female infants would be exposed on the Day of Judgment:

> When the female infant, buried alive, is questioned—for what crime was she killed; when the scrolls are laid open; when the World on High is unveiled; when the Blazing Fire is kindled to fierce heat; and when the Garden is brought near—Then shall each soul know what it has put forward [Qur'an 81:8–9].

Numerous other qur'anic passages and hadith echo themes of equality between men and women before God, the importance of kindness toward daughters and sons, and a woman's rights in marriage, divorce, and inheritance. Although there are many contested issues related to gender and Islam today, it is clear that the Qur'an and the teachings of Muhammad significantly elevated the rights and status of females and, in the process, they directly challenged the social status quo in seventh-century Arabia.

Predictably, Muhammad and the first Muslims were mocked and harassed. Had Muhammad not been a member of the ruling Quraysh tribe and enjoyed the protection of his powerful uncle, Abu Talib, he would undoubtedly have met with even more severe persecution from the outset. Meccan opposition to Muhammad grew steadily over the decade after he began uttering the revelations. Following the deaths of Muhammad's wife, Khadija, and his uncle, Abu Talib, Meccan leaders of the Quraysh determined to put an end to the fledgling movement. At that same time, Muhammad was approached by a delegation from

Yathrib (later named Medina)[9] some 200 miles to the north. They invited Muhammad and his followers to immigrate to Medina, where they could practice their religion freely if Muhammad would agree to be the arbitrator between feuding tribes in their city. Beginning in July of 622 CE, the small Muslim community began moving to Yathrib. Muhammad and his close friend, Abu Bakr, were the last to leave Mecca, just narrowly escaping a plot to kill the prophet.

The *hijra* ("flight" to Medina) in 622 CE occurred 12 years after Muhammad's first revelation. It marks the start of the Islamic calendar because the Islamic *ummah* ("community") was now unencumbered and the new Islamic state was established. Muhammad continued to receive the revelations that constitute the Qur'an until his death in 632 CE.

## Medina: The First Islamic State

Soon after reaching Medina, many of the Arab tribes there embraced Islam and Muhammad's religious, political, and military leadership. Muhammad had come to Medina to serve as an arbiter; he quickly became the leader of a new religious-political government. In the process of securing economic stability, keeping the peace, and adjudicating disputes within the city, Muhammad rendered many decisions. Detailed records from the decade in Medina show him to be decisive in matters of religion and often pragmatic in matters of governance. The new framework for society was fashioned around the ummah, a community bound by the religious faith and commitment of Muslims rather than by tribal affiliation and loyalty. As a result, the first Islamic state was fashioned under Muhammad's leadership in Medina (in what is now Saudi Arabia) between 622 and 632 CE. The authority for the new approach to religion and politics rests on the Qur'an and the sayings and actions of Muhammad. All subsequent efforts to construct Islamic states must build on interpretations of this foundation.

In subsequent centuries, when debate over tensions between religious and political authorities would erupt, leading scholars such as al-Ghazali (d. 1111) and Ibn Taymiyyah (d. 1328) cited Muhammad's concern for effective leaders to oversee the functions of the state. For example, Muhammad appointed and reappointed Khalid ibn al-Walid as commander of the Muslim armies despite his dissatisfaction with Khalid's religious behavior. Many influential early Muslims leaders surpassed Khalid in their knowledge of Islam and personal piety, but Muhammad must have decided that effective military leadership required skills apart from religious faith.

Another famous episode, the Treaty of Hudaybiyya, illustrates Muhammad's political pragmatism. In 628, when the Muslims of Medina had gained the upper hand over the Meccans, Muhammad led 1,500 Muslims on a pilgrimage back to Mecca. When the Meccans dispatched some 200 men to intercept them, Muhammad stopped short of Mecca and began a negotiation process. He agreed to terms whereby the Muslims would not make the pilgrimage that year and both sides would embrace a 10-year peace treaty. Muhammad returned the following year, entered Mecca peacefully, and cleansed the Kaaba of its many idols. Despite having a dominant position, Muhammad demonstrated the wisdom of diplomacy with non-Muslim adversaries even though it required him to agree to some provisions that were unfavorable. Consequently, even during the best circumstances—the time when the prophet is leading the emerging Islamic state—practical needs of a functioning government may take precedence over a religious ideal.[10]

## Relationships with Non-Muslims in Early Islam

When Muhammad assumed political authority in Medina, there were Arab as well as Jewish tribes living there, so the structures for governance also had to include provisions for the non-Muslims. A well-known passage in the Qur'an emphasizes the religious rights of individuals: "There is no compulsion in matters of religion" (Qur'an 2:256).

Muhammad promulgated a formal agreement between the Muslims and non-Muslims in Medina. Several early Islamic documents include versions of this "constitution" or "charter" of Medina.[11] It contained rules for diverse communities living together under the authority of God and God's messenger, Muhammad. Some key provisions outline the framework Muhammad established: to provide security for the community, Medina was to be free from violence and weapons; religious freedoms and security for women were guaranteed; a tax system was established to support the community's needs, especially in time of conflict with the Meccans; and a judicial system attended to peaceful resolution of disputes. The Jewish tribes were considered part of the community of believers. Each group would practice its religion without interference so long as the Jews did not inhibit the Muslims. Jews, for example, must pay taxes to support the cost of war against enemies of Islam, but they and other non-Muslims were not obligated to fight in the religious wars of the Muslims.

The Qur'an's affirmation of the People of the Book and the provisions for non-Muslims incorporated into the political structures in Medina are an important resource for interfaith relationships throughout Islamic history. The Qur'an recognizes religious diversity and even declares it part of God's plan.[12] At the same time, the formative period also includes components of violent confrontation between Muslims and non-Muslims. The broader theological understanding and affirmation of God's revelations to the People of the Book is set alongside the requirement to proclaim the message and stand up in defense of Islam when it is under assault. Two examples from the decade in Medina illustrate how difficult it can be to hold these two mandates together when there is deadly conflict that threatens the ummah. The two examples are poignantly relevant today: passages in the Qur'an that allow or require Muslims to fight, and the experiences of the three Jewish tribes in Medina.

In the aftermath of September 11, selected verses in the Qur'an have been quoted repeatedly in an effort to "prove" that it endorses or even requires the killing of Jews, Christians, and other non-Muslims. Here is an example of one of what are called the "sword verses":

> Fight those in the way of God who fight you, but do not be aggressive:
> God does not like aggressors.
> And fight those (who fight you) wherever you find them,
> And expel them from the place they had turned you out from.
> Oppression is worse than killing.
> Do not fight them by the Holy Mosque unless they fight you there.
> If they do, then slay them: such is the requital for unbelievers [Qur'an 2:190–91].

This passage and a few similar verses are often employed to justify the behavior of violent extremists, or by non-Muslims who wish to paint a picture of Islam as an inherently violent religion that teaches its adherents to kill unbelievers and infidels (including Jews and Christians). Such generic claims appear to contradict a multitude of passages that speak positively about Jews and Christians, as People of the Book who are also promised their reward in heaven.[13]

I have asked more than a hundred Muslim scholars and academicians personally how they interpret such texts. Most have replied by pointing to one or more leading commentators through the centuries. As is the case with many passages in the Bible—especially passages that appear harsh or even contradictory to well-known themes such as God's love for all of creation or the requirement to treat others as you would like to be treated[14]—there are several ways Muslims have interpreted and are applying such texts. Most interpreters focus on the occasion of the revelation, namely, a very specific incident when some nonbelievers among the Quraysh had broken a truce and were preparing to fight the Muslims. Other commentators and scholars claim a more general interpretation that applies to fighting against all infidels when Islam is under attack. Some add that this verse must be taken in the context of other verses where proportional response to those who are fighting Muslims is required.

It is common—extremely common—to find people in all religious communities who read their sacred texts selectively. When one lifts a line here or two sentences there from the page, one can make a sacred text support literally any position or theology imaginable. The world of the 21st century is awash with religious leaders and obedient believers who use sacred texts in this way. The consequences of such selective narrowness and the zealotry it reinforces are often deadly. The righteous slaughter by Christian crusaders and inquisitors as well as the massacre carried out by Baruch Goldstein at Abraham's tomb are chilling examples.

Muslims, like Jews and Christians, who claim a sacred text face the challenges of understanding and interpreting the whole text. The ceaseless production of numerous, multivolume commentaries on the Bible and Qur'an right up to this day illustrates that this process of interpretation is ongoing. It is easy enough to declare the "truth" and then find sacred texts to support the claim; it is far more daunting to wrestle with the entire text and seek to discern the meaning and contemporary application of the truths one believes are contained therein.

The fate of the three Jewish tribes in Medina proved to be grim. Following the first major military victory of the Muslims in Medina over the Meccans in 624, the weakest Jewish tribe, the Qaynuqa, was forced to leave Medina, taking some of their possessions with them to Syria. Two years later, a second tribe, the Nadir, was attacked by the Muslims for failing to come to their aid in the second major battle with the Meccans. There was no clear victor in this battle, but Muhammad was injured and the Nadir were accused of plotting against the prophet of Islam. They negotiated terms for their departure with their camels and movable goods. The Muslims seized and divided up the Nadir's land. Finally, the third tribe, the Qurayza, was accused of comporting with the enemy in the last great battle between the Muslims and Meccans in 627. Although scholars have differed on whether and to what extent the Qurayza were guilty of treason, they were declared guilty by a Muslim leader appointed for the task by Muhammad. The judgment was extremely harsh: the men of the Qurayza were beheaded in the central marketplace of Medina, their property was seized, and the women and children were sold off into slavery.[15]

A paradigm emerges from these early years. People of the Book living under Islamic rule have their rights and should be protected, unless they are guilty of joining forces with the enemies who are attacking Islam and Muslims. In this situation, Muslims are allowed, or even required, to fight back in defense of Islam. A great deal depends, then, on the interpretation of what constitutes an attack on Islam and what constitutes "defense." The presence of large Jewish communities in Persia (Iran), Mesopotamia (Iraq), Syria and Lebanon, Palestine, Egypt, the Magreb (especially Morocco), and Islamic Spain throughout Islamic history is instructive. Clearly, the vast majority of Muslims—at least prior to the creation of the state of Israel in 1948—did not consider the Jewish presence in their midst as a threat that required a military response.

## The Crisis of Leadership in Early Islam

Under Muhammad's guidance, foundational Islamic political structures took shape in Medina that have several distinctive characteristics. First, the prophet put into place a wholly new structure for society that made adherence to Islam, not tribal affiliation, the organizing principle. Second, the authority guiding the Islamic state was derived from the Qur'an and the teachings of Muhammad. Clear guidelines for religious practice were intertwined with pragmatic approaches to the daily affairs of governance. Finally, the first community offered both a model for peaceful coexistence with non-Muslims and a precedent for violent confrontation with whoever is perceived to threaten the Muslims. Thus these formative years established a basis on which various Muslim regimes could build and adapt amid diverse circumstances over many centuries. Nevertheless, Muslims have been far from united on how best to structure and implement an Islamic governmental system once Muhammad was no longer on the scene. These challenges were vividly manifest in the crisis precipitated by the unexpected death of the prophet in 632.

When Muhammad died after a short illness, Muslims were divided as to whether there were specifics about who should succeed him. Sunni Muslims (from *ahl al-sunnah*, "the people who follow the customs of the prophet") believed he left no instruction, but the less numerous Shi'ite Muslims (from the Arabic phrase *shi'at Ali*, "partisans of Ali") believed that Muhammad specifically designated Ali, his first cousin and son-in-law, to be his successor or caliph. Ali was the first male convert to Islam, a devout defender of the faith and the father of Muhammad's grandsons, Hasan and Hussein. The Shi'ites cite a hadith from the last year of Muhammad's life: "Anyone for whom I am the *mawla*, Ali is his *mawla* too." The term *mawla* can mean "master," "patron," "friend," or "client." The Shi'ites take it to mean master. Most authoritative Sunni collections of hadith don't include this saying. Those Sunnis who accept the authenticity of the utterance simply interpret it to refer to Muhammad's close relationship with Ali.

Muhammad's death produced a crisis of leadership. A small group of prominent Muslims affirmed the role of Abu Bakr (the second male convert and the father of Muhammad's beloved last wife, Aisha), not Ali. Abu Bakr assumed the title "successor of the messenger of God" (*khalifat rasul Allah*) or caliph. Most Muslims at the time deemed Abu Bakr the person best qualified to lead the community, a position reinforced by Muhammad's appointment of Abu Bakr as the leader of the daily prayers during the last days of Muhammad's illness.[16] As successor to Muhammad, he exercised authority as leader of the community, but he was not a prophet; the role of prophet ended with Muhammad.

Tension between the Islamic ideals of piety and egalitarianism and the deeply rooted traditional cultural bias toward blood kinship and tribal hierarchy is woven into this pivotal decision about leadership. These competing forces have continued to animate debates and decisions for centuries.

Abu Bakr died two years after Muhammad, and Umar ibn al-Khattab, who had been a companion of the prophet and close advisor of Abu Bakr, became the second caliph. In a story line reminiscent of the Apostle Paul, Umar was a fierce opponent of Islam prior to his sudden conversion in 618. He then became the staunchest advocate of the faith as well as one of the most accomplished military leaders. Under his leadership (634–644), the Muslim armies moved out of Arabia in dramatic fashion. They conquered Jerusalem and Damascus to the north, Egypt in the west, and Mesopotamia—the Tigris and Euphrates valley—in the east. The successful military campaigns and rapid expansion presented a host of organizational and administrative challenges that required new institutions to maintain political authority over its territory. Asma Afsaruddin, a scholar of early Islamic history, illustrates this point with Umar's policy on booty from conquest:

> One of the major innovations undertaken by Umar during his tenure as caliph was the institution of the state register of pensions known as the *diwan* . . . in order to effectively and equitably disburse the increasing revenues pouring into the state treasury. . . . Those who were among the earliest converts to Islam and had fought in the early battles were given larger stipends. . . . Abu Bakr and Ali believed in complete equality in the disbursement of pensions while Umar subscribed to a preferential system.[17]

There is little indication that non-Muslim peoples in the conquered territories were expected to embrace Islam. A range of factors contributed to some non-Muslims shifting allegiance to Islam, among them the compelling message of Islam, intermarriage, and the desire to share in the military, political, and economic success this movement enjoyed. For the most part, however, non-Muslims were largely free to function within their own communities, so long as they paid a specified tax (called *jizya*) to the ruling Muslim authorities. Numerous stories from this period attest to Umar's generous attitude toward Jews and Christians.

Contrary to the 21st-century view promulgated by some highly visible Christian and Muslim leaders, Islam does not teach its followers to label Jews and Christians as infidels and then seek to kill them. Qur'anic affirmation of the People of the Book and the attitudes and actions of Umar and other caliphs help explain how large numbers of Jews were able to live in Iraq, Iran, Egypt, Morocco, Palestine, and elsewhere for more than 1,400 years. Similarly, the presence of 15–17 million indigenous Arabic-speaking Christians in the Middle East today indicates a long history of accommodation and cooperation rather than constant military assault or forced conversion by the overwhelming Muslim majority.

An assassin mortally wounded Umar in 644. In the days before his death, he created a six-person *shura* ("advisory council") to select the next caliph. The two finalists, Ali and Uthman ibn Affan, were both members of the shura. Ali was once more bypassed when Uthman, another early convert and prominent member of the Umayyad clan, was named the third caliph. In the view of many Muslims today, Uthman's election illustrates that a form of democracy was practiced in the first decades of Islam.

As it had with his two predecessors, the rapidly changing landscape required Uthman to devise rules of political conduct. In an effort to exercise greater control over the provinces of Egypt, Syria, and Iraq, for instance, Uthman appointed relatives to top positions in these regions. Some Muslims were willing to accept his authority, but historical records reveal that many others strongly disagreed with him on various matters. In the 12th year of his tenure, anger against Uthman peaked when several hundred disgruntled Arabs from Egypt and Iraq challenged the aging caliph. Fifty days of heated confrontation ended when a group of Egyptians assassinated Uthman in June of 656 as he sat reciting the Qur'an in the mosque at Medina.[18]

Amidst the turmoil following Uthman's death, Ali finally assumed leadership of the community as the fourth caliph. His five-year tenure was tumultuous. A concern for egalitarianism led him to reverse the

policy of Umar and Uthman on the pensions (*diwan*). He declared that
everyone entitled to a government stipend would receive the same
amount regardless of when the person had embraced Islam or how many
wars he had fought. Although this move endeared Ali to many, it also
embittered many others who had enjoyed privileged positions in the
early decades of Islam. Ali encountered other strong opposition from
within the community as well. Two well-respected leaders headed a
group demanding that Uthman's death be avenged. With the support of
Muhammad's wife Aisha, they mounted a force to challenge Ali, who
was busy consolidating his control in the garrison towns of southern
Iraq. In December 656, six months after Uthman's death, the two
Muslim armies clashed near the Iraqi town of Basra. Ali's army prevailed
decisively, but this was not the end of the civil conflict. Ali moved from
Medina to Kufa in Iraq. Powerful opposition remained, however, in
another emerging center of power: Syria.

Mu'awiya, whom Uthman had appointed governor in Syria, continued to insist that the assassins of the third caliph be prosecuted.
Mu'awiya refused to recognize Ali's leadership and Ali refused to acqui-
esce to Mu'awiya's demand. In 657 their respective armies met at Siffin
in Iraq. Following efforts to negotiate, hostilities broke out. Almost
immediately, Mu'wiya's men raised copies of the Qur'an on their swords
and called for arbitration. Ali agreed. Even though the negotiation
dragged on unproductively for months, the events undermined Ali's
claim to the caliphate. Some of his own supporters turned on him, and
he pursued them vigorously. Ali won some short-term victories, but his
regime continued to weaken. Ultimately, like his two predecessors, Ali
was assassinated in 661.

Upon Ali's death, Mu'awiya proclaimed himself the Caliph and
promptly moved the seat of government to Damascus in Syria. Just 29
years after the death of Muhammad, the "golden era" or what most
Muslims call the period of the *rashidun* ("the Rightly Guided Caliphs")
had come to an end. The golden era of the first four caliphs was far from
tranquil, though. Rapid territorial expansion, demands of political necessity, and bitter internal divisions shaped these initial decades. The earliest
Muslims disagreed about how the caliph should be chosen, the limits of
his power, and how faithful adherents should respond if the caliph was
thought to be acting unjustly. Even so, Muslims throughout the centuries
and today look to the rule of Muhammad and the rashidun for prece-
dents and guidance in devising authentic Islamic forms of government in
vastly different settings.

## The Umayyad and Abbasid Dynasties

With the ascent of Mu'awiya, who was a Sunni Muslim and part of the Umayyad clan, the question of succession was put to rest. For the next 90 years, the caliphate would be passed on from father to son. Ali's oldest son and Muhammad's grandson, Hasan, posed a modest challenge to Mu'awiya's authority but did not threaten or challenge the new regime as his younger brother, Hussein, would in subsequent decades.[19]

While Mu'awiya expanded his power from Damascus, the Shi'ite Muslims believed legitimate leadership belonged with the descendants of the prophet, not with the current rulers. They continued to strengthen their ranks in the military towns in southern Iraq. Hussein emerged as their leader. With the passing of Mu'awiya, his son, Yazid, became the new caliph in 680 and the long-standing civil strife erupted into war. In 680, Yazid's forces slaughtered the outnumbered Shi'ites; Hussein, the grandson of Muhammad, was beheaded in the battle at Karbala. The slaying of Muhammad's grandson by Muslims less than 50 years after the prophet's death forever changed Islam. The commemoration of this disaster, known as Ashura, became the most sacred day in the religious calendar for the Shi'ites. They continue to view the martyrdom of Hussein at the hands of Yazid as both a reminder of temporal injustice and a powerful symbol of redemptive suffering. After this defeat, the political power of the Shi'a posed no immediate threat to the Umayyad dynasty. The Shi'ites continued to look to Muhammad's direct descendants as their leader or imam. Because the Shi'ite imams were believed to be guided by a divine light within, their teachings added another type of authority within this minority Muslim community. What began as a simple question of succession when Muhammad died developed over time into branches of Islam with their own theological understandings and some distinct practices.

The Umayyad dynasty governed over the most rapid expansion of an empire the world had ever seen. By the year 732—a hundred years after Muhammad—Muslim armies had moved across North Africa to Morocco and up into Spain, all the way to the Pyrenees Mountains on the border of France. At the same time, the Muslim military expansion to the east moved through Persia (Iran) and progressed all the way to modern-day Pakistan. The move to Damascus facilitated their ability to manage the multiple demands of such a vast empire.

In addition to its Jewish inhabitants, Damascus was a major center for Orthodox Christianity for six centuries prior to the coming of Islam.

Jews and Christians continued to live and practice their religion throughout the reign of the Umayyad dynasty. There are a number of written sources revealing a range of responses to the early Arab conquests. Some offer a harsh critique of the Arabs; some express gratitude and relief at being liberated from oppressive rule by the Byzantines.[20] The first coherent treatment of Islam by a major Christian thinker appears at this time. John of Damascus (d. 750) lived in proximity to the Umayyad court. It is fascinating to read how he critiques Islam as a kind of Christian heresy. He doesn't perceive Islam as a new religion but as a type of Christianity with heretical teachings. He points to what Christianity and Islam have in common: belief in God, Abraham, Moses, David, and the prophets; angels; Mary and the virgin birth of Jesus; a coming Day of Judgment; and heaven and hell. But he saw rejection of the divinity of Christ and the doctrine of the Trinity as grave distortions. John of Damascus helps us see Christians living and functioning at the very center of the Islamic state.[21] As we have seen before, at various times Muslims treated other People of the Book as followers of true, revealed religions, though operating without the perfected revelation afforded by Islam.

The Umayyad dynasty brought organization and stability to an expanding empire that ruled over many non-Muslim inhabitants. They embarked on a building campaign that included two of the most magnificent structures on earth today: the Great Umayyad Mosque in Damascus and the Dome of the Rock in Jerusalem. Their rule included both effective and corrupt leaders on all levels. Those who opposed the Umayyad rulers decried them for abandoning Islamic principles and returning to a tribal form of dynastic rule in pursuit of the earthly kingdom. Critics cited their arrogance for changing the title of the caliph from "Successor to the Messenger of God" (*khalifat rasul Allah*) to "Deputy of God" (*khalifat Allah*). The massacre at Karbala in 680, however, was the most egregious transgression in the view of many. Memories of this outrage against the grandson of the prophet continued to spark civil conflict and revolutionary movements throughout the 90 years of Umayyad rule.

Between 747 and 750, the discontent within the Umayyad empire coalesced into a revolutionary movement to topple the regime. The Shi'ites loyal to Ali and the family of the prophet allied with a strong military force in Persia (Iran) that rallied around another family with deep roots in Mecca. The revolutionaries succeeded in both toppling the Umayyad dynasty and establishing Abu 'l-Abbas, a descendant of an uncle of Muhammad, as the new caliph in Iraq, beginning the reign of the

Abbasid dynasty. He presided over the systematic hunting down and kill-ing of all but one member of the ruling Umayyad clan. The one who got away, Abd al-Rahman, was a young man who made his way across North Africa and into Spain. Less than a decade later, Abd al-Rahman estab-lished an Umayyad regime to rival the Abbasids—later called a caliphate—in Spain. This marked the beginning of a truly remarkable civilization where culture and interreligious cooperation flourished in Spain, a phe-nomenon we will discuss later in this chapter.

Establishment of the new Abbasid dynasty effectively marginalized the Shi'ites once more. Those direct descendants of Muhammad who many believed were uniquely guided by God had helped overthrow the Umay-yads, but were yet again on the outside looking in. The Abbasids consoli-dated their power and began what would become an unbroken line of dynastic rule based in Baghdad for more than three centuries. Between the eighth and eleventh centuries CE (the second through fifth centuries of Islam), the structure of Islamic sciences and legal systems and the brilliant Islamic civilization flourished. In a famous hadith, Muhammad called on believers to "seek knowledge wherever you may find it . . . even unto China." The Muslims heeded his call. The quest for knowledge expanded exponentially as Muslims passionately pursued theology, philosophy, mathematics, medicine, horticulture, astronomy, navigation, architecture, and other disciplines. During the so-called Dark Ages in Europe, when doctors were treating people with leeches, Muslim physicians in Baghdad were charting the circulatory and nervous system and performing delicate operations. As with other scholarly endeavors, Muslims discovered, clari-fied, and substantially enriched mathematics through innovation. Algebra, for instance, is an Arabic term. The number system we use today—Arabic numerals—reflects but one of many ways Western civilization is deeply indebted to Islamic scholarly achievements during the centuries when Islam dominated the world.[22]

During the reign of Harun al-Rashid (786–809), the fifth Abbasid caliph, the court was at the height of its splendor. He is remembered as an ideal monarch in the stories of the *Thousand and One Nights*. A patron of the arts and supporter of the great cultural renaissance under way in Baghdad, Harun al-Rashid's court strongly resembled the monar-chy of the earlier Sassanian and Persian rulers. At the same time, he, and subsequent caliphs, left no doubt about their power over life and death: an executioner routinely stood at the ready behind the ruler's throne. The relationship between religion and political rule had undergone consider-able transformation in the 150 years since the Muslims first expanded beyond Arabia. In the complex world of the Abbasid empire, Harun al-Rashid could not function as the religious, political, military, and economic leader, as was possible during the caliphate of Umar. Historian Marshall G. S. Hodgson describes the changing organization of government under Harun al-Rashid and his second son, al-Ma'mun (816–833), in this way:

> Under the caliph, the government was now largely delegated to administrators, a vizier as financial chief and generally head of government, and his secretaries in their many bureaus. The caliph was not expected necessarily to take a personal role in government, but rather to be a court of ultimate appeal. . . . Al-Rashid's son, who took the duties of government very seriously, summed up those duties under three heads: maintenance of justice in the courts, of security in the streets and highways, and of defense on the frontiers. That is, government had no concern with the positive social ordering, with actively creating conditions for the good life (this was left to family tradition or to the efforts of the *'ulama*, according to taste); it was simply to guarantee security.[23]

In addition to the quest for knowledge we have already mentioned, scholarly studies within Islam both expanded and deepened during the Abbasid dynasty. During this time, the hadith, so essential for doctrine, faith, practice, and government, were carefully organized and evaluated by the recognized scholars known as the *'ulama*. The scholars of the Qur'an and hadith became the guardians of orthodox teaching and the driving force behind the formalization of shariah (Islamic law). During the Abbasid period, the recognized Sunni schools of Islamic law were developed into four major branches. The differences in the legal schools depended on important factors such as the degree to which Muslims were bound by the decisions of the early companions of the prophet. Some allowed more flexibility in applying principles of jurisprudence as scholars applied analogy and developed consensus around contemporary issues. Contrary to the popular media images taken from eye-for-an-eye punishments meted out by the Taliban in Afghanistan, shariah law has always been a broad term encompassing a work in progress. Shariah can refer to different aspects of "law," ranging from personal religious morality to the "ideal" of God's eternal, unchanging prescriptions for human behavior. Muslims throughout the centuries and today have affirmed that even when shariah is thought of in terms of God's eternal prescriptions for human behavior, Muslims must continuously work out the details for rules to govern how they should live and their societies function. Muslim scholars have always recognized that changing times demanded new rules and appropriate adaptations.[24] Alongside the major legal schools within Sunni Islam, the Shi'ites developed legal traditions consistent with the ongoing interpretations of the line of imams, whom they believed were guided by God as infallible interpreters of the Qur'an and the requirements of Islam. This process continues today, with the most venerated Shi'ite leaders providing guidance and legal counsel on all types of issues confronting Muslims.

We know a great deal about the history of Abbasid rule and the rival regimes that later sprang up in parts of the empire. In addition to the Umayyad-led caliphate based in Spain, for example, the Fatimids, a powerful regime based in Egypt, held power over large portions of the Islamic lands across North Africa, Syria, and the Arabian peninsula from 909 to 1171. They were Shi'ites who took their name from Fatima, the daughter of Muhammad, wife of Ali, and mother of Hasan and Hussein. Under the Fatimids, Cairo became a cultural and academic center of the Muslim world during this time. They established al-Azhar, the first university in the Western world, which continues to hold a place of prominence for Islamic studies and training religious leaders to this day. When the first crusaders reached Jerusalem at the end of the 11th century, the Muslims they encountered were under Fatimid rule. Three-quarters of a century later, the legendary Muslim general Salah al-Din (Saladin) recaptured Jerusalem and also displaced the Fatimids. Salah al-Din then established a new Sunni regime, the Ayyubids (1171–1250). The end of an era loomed just ahead; 626 years after the death of the prophet, Mongol armies stormed through the region in 1258.

The ninth through the twelfth centuries were a richly diverse time in Islamic history, as numerous studies of leading Muslim philosophers, theologians, historians, and scholars have made clear. Authoritative collections of hadith, major legal schools, splintered groups among the Shi'ites, the emergence of the mystical tradition of Sufism, and the stunning intellectual and cultural contributions of Muslims reflect far different dynamics than those shaping the earliest decades of Islam.[25]

## Islam in Spain and Beyond

While the primary focus of the Islamic world centered on the cultural, economic, and scholarly achievements of the Abbasid dynasty, the Umayyad legacy took root and blossomed in distant Spain. The only survivor of the Abbasid takeover, Abd al-Rahman, established a provincial regime in Cordoba in 756. Although many under his rule considered him the legitimate caliph, it would be another two centuries before his descendants formally claimed that title. For the next 300 years, Spain remained under Umayyad rule, forever shaping the history of Europe and its civilization. Visitors to Cordoba, Granada, and Seville can still witness the architectural splendor of Islamic Spain. What is less widely known or explored, however, is the story of interfaith cooperation and coexistence that made Spain so distinctive. Borrowing from a long standing designation of Cordoba, Maria Rosa Menocal describes this era of Islamic Spain as "the ornament of the world." In spite of their differences and episodes of communal conflict, Muslim leaders created and nurtured a tolerant, respectful culture in which Jews and Christians could also flourish. Islamic Spain produced Jewish luminaries such as Moses Maimonides (the "second" Moses) and Judah Halevi, a Spanish Jewish physician, poet, and philosopher. Menocal summarizes an environment where conflicting ideologies and theologies created a synergy nourishing all communities:

> It was there that profoundly Arabized Jews rediscovered and reinvented Hebrew; there that Christians embraced nearly every aspect of Arabic style—from the intellectual style of philosophy to the architectural style of mosques . . . there that men of unshakable faith, like Abelard and Maimonides and Averroes, saw no contradiction in pursuing the truth, whether philosophical or scientific or religious, across confessional lines. This vision of a culture of tolerance recognized that incongruity in the shaping of individuals as well as their cultures was enriching and productive.[26]

In the early 10th century, when Abbasids ruled in Baghdad and the Fatimids controlled North Africa, parts of Arabia and Syria, Abd al-Rahman III, the Umayyad caliph who ruled for 40 years in Cordoba, elevated Hasdai ibn Sheprut, a brilliantly well-educated Jew, to *vizier*, the top position in his government because he was determined to be the best person for the multiple skills the job required. As People of the Book, Jews in Spain had almost unlimited opportunities for education and economic advancement, even as they, and the Christians, maintained their religious practices and communities.

The story of Jews, Christians, and other non-Muslims living under Islamic rule is, of course, multifaceted. One can easily find numerous examples of conflict and persecution in particular settings. The dynamic relationships could improve or worsen depending on the Muslim leaders or as external circumstances varied (for example, during the centuries of the crusades and during the sectarian strife within Iraq in the years following the war that began in 2003). Despite numerous difficulties and hardships, however, we find many examples of Jews and Christians flourishing during centuries of Muslim rule in Spain, in Egypt, in Palestine, and in Mesopotamia.[27] This long history of coexistence contrasts sharply with the uninformed and widely propagated claims that the Qur'an teaches Muslims to convert or kill Christians and Jews. If this is what the Qur'an teaches or Islam demands, as many preachers and pundits today assert, it appears the overwhelming majority of Muslims throughout the centuries failed to get the message.

As with all great civilizations in world history, the grandeur of Islamic civilization did not last. The extraordinary political, economic, and military power that stretched from Spain to India was fractured prior to the Mongol invasion and visibly in decline thereafter. In the past 500 years, new and powerful Islamic empires have arisen in portions of the previously controlled lands: the Ottoman Empire, the Safavid Dynasty, and the Mughul Empire. Distinctive approaches to government that drew on the connections between religion and politics can be seen in these more recent Islamic regimes.

The origins of the Ottoman Empire can be traced to the 13th century, but it emerged as a formidable power based in Istanbul beginning in 1453. Over the course of the next two centuries, Ottoman rule covered a vast stretch of land in what is now Hungary, Bulgaria, Rumania, the Ukraine, Greece, Turkey, Syria, Jordan, Lebanon, Israel/Palestine, Egypt, Libya, Algeria, Tunisia, Yemen, and parts of Iran and Iraq. The Ottoman sultans, sometimes called caliphs, generally enjoyed long reigns and were then succeeded by one of their sons. In the 17th century, the pattern of succession changed, whereby the oldest member of the ruling family would replace the caliph. The empire developed an extensive bureaucratic system led by viziers who controlled the army and navy, provincial governments, and all aspects of civil service. These viziers reported to the Grand Vizier who effectively ran the government.

The Ottomans took responsibility for the care and protection of Islamic sacred places (Mecca, Medina, and Jerusalem) and practices such as the annual pilgrimage (*hajj*) to Mecca. They developed and implemented Islamic structures to maintain shariah law through a religious structure for the religious scholars that somewhat paralleled the political organization. The legal religious system included judges in cities and local settings (*qadi*) and regional interpreters of shariah (*mufti*) to adjudicate religious matters. These systems still function today. Officially recognized Muslim legal officials are those who can issue fatwas ("legal opinions") on a range of issues. Over the course of the past three decades, I have had numerous meetings with several of these well-educated and thoughtful Sunni religious leaders—the muftis of Jerusalem, Beirut, and Syria—both individually and with groups of religious leaders.

Jews and Christians within the Ottoman Empire were *dhimmi,* "protected people." As such, they were subject to special taxes (*jizya*). Over the course of the centuries, many developments and changes took place within the empire and within these religious communities. The rich mixture of Christian communities in the Middle East today—from Roman Catholic and Greek Orthodox to the various Oriental Orthodox churches (Armenians, Copts, and Syrian Orthodox) and "uniate" churches (Greek Catholic, Armenian Catholic, Coptic Catholic, Maronite, and others)—were able to grow. The Ottomans implemented a system that recognized the head of each religious community and permitted structure for the management of its religious affairs.[28]

As the Ottomans engaged and battled European powers to the west, the Shi'ite Safavid Dynasty in Iran arose in the 16th century to challenge them on the eastern frontiers. When Ismail I assumed power and took the title of shah in 1501, he implemented a policy of forced conversion. Sunni 'ulama either embraced Shi'ism or were exiled or killed. Ismail I and his successors steadily consolidated their hold on Iran and parts of Iraq during subsequent decades. The most powerful of the Safavid rulers was Shah Abbas, who assumed the throne at age 16 and reigned for more than four decades (1587–1629). The Safavids established the largest branch of Shi'ite Islam, the *ithna'ashari* (Twelver) school, as the official religion of their empire. This remains the dominant form of Islam in Iran today. The shah became the head of a feudal theocracy and claimed direct descent from the family of the prophet. Although this lineage is widely disputed, the Shi'ites were no longer on the outside looking in. The Safavids continually battled the Ottomans over portions of present-day Iraq. Though their regime ended in 1760 after a century of decline, the Safavids permanently changed the landscape and their dynasty foreshadowed many of the dynamics that have played out in Iran and Iraq since the late 1970s, when both the Iranian revolution and Saddam Hussein (a Sunni Muslim whom the Ayatollah Khomeini often called "Yazid," comparing him to the Umayyad caliph responsible for the beheading of the prophet's grandson in 680) moved to center stage at the center of the world's most important and volatile oil-producing regions.

Farther east, in 1526 the Mughul Empire was established in India, where it continued to rule decisively for two centuries and even into the mid-19th century, though the latter rulers were effectively puppets for the British colonial power. The Mughuls reigned over a majority Hindu population and several minority religious communities, most notably Sikhs, Christians, and Zoroastrians. Some of the Mughul rulers were tolerant, and some were highly intolerant of religious diversity. They implemented a well-organized central administration, a single currency, and a system of roads. The Mughul Empire infused the subcontinent with Persian literary and artistic traditions. Their most lasting visible legacy, of course, is seen in the sublime architecture of the Taj Mahal in Agra.

Although the Muslims in the Indian subcontinent were the numerical minority, they constituted a massive population. In the 20th century, when India gained independence from British rule, it was divided into three separate countries: India, Pakistan, and Bangladesh. The Islamic populations today number well over 130 million in each of these three nations, making them the second-, third-, and fourth-largest national groupings of Muslims (Indonesia being the most populous Muslim country).

## Lessons from Islamic History

From this overview of the basis for Islamic approaches to religion and politics and the regimes that have shaped the predominantly Muslim world, we can see the model begun during the life of Muhammad that, under the leadership of the first four "Rightly Guided Caliphs," quickly gave way to various forms of dynastic rule. Throughout their history, Muslims have maintained some acknowledgment of the ideal of a comprehensive and authoritative approach to religion and political rule, but pragmatism and flexibility have dominated the lived reality of Islamic rule. Religious and political systems intertwined in various ways as circumstances arose that required new institutional structures and mechanisms for clarifying orthodox doctrine and legal requirements of Islam. Islamic history reveals that there has been no definitive or characteristic political system. Forms and structures of government varied over time in different parts of the central Islamic lands.

One common theme that is discernible, however, is the necessity of articulating and adjudicating shariah and the authoritative teachings of Shi'ite imams. In other words, whatever the structure of government, Muslims maintain that it should be informed by and responsive to a recognized version of Islamic law. Still, there has always been substantial disagreement over the shape and interpretation of shariah—and that disagreement continues today, as we will see when we turn our attention in the next chapter to the contemporary struggle for the soul of Islam. Understanding the foundational sources of authority and the primary dynamics that have persisted throughout Islamic history helps enable those of us who are not Muslim to better comprehend the hopes, dreams, and passions guiding many contemporary Muslim individuals and groups.

7

# MUSLIM VS. MUSLIM

## THE STRUGGLE FOR THE SOUL OF ISLAM

IN THE DECADE SINCE THE TERRORIST attacks on September 11, 2001, we have been assaulted by grisly images of deadly suicide bombings and videotaped beheadings of hapless American or British hostages. These horrific images combine with those forever etched in our minds of that fateful day in 2001: airplanes crashing into the World Trade Center Towers, trapped victims jumping to their deaths, the crumbling of the massive burning buildings as desperate people scrambled to escape, and the aftermath of passenger planes slamming into the Pentagon and a field in Pennsylvania. Weaving these terrible events together were the claims of violent extremists who said they took their inspiration from and were acting in the name of Islam. It is not at all surprising that many Americans have come to see Islam and its adherents as somehow inherently violent and menacing.

Those Americans who take the trouble to go beyond the most dramatic and sensational media images see other faces of contemporary Islam: Muslim religious leaders in the United States and elsewhere who condemn violence and terrorism, thoughtful Muslim political leaders such as King Abdullah II of Jordan and Palestinian Authority President Mahmoud Abbas pursuing a durable peace process with Israel, and democratic elections in Turkey, Indonesia, Pakistan, and many other predominantly Muslim countries. The positive images of democratic elections in Iraq are juxtaposed with other scenes of violence targeting civilians or rival Muslim groups.

All these events and upheavals of the past decade highlight the ongoing political struggle for the soul of Islam. Muslims constitute the majority in more than 50 countries where the government structure may be parliamentary democracy, authoritarian or theocratic republic, absolute monarchy, or military junta. The substantial majority of these countries already include some form of participatory democracy. Although the most radical views and violent actions invariably dominate media attention, there are many Islamic approaches to religion and politics, all influenced by poorly perceived blends of real and imagined understandings of Islamic history, a sincere appeal to and cynical exploitation of religious sentiments, the experience and legacy of colonialism, the 20th-century rise of the nation-state system, and raw pursuit of power.

The next two chapters present a framework for understanding these factors and influences shaping the contentious disputes about religion and politics in contemporary Islamic countries. Before turning our attention to two case studies (Iran and Iraq), we first consider several central factors that help clarify what is going on in many Islamic countries and why. Understanding more about the roots of Islamic revival and renewal movements during and after the experience of colonialism is essential. So too is exploration of alternative visions for religion and politics in 21st-century Islam—including the role of shariah law—that are being advanced by Muslim scholars and religious leaders today. We begin, however, with consideration of an often-cited but poorly understood theory, the so-called clash of civilizations.

## A Clash of Civilizations?

Many political and religious leaders and commentators, and some scholars in North America today, have explained the tumultuous situation all over the world as a "clash of civilizations." Because we have heard it so often from so many sources, it may seem to describe how Western culture has been interacting with Middle Eastern and Islamic cultures. But it reinforces a simplistic and dangerously inaccurate perspective on more complex and frequently explosive developments. Instead of casually latching on to such explanations, many of us need to think more deeply about the political struggle for the soul of Islam and the impact on international relations. When it comes to the clash-of-civilizations hypothesis, we in the West need to "unlearn" some of what we think we know about turbulent events within many Muslim lands today. No doubt, Muslims in many countries are deeply frustrated and even hostile, but the explanations for those reactions are not fundamentally rooted in or explained by a so-called clash of civilizations.

This way of looking at international conflict began with an article in 1993, published by Harvard professor Samuel Huntington in *Foreign*

*Affairs*: "The Clash of Civilizations?" He questioned whether world politics were entering a new phase. Three years later, he turned that article into a book and removed the question mark: *The Clash of Civilizations and the Making of World Order*. Huntington insisted that the principal clash was between Western and non-Western societies, and he focused on Islam. Fundamentally, his argument recycles the Cold War thesis, now positing how the future conflict will not be so much economic and social as it will be ideological. Islam and China are seen as ascendant world forces that are already threatening the West.

Huntington concludes his book with a description of what the West must do to keep its opponents divided. The West, he argued, must exploit differences and conflicts among Islamic states, while at the same time strengthening international interests and involvements that reflect and legitimize Western interests and values. He argued for an aggressively interventionist stance toward much of the world.[1]

Although Huntington popularized this view of civilization and conflict, it was Princeton's Bernard Lewis who first put forward this line of thought. In a 1990 *Atlantic Monthly* article, "The Roots of Muslim Rage," Lewis articulated his thesis:

> It should by now be clear that we are facing a mood and movement far transcending the level of issues and policies of the government that pursues them. This is no less than a clash of civilizations—the perhaps irrational but surely historic reaction of an ancient rival against our Judeo-Christian heritage and the secular present; and the worldwide expansion of both. It is crucially important that we on our side should not be provoked into an equally historic but also equally irrational reaction against that rival.[2]

The late Edward Said, a Palestinian author and professor at Columbia University, was an early and forceful critic of this clash-of-civilizations concept. Said pointed out a fundamental flaw in an approach that employed sweeping generalizations about 1.5 billion Muslims scattered over five continents, speaking dozens of languages, and influenced by vastly different traditions and histories. Both Lewis and Huntington present Muslims as somehow all uniformly enraged and Western civilization as no more complex than a simple declarative sentence. Their theory simplistically presupposes that "the Islamic world" and "the West" are monolithic and homogeneous entities. They are neither.

Nor is anti-Westernism the defining quality of Islam. As we saw in the previous chapter, Muslims have contributed enormously to Western civilization as we know it. Indeed, Western civilization is very much a product of a Judeo-Christian-Islamic heritage, along with Greek and other influences woven in. While Europe was languishing in the dark ages for centuries, Muslims led the world as a most advanced and sophisticated civilization, to which we can trace many the roots of knowledge of mathematics, medicine, philosophy, and chemistry. Muslim scholars learned from various peoples and cultures they encountered and then incorporated, nurtured, developed, and advanced what was already known in India, China, and elsewhere.

Contrary to popular understanding in America, Islam is not and never has been an anti-intellectual tradition. Scholarly pursuits have generally been highly important within Islam. Recall the famous hadith in which Muhammad advises Muslims to "seek knowledge wherever you may find it, even unto China." Much of what we know about Greek philosophy, for instance, was lost in the West by the middle of the sixth century CE, but Muslim scholars discovered and reintroduced Greek thought to Europe via Islamic Spain. Saint Thomas Aquinas and other great thinkers of the Middle Ages openly acknowledged their indebtedness to the contributions of their Islamic counterparts.

Lewis acknowledges the rich history of Islamic scholarly pursuits and contributions. But he argues that Islam—unlike the Christian West—never modernized itself and seemingly failed to distinguish between religion and the state. Lewis presented his thesis in a best-selling book, *What Went Wrong? The Clash Between Islam and Modernity in the Middle East.*[3] A major flaw in his argument is that he essentially dismisses the impact of extended European colonial rule and more recent superpower decisions and actions that have affected subjugated Muslim majorities. In the immediate aftermath of September 11, when the dominant media question was "Why do they hate us?" this clash-of-civilizations approach conveniently fit a simplistic "us versus them" worldview. Many Americans—including many political leaders—were all too eager to embrace a theory that presented "Islam" and "the West" as monolithic, adversarial entities. Embracing such a framework for understanding is not only flawed and misleading; it is also self-serving for the superpower in question.

## Renewal and Reform Movements in Islam

The omission of the role of colonial powers and later superpowers in the relations between Islamic peoples and the West is serious indeed. As we saw in the previous chapter, the once-dominant central Islamic lands experienced uneven decline and fragmentation after the Mongol invasion in the 13th century and, later, the emergence of Western Europe. During the 19th and early 20th centuries, the global reach of European colonial powers—the British, French, Dutch, and Portuguese—systematically seized control of most Muslim-majority lands. Eventually, even the Mughul Empire in India, the Safavid Dynasty in Iran, and the Ottoman Empire in the Middle East gave way to Europe's imperial rulers. The impact and legacies of colonialism are essential in comprehending attitudes and behaviors of Muslims in many lands today, including influential Islamic revival and reform movements that emerged before and especially during times of colonial rule in the 18th and 19th centuries. Reform movements emerged as Muslims feared that European political and economic domination was threatening the cultural and religious values of their Islamic societies. Islam had once led the world, but something had gone wrong. Why, they asked, could Islam not once again be the basis for a comprehensive system? As we will see below, reformers feared similar and distinct influences from colonial rulers. Identifying selected major figures and reform movements illustrates the diverse responses to perceived threats against traditional Islam and clarifies key elements that are central in contemporary debate about the future of Islam.

Renewal and reform are deeply important to Muslims. Muhammad, in fact, was a prophet who (like all prophets) called the community of faith back to God's path. A well-known hadith affirms that "God will send to this umma [the Muslim community] at the head of each century those who will renew its faith for it."[4] Islamic history includes prolific scholars, such as al-Ghazali and Ibn Taymiyya, who claimed this mantle and shaped the thinking and behavior in major segments of the Islamic world.

One of the most important reform movements took root in the Arabian peninsula through the combined efforts of Muhammad ibn Abd al-Wahhab (1702–1791) and Muhammad ibn Sa'ud (d. 1765). Abd al-Wahhab advocated a rigid version of Islamic law. His call to return to the basics of the Qur'an and early Islam fueled a vigorous attack on what he deemed heretical teachings and practices of Shi'ites (e.g., the cult of imams, pilgrimage to various "sacred" places), Sufi mystics (veneration of saints), and less stringent applications of Islamic law among many Sunnis. While Muhammad ibn Abd al-Wahhab lent the religious guidance, Ibn Sa'ud was the political leader in what became the Saudi royal family. This combination shaped the religious and political landscape that continues to this day in the Kingdom of Saudi Arabia. Numerically, the Saudis represent a tiny fraction of the larger Sunni Muslim community. But the influence of their narrow sectarian approach within the most conservative of four recognized schools of Islamic law has been massive.[5] Resources from oil revenues have enabled Saudi Arabia to fund the training of religious leaders, build mosques and schools, and furnish educational materials for Muslims all over the world. All of this material support carries with it the strict and highly conservative interpretation of Islam prevalent in Saudi Arabia today. Muslims who embrace this approach are often called Wahhabis or Salafis (the latter a term that refers to the first three generations of Muslims who, they believe, practiced the pure form of Islam).

Jamal al-Din al-Afghani (1839–1897) was another highly influential reformer who traveled widely, urging Muslims to recognize and expel dangerous Western influences from their lands. In addition to his anti-imperialist message, he preached reform and renewal based on traditional Islamic principles and the insights of modern science and enlightened thought. In his view, the cultural influences (such as consumption of alcohol) of the dominant European colonial powers were insidiously infecting the Islamic community, but enlightened scientific advances could be put to use.

At the same time, a prominent Muslim thinker in India, Sayyid Ahmad Khan (1817–1898), embraced a very different approach. Ahmad Khan advocated Western methods and models of education over the traditional Islamic *madrasa* (school) system. He founded the influential Muslim University of Aligarh. In addition to changing education, he worked tirelessly for social reforms. His sympathetic embrace of the West led al-Afghani and others to reject his views. The legacy of his educational reform movement can be seen in inclusion of the physical sciences, state-of-the-art technology, economics, business administration, and so forth in most Islamic countries today.

In Egypt, Muhammad Abduh (1849–1905) was an exceptionally gifted thinker who arose from poor, humble beginnings to later become a leading figure at al-Azhar University in Cairo. Abduh was in personal contact with al-Afghani and shared al-Afghani's view that strengthening authentic Islam required the removal of Western power and influence in Islamic lands. Like some other reformers, Abduh believed that Islam was progressive, able to incorporate science, advances in health care, and other new methodologies without losing moral and ethical standards at the heart of their religion. He was a reformer who worked for the betterment of society, most notably his home country of Egypt, but also beyond.

Muhammad Abduh, Ahmad Khan, and al-Afghani illustrate different and widely debated Muslim responses to the challenges posed by the changing world of the late 19th and early 20th centuries. In distinctive ways, they called and worked for reform within predominantly Muslim lands that were under the control of European colonial powers.

In addition, they planted seeds for various movements for Islamic reform that have taken root and sprouted and are now shaping major contours of thought and action across the Muslim world. Two other important figures in Egypt must be mentioned for their powerful roles in shaping the contemporary struggle for the soul of Islam. Hassan al-Banna (1906–1949) was the Egyptian activist who founded the Muslim Brotherhood in 1928. He argued that Western influences such as secularism, materialism, use of alcohol, and questionable ethical standards presented a direct threat to Islam. Many Egyptians appreciated his charismatic effort to call the faithful back to traditional Islam through study, devotional piety, and social activism, so much so that over time the Egyptian government perceived this movement as a threat. As the home to al-Azhar University, Cairo has been a spiritual and intellectual center of the Islamic world for a millennium. Religious leaders and reformers have often been viewed as a threat to those in power down through the centuries. Al-Banna and numerous subsequent leaders were suppressed and jailed, fueling a view among Egyptians and others that the government was corrupt and not truly Islamic. From the late 1940s until the 1980s, the Muslim Brotherhood recruited followers and often worked underground; at times, however, the Egyptian government has permitted closely watched representatives of the Muslim Brotherhood to hold seats in the Parliament.

Sayyid Qutb (1906–1966) was a leading thinker and writer within the Muslim Brotherhood. Qutb, who was well educated and spent an extended period of time in the United States, argued all Islamic societies had lost their way and compared the mid-20th century to the "times of ignorance" (the term all Muslims know as *jahiliyyah*) that preceded the prophet Muhammad. He called for a return to the Qur'an, which, he believed, should be the basis for Islamic government, and to shariah law. His books *Social Justice in Islam* and *Milestones* were and continue to be widely read sources of inspiration for Islamic revival movements, including some whose blueprint for change leads to violent extremism. Khalid al-Islambuli, the leader of al-Jihad (the group that assassinated Egyptian President Anwar Sadat in 1981), was inspired by Sayyid Qutb's unambiguous call to action.

The people and movements noted here represent a range of approaches to revival and reform in recent centuries. Although all of them sought to energize and revitalize their societies in religious, social, and political terms, they differ in their understandings of which elements are essential to the life of "true" Islam. They are not the only reform movements; in fact there have been explicitly secular efforts to separate religion from politics. Contemporary Islam is a tapestry woven from many similar and different threads.[6]

With the end of colonialism during the first half of the 20th century, the political landscape in Muslim majority lands changed dramatically. British domination of the Indian subcontinent and parts of the Middle East gave way to new, independent countries such as India, Pakistan, Bangladesh, Egypt, and Israel. When Dutch control of the East Indies (what is now known as Southeast Asia) ended, the most populous Muslim country and fourth-largest country in the world was established: the Republic of Indonesia. Similarly, with the end of French colonial rule in North Africa and parts of the Middle East, the countries of Morocco, Tunisia, Algeria, Syria, and Lebanon were born. The departing colonial powers did not simply walk away and wish the indigenous people well with their new nation-states. Rather, they often sought to protect their perceived "interests" in natural resources such as oil and in military arrangements that ensured their continued hegemony.

The decades-long processes that created today's nation-states defy simple analysis. In many settings, the lines defining national boundaries were artificial and thus created enormous problems. For example, the Kurdish people were divided among five countries (Turkey, Syria, Iraq, Iran, and the former Soviet Union). Tribal people bound by language, religion, and history suddenly were now citizens of different countries. Study the difficult 20th-century history of the Kurds and you can see how it is intertwined with the legacies of colonial rule. In many settings, indigenous Muslims were technically running their own countries, but the colonial powers constrained their opportunity to debate and shape the governmental structures. Monarchies were common. In Egypt and Iraq, the kings were deposed in military coups, but the legacies of colonialism or external influence and domination of post-World War II superpowers continued. Even when some forms of participatory government were woven into the first phases of independent, indigenous rule, in many cases militarily strong leaders maintained their power by force, not through popular choice.

Understanding the major, interconnected, and often convoluted forces shaping developments in segments of the predominantly Muslim world and in any given country does not do much to clarify what it would mean to establish a viable government imbued with Islamic principles and laws. It does, however, enable us to recognize that the context of the history of specific places and populations is central to that understanding. Algeria is not Afghanistan; Iran is not Indonesia; Pakistan is not Palestine. The history of colonial and superpower influence and domination plays an important role, as it has done in Israel/Palestine, Iran, and Iraq. But there are other ingredients in the ongoing upheaval and conflict: economic exploitation by a small ruling elite, human rights abuses, and a history of internecine conflicts. To make sense of a country, we have to be willing to move beyond generalities and enter into the denser thicket of particulars shaping people and events in each specific setting.

## What 1.5 Billion Muslims Really Think

Between 2001 and 2007, the Gallup organization conducted the single most comprehensive study ever done of Muslim attitudes and beliefs worldwide. Gallup gathered data from tens of thousands of people through hour-long interviews with citizens in some 35 countries with majority or large minority Muslim populations. Their sample represented 90% of the population.[7] The study sought to gain insight into dominant views within various Muslim countries as well as clarify how those views intersect with international relations and views about Islam in the West. The Gallup findings, published in the 2007 book *Who Speaks for Islam? What a Billion Muslims Really Think,* offered a wealth of information about topics such as attitudes toward the United States, the legitimacy of violence and suicide bombings, issues of gender in Islam, and hopes for changes in different countries. These findings illuminate the rich diversity of people and opinions engaged in the struggle for the soul of Islam.

Contemporary Muslim attitudes toward the West (the United States, Canada, Western Europe, Australia, and New Zealand) contradict the oft-repeated mantra that "they (Muslims) hate us because of our freedom." Most, in fact, admire the West because of democracy, technology, and visible concern for human rights. Muslims say that perceived moral decay and the breakdown of traditional values are the least admirable qualities about the West. They see the dominant cultural influence of the West as undermining and corrupting Islamic moral and ethical standards. When the study focused on specific Western countries, distinctly different perspectives clearly emerged. The United States is largely viewed as aggressive, generally hostile toward Islam, morally decadent, and hypocritical about its support for genuine democracy in Islamic lands. France and Germany, on the other hand, were viewed far more favorably.[8]

One of the most significant insights from the Gallup data is that both politically radical and moderate Muslims are concerned about the same issues. The more radical responses to perceived political and economic domination and corruption of Islamic moral standards come from differences in "prioritization, intensity of feeling, degree of politicization, and alienation." Everyone hopes for improved economic conditions and opportunities. The more moderate Muslims place high priority on improvements in educational systems, while the more politically radicalized emphasize "promoting democratic ideals and freedom of speech, enhancing their country's international status, earning more respect, and playing more important regional and international roles."[9] These views of the more radicalized Muslims connect directly to their frustrations about leaders who have stayed in power by force rather than popular will, and at times thanks to U.S. support. Add in widespread convictions about the United States being aggressive, generally hostile to Islam, and disingenuous about its support for genuine democracy in Islamic countries, and you have an explosive combination. The Gallup study estimates that approximately 7% of the global Muslim population can be classified as "politically radicalized." Though a small percentage, in a population of some 1.5 billion 7% is well over 90 million people. If only a fraction of those people continue to feel dominated, occupied, exploited, and disrespected by their own governments or by an external superpower like the United States, the potential for disaster is high. In a post–September 11 world, we know with certainty that it doesn't take many people to wreak havoc on a global scale. Inspired by the writings of Sayyid Qutb and a Wahhabi-like call to return to "true" Islam, some of the most radical activists conclude that violent confrontation is the only way to achieve the changes they desire.

The Gallup study revealed that Muslims who endorsed the September 11 attacks and justify suicide bombings that may kill civilians (the 7% politically radicalized group) are no more actively religious or visibly observant than the general Muslim population; among moderates and radicals alike, approximately 90% say religion is very important in their daily lives. The vast majority of Muslims reject actions that might harm civilians as un-Islamic. Many cite the well-known passage in the Qur'an (5:32) that says killing one innocent person is like killing the whole world. The poll appears to endorse conclusions reached by Robert Pape's study of every suicide bombing in the world between 1980 and 2004, *Dying to Win*; the overwhelming majority of suicide-terrorist attacks are not driven by religion but by military strategies aimed at compelling an occupying force to withdraw from what terrorists view as their homeland.[10] This insight helps explain why several well-respected Muslim leaders who otherwise condemn suicide bombing have issued statements saying armed resistance (including suicide attacks) may be permissible when directed at Israelis.[11]

One of the painful and often public ways in which the internal struggle within Islam is taking place is seen in the area of women's rights and
opportunities in predominantly Muslim countries. In sharp contrast to
popular images of silently subservient and submissive women, the Gallup study reported that the large majority of Muslim women in virtually
every country believed they deserve the same legal rights as men, could
work in any job, and could serve at the highest levels of government.
The majority of Muslim women expressed admiration for gender parity
in the West, but they did not wish simply to emulate females in Europe
and the United States. Many said that the lack of modesty suggested a
degraded cultural status of Western women. In varying ways, most
Muslim women believed Islam was not an obstacle to their progress but
actually a crucial component. Citing examples of women using shariah
to combat injustice in the early centuries of Islam, many women believe
that shariah still embodies the resources for rectifying problems or
limitations and opposing unjust practices.

The aspirations of most Muslim women converge or conflict with
educational opportunities in some Islamic countries. Even when the percentage of women with postsecondary education is similar—as is the case
with 34% of Egyptian women and 32% of Saudi women—there are often
substantial differences in the opportunities available to them once they
graduate. The level of frustration among many Muslim women is understandably high, and changes are often slow in coming. I (and many female
and male colleagues I know personally) have engaged Muslim women and
men for years about these issues. Opportunity for women in postrevolu-
tionary Iran was a major issue. One of the most poignant expressions of the
inherent tensions came early in my work at the National Council of
Churches (NCC). During an official, government-sponsored visit to Saudi
Arabia in 1986, our four-person NCC delegation included one woman.
She was often separated during meals and meetings, where she spent hours
with Saudi women, many of whom had advanced degrees in various fields.
She discovered firsthand the anger over women's inability to drive cars, go
out without being accompanied by a male relative, vote, and so forth. But
these types of cultural limitations on women in Saudi Arabia pale in comparison to the deadly practices under the guise of "honor killings" and
"female circumcision in other predominantly Muslim countries."[12]

The policies concerning women implemented by the Taliban during the
1990s in Afghanistan drew the world's attention to the most rigid and
oppressive possibilities in the Wahhabi framework for government rule.
Severe limitations blocked educational and professional options for
females, while severe punishments were meted out to those who

challenged the authority of the Taliban. It is worth recalling that only three countries in the world—Saudi Arabia, Pakistan, and the United Arab Emirates—ever recognized the legitimacy of the Taliban rulers in Afghanistan during their reign between 1996 and 2001; more than 50 Muslim countries sided with the rest of the community of nations in deploring the Taliban's policies. Some of the same religious and cultural ethos expressed in Afghanistan can be found in portions of neighboring Pakistan. Greg Mortenson's extraordinary best-selling book *Three Cups of Tea* addresses directly the lack of educational opportunity for many girls in Pakistan and Afghanistan, even as he works to change the status quo.[13] But Pakistan is also the country where Benazir Bhutto, a Shi'ite woman, was twice elected prime minister (1988–1990 and 1993–1996) and was a leading candidate once again when she was assassinated during her 2007 campaign. In fact, four of the five most populous Muslim-majority countries have elected women to the top political office: Indonesia, Pakistan, Bangladesh, and Turkey. Egypt (the fourth largest) is the lone exception.

The picture of women in Islam that begins to come into focus reflects different histories and cultural traditions intertwining with Islam in a variety of ways. Some of the most vocal advocates who are challenging oppressive and sometimes lethal traditions are found among Muslim women now living in the West. Azizah al-Hibri, distinguished professor of law at the University of Richmond, is one such advocate. Al-Hibri, who heads an organization of Muslim women lawyers for human rights called Karamah, speaks and writes extensively on Muslim women's rights. Like many others, al-Hibri acknowledges multiple problems plaguing Muslim countries. The resources for fundamental change, she argues, are found within the Islamic legal tradition. The problem is not with Islam so much as it is with people in power.[14]

Although data like those from the Gallup study are useful, they don't tell the whole story of how the struggle for the soul of Islam will play out in the coming decades. When some of those engaged in the "debate" are prepared to kill those who disagree with them and terrorize the population by attacking civilians, police recruits, and religious leaders and sites, it is exceedingly hard to have genuine debate. Nonetheless, a vigorous debate is under way within many countries and internationally. Western media regularly highlight the views of the most politically radicalized advocates for a return to "pure" Islam, including a Taliban-like approach to shariah law. They do not cover Muslim religious and intellectual leaders, professionals, and popular preachers who seek to persuade Muslims toward a path of cooperation and integration in the world of the 21st century. Here are four such leading Muslim scholars and religious leaders who urge a different way.

## Moderate Muslim Voices

Just as the hard-line religious leaders and violent extremists find inspiration in puritanical reformers such as Muhammad ibn Abd al-Wahhab and Sayyid Qutb, so too can we link contemporary advocates for a dynamic, progressive Islam to the pioneering work of figures such as Jamal al-Din al-Afghani, Sayyid Ahmad Khan, and Muhammad Abduh. In their own ways, these leaders sought to renew Islam in the modern era by both affirming unchanging principles and values revealed by God and adapting social, economic, and political structures in the context of the knowledge and circumstances of modern life.

Tariq Ramadan was born and educated in Geneva, where his family lived after his father was exiled as a leader in the Muslim Brotherhood, the organization founded in Egypt by Ramadan's grandfather, Hassan al-Banna. He also studied Islamic theology at al-Azhar University in Cairo. A prolific writer, Ramadan was ranked 49th in a 2009 *Foreign Policy* magazine poll of the top 100 intellectuals in the world.[15] Beginning in 2004, Ramadan became widely known and read in the American academic community. After he accepted a tenured professorship in religion and peacemaking at Notre Dame University's Institute for International Peace Studies, he was denied a visa on the grounds that he had contributed to a charitable organization the U.S. State Department later determined had directed some resources for the Palestinian organization HAMAS. Despite widespread protests from universities and scholars of religion across the United States, the travel ban was not lifted for Ramadan until 2010. Because he could not come to Notre Dame, Ramadan accepted a chaired professorship in Islamic studies at Oxford University.

Ramadan's perspectives are easily accessible through his more than 20 books and numerous articles and interviews that can be located via the Internet. He advocates a continuous process of rereading the Qur'an and hadith with a new mind and eyes because these are always influenced by one's contemporary social, political, and scientific environment. Muslims can and should be faithful to religious principles; but, he insists:

> Faithfulness to principles cannot involve faithfulness to historical models because times change, societies and political and economic systems become more complex, and in every age, it is in fact necessary to think of a model appropriate to each social and cultural reality.[16]

Ramadan believes that Western Muslims must fashion a Western Islam, just as there are variations of African Islam and Asian Islam. In other words, European Muslims should look anew at the fundamental sources of Islamic authority and interpret them in the context of their cultural setting in Europe.[17] His 2004 book *Western Muslims and the Future of Islam* is perhaps his best-known work.[18] Like other reformers, Ramadan constantly explores and expounds on the interplay between the traditional bases for Islamic law and theology (the Qur'an, Hadith, and established consensus of scholars) and the imperative to reread and interpret sacred texts in changing circumstances. This approach is not unique; it is central in all the major religious traditions that have stood the test of time. In a real sense, Islam and other major religions enmeshed in social and political systems are always works in progress, but fundamentalists are threatened by such flexibility and often disparage reform-minded thinkers, a subject we will examine in Chapter 9.

Ramadan was among the first prominent Muslims to condemn the terrorist attacks of September 11. He has repeatedly and forcefully denounced terrorism, including suicide bombing. Like most thoughtful analysts, Ramadan states clearly that violent extremism is never justifiable, but it is sometimes understandable why a few people feel compelled to lash out in such despicable ways. The effort to understand the sources of anger and frustration fueling such violence has led some critics to charge that Ramadan is really a wolf in sheep's clothing and not the advocate for cooperation and integration between Islam and the West he claims to be. Meanwhile, his affirmation of religious freedom and broader respect for human rights in the West, coupled with sharp criticism of many repressive regimes, has rendered him unwelcome in several Muslim countries.

In 2010, Imam Feisal Abdul Rauf became unexpectedly famous. Born in Kuwait and educated in England, Egypt, Malaysia, and the United States, Rauf is the leader of a mosque just 12 blocks from the World Trade Center site in lower Manhattan and a well-known advocate for interfaith dialogue and cooperation. He was interviewed on numerous national television and radio programs in the weeks and months following September 11. Rauf then and subsequently has repeatedly denounced violence and extremism. His media interviews, books, and public presentations can be easily accessed by anyone who wishes to know his views. Even so, Rauf and his spouse, Daisy Khan, became the focus of national and international attention when their initiative to build an Islamic community center (with a place for Muslims to pray) was vilified—by some national politicians, some Christian religious leaders, and some family members of those who perished on September 11—as the "Ground Zero Mosque," calling it an affront to the victims of the attack.[19]

Imam Rauf's 2004 book *What's Right with Islam: A New Vision for Muslims and the West* spells out in detail where he believes the relationships have broken down and how to rectify the rupture. He argues passionately that fundamental Islamic principles are consistent with the values of a democratic and pluralist society such as the United States. Although dialogue and cooperation are practical necessities, Rauf insists that the history of Islam—manifest in the advanced civilizations in the golden ages of Baghdad and Cordoba—shares values and ethics with the other Abrahamic religions of Judaism and Christianity. His book draws details from the Qur'an and traditions of the Prophet that Rauf argues lay the foundation for the pluralist society we need, a society in which all religious voices are welcome and given maximum freedom.[20]

Islamic law figures prominently in the reformist approach proffered by Rauf. In 1999, he published a book titled *What Every Muslim Should Know About the Shari'ah*. Contrary to the image of Islamic law associated with severe punishments meted out in Saudi Arabia or by the Taliban in Afghanistan, Rauf explains how shariah provides a constructive framework that enables Muslims to practice Islam ("submission to God's will") as fully as possible. Reformers such as Tariq Ramadan and Imam Rauf, as well as Muslim human rights advocates such as Azizah al-Hibri, must frame their positions in the context of Islamic law and theology. Two other influential Muslim writers— Khaled Abou El Fadl and Abdullahi Ahmed an-Na'im—now living in the United States are at the center of the effort to reformulate Islamic law so as to both preserve the integrity of the tradition and offer a viable framework for the future.

Khaled Abou El Fadl was born in Kuwait. His theological and academic education included time in Kuwait and Egypt in addition to undergraduate and graduate degrees from Yale, the University of Pennsylvania, and Princeton. A chaired professor at the UCLA Law School, El Fadl has authored 14 books and more than 100 articles on Islamic law and the core values and emphasis on beauty in Islam. He has appeared on many national television programs and received numerous awards for his work in the area of human rights.

The title of his 2005 book, *The Great Theft: Wrestling Islam from the Extremists,* leaves little doubt that he believes there is a struggle for the soul of Islam playing out in the first decades of the 21st century. El Fadl presents a passionate case against the narrow sectarianism of the Wahhabi-inspired interpretation and implementation of Islamic law.

He forcefully asserts that this extremist view is a deeply flawed approach to an "imagined Islam" that is inconsistent with the tradition's rich and diverse history. El Fadl asserts that Wahhabism is a fringe puritanical movement that would be largely inconsequential today apart from the massive infusion of Saudi petro dollars and influence during the past half-century. He explains and laments this "grand theft" of Islam and articulates a hopeful alternative based on classical, moderate positions on the nature of law and morality, democracy and human rights, gender issues, interaction with non-Muslims, and Islamic approaches to warfare and terrorism.[21]

El Fadl is an accomplished scholar and Islamic jurisprudent. Although many Muslims around the world affirm his understanding of Islamic history, they are less ready to accept his efforts to refine and modernize approaches to Islamic law. Muslim reformers, like their counterparts in Judaism and Christianity, are inevitably challenged by a segment of the religious establishment who perceive the call for reform as a threat to its position or the status quo. Many Muslims easily confuse understanding of the Qur'an as the literal Word of God with inflexible, literal interpretations of the text and tradition. These are the challenges that also confront Abdullahi Ahmed an-Na'im, author of *Islam and the Secular State: Negotiating the Future of Shari'a*.[22]

Originally from the Sudan, Abdullahi Ahmed an-Na'im is a naturalized American citizen who holds a distinguished chair at the Emory University School of Law, where he also serves as director of the Religion and Human Rights Program. He is well known for his international work in human rights and gained a more popular following in the United States after being profiled in a lengthy 2006 article published on the fifth anniversary of September 11 in the *New Yorker*.[23] An-Na'im is convinced that the 21st century demands a new approach to shariah as a comprehensive guide to good conduct by Muslims. Rather than see the secular state as the enemy of Islam, he asserts that it is the indispensable vehicle for reclaiming the best of Islam in the service of human rights, women's rights, civility in society, and healthy pluralism. In his view, the state should be neutral with regard to enforcing religious values and concepts. After detailing why Muslims today need a secular approach to government, he positions his argument for religion and politics in Islam in an historical perspective. He then illustrates the value of his approach by close case studies of India, Indonesia, and Turkey. An-Na'im has been angrily criticized in some quarters but also warmly received by many Muslims, including some very conservative religious leaders who are wary of how they see their religion being politicized today.

Much more can be said about these few examples and many more contemporary Muslim reformers. Anyone who wishes to move beyond dramatic headlines and sound bites in order to learn more about the range of perspectives on the future of Islam will readily discover just how vigorous and substantial these debates are today.

While some Islamist leaders speak in grandiose terms about a new form of global Islamic rule, the vast majority of Muslims operate within the framework of the nation-state system. And despite widespread frustration in many countries, the overwhelming majority of Muslims reject violence and extremism as appropriate means for achieving needed reforms. Most Muslims believe that Islam can be a foundation or basis for an effective government structure. Unlike most non-Muslim Americans, Muslims know their history and believe that Islam once again can supply a societal framework for a comprehensive way of life. But there is a major disconnection between this affirmation of Islamic history along with a generic hope for the future and the actual functional structure for an Islamic government in a given country. There is nothing approaching a consensus on what precisely should constitute an Islamic state in the 21st century.

The desire to draw or build on Islam in order to fashion viable 21st-century political, economic, and social structures is real and widespread. For many if not most Muslims, the way forward includes a combination that embraces the modern world and rejection of negative Western influences—immoral behavior, pornography, economic exploitation, and crass materialism are at the top of the list—perceived and experienced as a threat to traditional Islamic values. Muslims are not alone in their concerns about these influences. Many Christian and Jewish leaders in the West echo the same fears and frustrations. How many religious leaders or practitioners, after all, would celebrate pernicious spread of pornography or the greed and lust for material gain that led us into the global recession beginning in 2008? To frame what has happened and will continue to unfold in many parts of the predominantly Muslim countries in the coming decade or two as a clash of civilizations is mistaken, and also dangerously misleading. A more thoughtful approach is essential. This is particularly true for two pivotal countries that are at the center of regional and global economic, political, military, and religious developments: Iran and Iraq.

# 8

# IRAN AND IRAQ

### AXIS OF EVIL OR HARBINGER OF HOPE?

ON MARCH 7, 2010, APPROXIMATELY TWO-THIRDS of the eligible voters in Iraq went to the polls to participate in what was expected to be a closely contested national parliamentary election. Various Shi'ite, Sunni, and Kurdish parties and candidates—most explicitly religious, some more notably secular—were vying for a major stake in the next government. By many accounts, the election process was significantly less chaotic than in previous elections. Even so, seven years after Saddam Hussein was toppled and new government structures were developed, in a series of election-day attacks 38 people were killed and dozens more seriously injured in Baghdad alone.[1]

During the nine months preceding these Iraqi elections, world attention was focused on presidential elections in two neighboring countries to the east of Iraq: Iran and Afghanistan. In different ways, elections in these two countries revealed how deeply large segments of the population were disenfranchised by "democratic" processes that were visibly rife with fraud and corruption. In Iran, massive numbers of angry citizens repeatedly took to the streets in courageous protests over many months. Meanwhile in Afghanistan, as the administration of President Obama decided to send in 30,000 more soldiers in the ninth year of the war, the 2009 Afghani presidential election raised serious questions about the legitimacy of President Hamid Karzai's government. The concerns were mitigated by two realities on the ground: there was no viable alternative to Karzai, and most of the fragmented tribal regions appeared to be largely unaffected by a "national" government whose authority was concentrated primarily in the capital city of Kabul. Widen the circle further—east to Pakistan and west to Israel/Palestine, Saudi Arabia, and Egypt—and one can see distinct and interrelated dynamics shaping tumultuous events at the intersection of religion and politics in these Muslim-majority lands.

The 2009 elections in Iran and Iraq were part of an ongoing series of turbulent developments in these neighboring countries. Both have been prominent in the Western media for three decades, most obviously since the events of September 11 and subsequent U.S.-led wars in Iraq and Afghanistan. A portion of the convoluted and sometimes deadly developments in both Iran and Iraq can be framed within the broader context of the contemporary struggle for the soul of Islam. But a great deal of the confused and confusing dynamics must be understood in the context of their close ties—their geography and their majority Shi'ite populations— yet clearly different histories.

I've chosen to focus on Iran and Iraq because they have been and will continue to be of paramount concern. Along with North Korea, Iran and Iraq were identified in President George W. Bush's 2002 State of the Union address as the "Axis of Evil" in the world. Iran and Iraq have not only been at the center of political, military, and economic attention for the past three decades, they have also undergone dramatic changes. They can help us develop a more accurate perspective on the contemporary interplay of Islam and politics. Both Iran and Iraq are rooted in 1,400 years of Islamic history. Both modern countries have been shaped by their experiences of colonialism and domination by superpowers. And both nations have drawn heavily on Islam in their efforts to fashion viable new political structures. Most tellingly, both show us there is no one template for an Islamic state today. As nations that are works in progress, they illustrate reasons for hope and the potential for disaster looming just ahead. What happens within these countries in the coming decade will have a profound impact throughout the Middle East, as well as powerful global ramifications.

## Can You Tell a Sunni from a Shi'ite?

The largest religious communities in Iran and Iraq are Shi'ite Muslims. Shi'ites constitute approximately 15% of the global Muslim population, but in the arc stretching from Pakistan through Afghanistan, Iran, Iraq, Bahrain, the Gulf states, Syria, and into Lebanon the Shi'ites make up well over 40% (some estimates range up to 50%) of Muslims. Sunni Muslim populations dominate in many of the most populous countries in Asia and Africa, such as Indonesia, Bangladesh, India, Egypt, and

Nigeria. As we have seen in earlier chapters, historical and theological differences between Sunni and Shi'ite factions that developed through the centuries are significant in understanding developments and future prospects in Iran and Iraq. What began as a disagreement over the legitimate leadership following Muhammad's death grew over time into theological divisions and hostility erupting at times in civil war. In many settings, Sunnis and Shi'ites lived harmoniously; in others—such as Arabia in the centuries since adoption of Wahhabi reforms—the animosity was unambiguous.

In the aftermath of Saddam Hussein's fall from power and the war in Afghanistan, new links between a more powerful Iran and other Shi'ites are shifting the balance of power and contributing to new approaches to religion and politics.[2] Comprehending variations within Islam and between the demographics in Iran and Iraq requires exploring the dense thicket of particulars.

A stunning opinion piece in the October 17, 2006, edition of the *New York Times* underscored how little many top decision makers knew about some of the most basic elements in the explosive mix of religion and politics in Iraq and Iran. The article, entitled "Can You Tell a Sunni from a Shi'ite?" was published three and a half years after the war in Iraq began and innumerable stories had focused on the Shi'ite majority in elections, the role of Shi'ite clergy in the revision of Iraq's Constitution, relationships with neighboring Iran, and violent clashes (bordering on civil war) not only between Shi'ites and Sunnis but also among Shi'ite factions in Iraq. The article, written by Jeff Stein, the national security editor at *Congressional Quarterly*, was inspired by a 2005 sketch from Comedy Central's *The Daily Show with Jon Stewart* in which various U.S. officials were shown to be utterly ignorant about Islam. With dismay and humor, Stein reported on months of interviews with Washington counterterrorism officials and congressional leaders, most of whom were baffled when asked which groups or Muslim leaders were Sunni or Shi'ite, or why it would be important to know.[3]

Shi'ites in Iraq constitute around 60% of the 31 million citizens; Sunnis represent 35%, with Christians and other communities collectively totaling roughly 5%. The size of these communities, their physical locations in relation to Iraq's oil reserves, and the recent history of the distribution of power and wealth in Saddam Hussein's Sunni-dominated regime are exceedingly important. Iran, on the other hand, with more than 70 million citizens, is more than 90% Shi'ite and only 8% Sunni Muslim. Iran is unique in that the largest branch of Shi'ite Islam has been the official religion of the country since the 16th century.[4]

## Before the Revolution

In the first chapter, we saw how the 1979 revolution in Iran produced a seismic shift at the intersection of religion and politics in Middle Eastern Muslim countries. The popular, largely nonviolent revolution that toppled the powerful shah jolted the region and sent tsunami shock waves all around the world. Following as it did on the 1974 Arab oil embargo and the 1976 civil war in Lebanon, this revolution signaled that many Muslims were awakening to their potential political and economic power as vehicles to change the status quo. The tipping point came in January 1979, when the shah went "on vacation" and Khomeini returned from Paris in February to lead the new government. Ten months later, on November 4, student militants stormed the U.S. embassy in Tehran and seized 53 American hostages in what would become the crisis that dominated media attention for the next 444 days. But neither the revolution nor the seizure of U.S. hostages happened in a vacuum. These events were rooted in Iranian history and internal political machinations even as they intertwined with other regional dynamics.

Ali Gheissari and Vali Nasr are two leading American scholars with deep ties to Iran. Their extensive field research explicates both the rise of the modern state and the fascinating evolution of the idea and practice of democracy in Iran. Their compelling book *Democracy in Iran: History and the Quest for Liberty* explores Iran's distinctive history and broader issues of political change in the Middle East, where the interplay among Islam, democracy, and state power is front and center. In Iran, the formal movement toward a nation-state and a constitutional form of government arose in the first decade of the 20th century. The Constitutional Revolution of 1906 created a parliamentary system that guided Iran for 20 years.

The Constitutional Revolution was perhaps the first movement of its kind in the Muslim world: an indigenous political reform movement directed at establishing accountable and representative government, one that would meet the demand for strong state institutions, rule of law, and individual rights.[5]

This initiative developed in response to corrupt rule by Safavid monarchs and their successors, as well as repeated European imperialist efforts to exploit Iran's economy. In the 1920s, a powerful military leader, Reza Khan, challenged Iran's parliamentary democracy and led a movement to concentrate power in a new executive office. By 1926, Reza Khan held the reins of power as the shah of Iran. He called for modernization and a stronger national identity even as he successfully shifted constitutional power away from the legislature toward the executive. He effectively became a monarch. In 1941, under relentless pressure from allied forces because of Iran's strategic location and close economic ties with Germany, he stepped down and his son, Muhammad Reza Pahlavi, became the new shah.

The ensuing decade was especially tumultuous for the weak young ruler. British and Soviet machinations, combined with long-standing exploitation from the Anglo-Iranian Oil Company, produced crisis after crisis. A new movement led by Prime Minister Mohammed Mossadeq and his National Front shifted the balance of power away from the shah. Between 1951 and 1953, Iran was at the center of world attention as Mossadeq led a democratic movement that rebuffed the British and nationalized Iran's extensive oil industry. Mossadeq's importance in both regional and global contexts was underscored when *Time* magazine named him "Man of the Year" in 1951. Although the British government vigorously protested the changes implemented by Mossadeq, they did not receive unqualified support from the administration of President Harry Truman. The situation changed abruptly with the U.S. presidential election of 1952. No sooner had Dwight Eisenhower assumed the presidency in 1953 than a CIA-led coup was launched. The popular, democratically elected Mossadeq was ousted and Muhammad Reza Pahlavi was restored to the Peacock Throne. In the process, long-standing British imperial involvement in Iran was replaced by the new global power, the United States.

Stephen Kinzer, an award-winning foreign correspondent for the *New York Times*, details the story of the 1953 coup in the context of 20th-century history before and after the restoration of the shah to power. Kinzer's superb book, *All the Shah's Men: An American Coup and the Roots of Middle East Terror,*[6] should be required reading for every member of Congress and any official in the executive branch who deals with U.S. foreign policy. Two other books already cited—Ray Takeyh's *Hidden Iran: Paradox and Power in the Islamic Republic* and Gheissari and Nasr's *Democracy in Iran*—should also be on a short list of essential reading for U.S. government officials and American citizens who want to move beyond sensational headlines toward a more accurate understanding of the vitally important country of Iran.

## Struggles in Iraq and Afghanistan

To the west in neighboring Iraq, Saddam Hussein seized power also in 1979, and in 1980 he launched what became a devastating 10-year war with Iran. This war wreaked havoc on both countries in human and economic terms; more than one million people were killed and untold numbers suffered from serious injuries during this war of attrition. At the same time, on the eastern border of Iran a loosely organized coalition of Muslim *mujahideen* ("fighters in the way of God") in Afghanistan vigorously resisted the occupying Soviet army and the Soviet-supported puppet regime ostensibly governing their rugged, fiercely tribal nation. Since this was still during the Cold War, the United States famously supplied military assistance to those Afghan "freedom fighters" struggling against the USSR.

In Iran, however, the Muslims who revolted against the shah and his patrons were labeled extremists, fanatics, or terrorists by the U.S. government and media. An old adage in political alliances was invoked: when "the enemy of my enemy is my friend," some striking and unsavory partnerships are possible. Consequently, in the 1980s the United States effectively supported both Saddam Hussein in Iraq and the mujahideen in Afghanistan. The folly of even tacit support of a thuggish dictator like Saddam Hussein was exposed after his 1990 invasion of Kuwait and the 1991 Gulf War that followed. Similarly, the wisdom of U.S. military training and material support for Afghan mujahideen was clearly short-sighted after the Taliban seized control of Afghanistan in 1994 and welcomed Osama bin Laden and al-Qaeda ("the base") to set up training camps and operational centers in their country.

Meanwhile, in November 1979 a heavily armed militant group took control of the grand mosque complex in Mecca, holding it for two weeks. This stunning assault on the symbolic center of Islam—Muslims pray five times a day toward the cube-shaped Kaaba and make pilgrimage there during the annual ritual of the hajj—revealed the growth of militant Islamist groups prepared to take forceful action. It also exposed the seething anger among some who despised the dominant Saudi regime, the official "guardian of the holy shrines." Fearing the spread of Iranian-inspired popular revolutions, the Saudi, Jordanian, and Egyptian governments linked arms with Saddam Hussein as the best way to thwart Iran. Although it proclaimed neutrality, the U.S. government also lent support to Iraq throughout the 1980s. Once again, short-term U.S. policies were predicated in large part on the theory that "the enemy of my enemy is my friend."

## From Revolution to Islamic Republic

In the midst of these chaotic developments, the successful revolutionaries in Iran had an unprecedented opportunity to devise and develop the framework for a contemporary Islamic state. The distinctive structure that emerged in Iran is a "theocratic republic," a new form of government. Various secularist and Marxist groups joined forces with Khomeini to overthrow the shah, so the first provisional government reflected their influence as well as the desires of many Iranian Muslims firmly committed to participatory government. The original draft constitution envisioned a strong presidency, an elected assembly, and safeguards for individual rights, closely mirroring Western parliamentary democracies, most notably France. However, Ayatollah Khomeini and other leading activist clerics who favored a more obviously Islamic state were convinced that the new government had to include religious authorities to oversee all its affairs. Iranian specialist Takeyh summarizes what happened during the first formative year of the new government:

> Soon after returning to Iran, Khomeini implored his allies to be vigilant and aggressive in their efforts to establish the theocratic order. . . . Through domination of the revolutionary committees overseeing local affairs, appropriation of the defunct regime's wealth, and mobilization of zealous supporters, Khomeini and his allies fashioned a parallel regime with more authority than the tentative and moderate provisional government. . . . In the midst of the enveloping turmoil [of the hostage crisis], Iran held elections for parliament and for the Assembly of Experts, which was to evaluate the draft constitution. . . . Islamist forces captured the majority of seats in the Assembly of Experts, ensuring them a commanding voice in the revision of the constitution. . . . The new constitution created the unprecedented theory of *velayat-e faqih* whereby a religious leader would oversee all national affairs. This office, designed for Khomeini himself, had virtually unlimited responsibilities and was empowered to command the armed forces and the newly created Revolutionary Guards. . . . A Guardian Council, composed mainly of clerics, was to vet all legislation, ensuring their conformity with Islamic strictures.[7]

Khomeini had envisioned and developed a new kind of Islamic state during his long exile in Iraq and France. Rather than return to the model employed by Muhammad during his 10 years of rule in Medina or duplicate key components that shaped the period of the "Rightly Guided Caliphs," he drew on the leadership of clergy in Shi'ite Islam and employed new structures that set up a supreme leader and qualified clerics as guardians of the people and true Islam.[8] These elements were designed to avoid or overcome corruption and threats to a true Islamic state already promoted a decade before in the writings of Ayatollah

Khomeini: oppression of the rights of the people by ruling classes, plundering of national resources, the influence of foreign powers, and the dangers posed by innovations that undermine Islamic law. The ayatollah clearly understood the frustration many Iranians felt about the shah's oppressive rule and economic exploitation, human rights abuses, and the long history of British and U.S. involvement in Iran.[9]

The theocratic republic is a hybrid framework drawing on both Khomeini's vision for a Shi'ite Islamic state and the previous century of popular support for participatory government. Major developments during the preceding century clearly frame the context in which to understand Khomeini, other religious leaders, revolutionary groups and leaders, as well as the masses who protested against the election fraud in 2009.

In the functional framework of the Islamic Republic of Iran today, the supreme leader and the Guardian Council (which selects and can theoretically remove the Supreme Leader) have the final word on most government affairs. But the Islamic Republic is not simply a totalitarian state run by clerical oligarchs. Elections for the country's president, parliament (the *majlis*), and municipal councils are cherished and generally effective components of the unusual mix. The structures devised in the Islamic Republic bear Khomeini's stamp but also reflect the complex and sometimes nuanced differences among multiple groups that helped depose the shah's regime. The American obsession with seemingly intransigent religious zealots such as Khomeini, his successor Ayatollah Ali Khamenei, and the current president, Mahmoud Ahmadinejad, fails to appreciate distinct ideological differences over religion and politics in Iran that continue to be debated vigorously. And the fault lines are not simply between the religious establishment and more secular Iranians; the reality is much more complex. In my engagements with numerous clerics and religiously devout Iranian citizens during the past three decades, many have openly and routinely expressed profound differences of opinion. The views of the late Grand Ayatollah Hussein Ali Montazeri underscore the point.

I met personally with Ayatollah Montazeri on two of three trips to Iran during the hostage crisis. Montazeri was a legendary figure whose imprisonment and torture for four years before the revolution validated his credentials.[10] He was the first chairman of the Assembly of Experts (in 1979), and the deputy supreme leader and designated heir to Khomeini (1985–1987) before he fell from favor because of his dissenting views. He was a driving force in shaping the new constitution and securing the position of supreme leader. He did not, however, support absolute rule for this person. Rather, he believed Khomeini and his successors should be the guiding advisor to the elected rulers. Montazeri was a consistent advocate for human rights and women's rights. He openly challenged policies designed to export revolution by training and arming various Muslim groups. He argued instead that Iran should lead other Muslims seeking change by example. He called for transparency in examining the successes and failures of the revolutionary government and boldly dissented from Khomeini's 1989 fatwa calling for the death of Salman Rushdie after publication of *The Satanic Verses*.

Western observers of Iran who looked behind headlines could discover Montazeri and other leading clerics at times sharply disagreeing with various major political leaders as diverse as Supreme Leader Ali Khamenei, Hashami Rafsanjani, Mir Hussein Mussavi, and presidents Muhammad Khatami and Mahmoud Ahmadinejad. But they were not calling for a revolution. These leaders were all intimately involved in the shaping of the theocratic republic that governs Iran today. They, like the masses who took to the streets under the banner of the "Green Movement," were insisting that Iran's policies should be improved and made more transparent under a leadership different from Ahmadinejad.

Prior to his death at age 87 in December 2009, Montazeri was a vocal supporter of those who took to the streets protesting Ahmadinejad's fraudulent reelection in June 2009. Beginning in 2007, Montazeri publicly criticized Ahmadinejad's incendiary approach to nuclear policies. The ayatollah supported Iran's right to develop nuclear energy, but he called Ahmadinejad's inflammatory behavior counterproductive: "One has to deal with the enemy with wisdom, not provoke it . . . [Ahmadinejad's behavior] only creates problems for the country."[11]

Two key points here are important to note. First, Montazeri, many other clerics, and the large majority of Iranians defend Iran's right to develop its nuclear energy capabilities. Most Iranians recoil when being told by the United States or other governments possessing nuclear power and weapons that Iran is not responsible enough to be trusted with nuclear power. Iranians point out that their country has not attacked or occupied others. What gives the United States or Israel or Great Britain or France the right to dictate such terms to Iran? The concern about Iran developing nuclear capabilities, however, is shared by neighboring Muslim countries and Israel. Nuclear power is not the issue; potential control of nuclear weapons by a regime whose president has made many incendiary statements about Israel is simply unacceptable. The second point related to Montazeri's position is that many Iranians strongly oppose the kind of defiant and incendiary rhetoric that often characterizes presentations by Ahmadinejad.

Ayatollah Montazeri was not an aberration. Rather, he represented the views of many religious Iranians who were calling for responsible, democratically elected leaders guided by the light of Shi'ite Islam. He and others embody long-standing debate within Iran about the relationship between state and society and the role of religious faith in politics.

## Even More Volatility

Besides those we have already discussed, there are many other major elements in the contemporary mix of religion and politics in Iran. A disconcerting number of Iranian leaders, for example, routinely display open hostility toward Israel and encourage material support for Sunni and Shi'ite groups whose history includes attacking both military and civilian targets in the Jewish state. President Ahmadinejad's highly publicized statements questioning the historical veracity of the Holocaust go well beyond bizarre and offensive. He and many others appear to focus on political Zionism and disregard Jews as human beings the Qur'an affirms as People of the Book. In the face of such aggressive and provocative rhetoric and behavior, Israeli leaders have been quite understandably focused on the potential that Iran might develop nuclear weapons. The Israeli government's preoccupation with a potentially nuclear Iran has been visible and vocal since 2007. The cover story of the September 2010 issue of the *Atlantic* magazine announced boldly that "Israel Is Getting Ready to Bomb Iran" and explained how, why, and what it might mean. But the impression that Israel and Iran have been and are mortal enemies is inaccurate. In fact, there is a long history of alliances and quiet cooperation, including secret arms deals beginning in 1981 that led into the infamous Iran-Contra scandal[12] during the Reagan administration. It appears that Iranian government rhetoric and behavior are politically tied to perceived national interests. Attacking Israel as an agent of U.S. imperialism and supporting the Palestinians is a frequently employed strategy in many Muslim countries today. It not only bolsters Islamic credentials but also deflects their people's attention from internal problems. As we will see, Saddam Hussein adopted a similar strategy.[13]

Government application of a particularly strict version of Islamic ideology can also be linked to other serious problems in the Islamic Republic. Afar Nafisi's best-selling book *Reading Lolita in Tehran* highlights restrictions on free speech, women's rights, and the rights of minority religious communities. Protests after the 2009 election shone an international spotlight on issues of free speech, free and fair elections, interrogation techniques that were sometimes extremely harsh, and dismal prison conditions. Three decades after the revolution, Iran is very much a work in progress with enormous problems, competing centers of power, and great diversity among its more than 70 million citizens.

## Perceptions and Realities

This brief overview enables us to see how the gap between perceptions about and realities within Iran is often substantial. Interpretation of current events and statements on the part of religious or political leaders requires historical perspective and contextual analysis. Iran is a land steeped in more than 4,000 years of continuous civilization. It has been a creative and productive center of Islamic civilization for nearly 1,400 years. And, as we have seen, the more recent history of this country includes concerted efforts toward democratic rule led by progressive Muslim leaders and young Iranians who feel strongly that more openness to the world and free and fair elections are essential ingredients for Iran's long-term future. Anyone who makes an effort to get behind such simplistic propositions as "If Ahmadinejad said it, all Iranians must believe it" will readily discover that it is a complex nation full of paradox. Iran has a young population (two-thirds are under 30) and its citizens are politically engaged and active; more than 80% vote in national elections (compared to roughly 50% in the United States voting in presidential election years). Iranians are increasingly connected to the wider world, and many clearly want constructive changes in their government. Few, however, see Islam itself as the problem.

Having followed events in Iran closely since the late 1970s, I remain hopeful. Convoluted and converging forces helping to shape events in this ancient land have far less to do with any clash of civilizations than with an internal and regional struggle for the political soul of Islam. If Iran's nuclear program and apparent support for groups confronting Israel directly do not result in Israeli or American military actions in Iran, it is quite possible that political reform and structural modifications there may position the country to be a constructive model for participatory government in an Islamic state and a cooperative member of the community of nations in the 21st century.

# The Republic of Iraq

On May 5, 2003, I was a guest on the National Public Radio program *Fresh Air*, which aired four days after the now-infamous speech in which President George W. Bush stood on the deck of an aircraft carrier with the "Mission Accomplished" banner behind him to celebrate the success of the military victories in Iraq. In the midst of national euphoria following the toppling of Saddam Hussein's regime and the presumed victory in Iraq, host Terry Gross talked to Albert Mohler, president of the Southern Baptist Seminary in Louisville, Kentucky, and me. Molher and many other prominent evangelical leaders in the United States were urgently insisting that a large wave of Christian missionaries go into that war-torn land to preach the Good News of salvation to its inhabitants and help meet their basic needs. The national radio program expanded on the *Time* magazine cover story in which Mohler and I had been quoted as Baptists with diametrically opposed views.

In my comments, I emphasized that the conflict in Iraq was nowhere near over and stressed that dispatching Christian missionaries to Iraq—however well-intentioned—would be like lighting a match in a room full of explosives. In the shadow of the Crusades and colonial domination, with deep divisions between and among Sunnis, Shi'ites, and Kurds and pent-up hostility toward many who benefited from Saddam's harsh rule, sending in Christian missionaries was the last thing to do in a land occupied by U.S. troops.[14] In addition to revealing ignorance about Iraqi history, Mohler and others seemed unaware that approximately 700,000 Christians were Iraqi citizens in 2003—Armenians, Assyrians, Catholics, and others. The Christian presence in the Tigris and Euphrates valley can be traced back to the first century.

The euphoria of assumed victory in Iraq faded quickly, and a sobering reality began to set in. Saddam Hussein had no weapons of mass destruction as America had told the world, and the leaders of al-Qaeda who perpetrated the terrorist attacks on September 11, 2001, had escaped Afghanistan to neighboring Pakistan.

Five and a half years later, the extraordinary human, economic, and political toll of the war in Iraq—for the United States, the people of Iraq, and others in the region—was a focal point of the successful presidential campaign of Barack Obama. How could the Bush administration have gotten it so wrong? Clearly, many Iraqis were pleased to see the end of Saddam Hussein's brutal rule. But the Bush administration's prediction of a new, capitalist, democratic society in Iraq was unrealistic to say the least. Assurances that Iraqi oil revenues would pay for most of the costs of putting the country back together under democratic leadership could not have been more wrong. Within months, religion had become an exceedingly lethal force as civil war erupted between Sunni and Shi'ite factions. Attacks on sacred sites and despicable forms of intra-Islamic warfare prompted a mass migration in which many Iraqis fled to neighboring

Jordan and Syria while many others relocated to respective Sunni or Shi'ite segregated strongholds. Conflict among Shi'ite factions erupted, while the largely separatist Sunni Kurds in the north favored a political solution creating three states, one of which would be an independent or autonomous Kurdish homeland. Why was this happening? The U.S. military quickly went from being the liberator from Saddam's oppression to a foreign occupying force that many segments of Iraqi society viewed warily or explicitly as the enemy.

Virtually all the Middle East experts I know opposed the relentless march to war in Iraq (as did almost all European governments); many of us identified and warned of the ensuing quagmire. Were we clairvoyant? Hardly. A working knowledge of the history of this land and the contemporary political struggle for influence and leadership among Sunnis, Shi'ites, and Kurds equipped us to predict much of what was likely to occur in this explosive, artificially created nation. Iraq, the Tigris and Euphrates valley, was the home of an ancient civilization. As we noted in Chapter 6, Baghdad was the capital of the Abbasid dynasty and the center of the rich intellectual and artistic Islamic civilization for centuries. Southern Iraq contained several of the most sacred sites for Shi'ite Muslims, who were the dominant majority in that region. Different factions within the Ottoman Empire controlled the area between the 16th and early 20th centuries. Contemporary Iraq was carved out of the Ottoman Empire by the British, French, and Russians following World War I.[15] After the war, the League of Nations granted the area to the British as a mandate. The borders of Iraq were cobbled together by including the Kurds in the north and the Shi'ites in the south, both of which had argued and fought for independence. In 1932, the British made this area an independent monarchy but negotiated military and transit rights for their forces and special access to Iraq's petroleum reserves. A military coup in 1958 ended the monarchy. Ten years later, another successful coup placed the Baathist Socialist Party in charge. Saddam Hussein rose in the ranks of party leadership and assumed control of the presidency and the Revolutionary Command Council in July 1979. The following year, he declared war and attacked Iran.[16]

## The Saddam Hussein Era

The Baath party in Iraq and in neighboring Syria was secular in orientation. Although both Saddam Hussein and Hafiz al-Assad in Syria were rulers who systematically smashed any potential opposition, their secular governments afforded more freedoms and protections for minority communities than was the case in most of the other Muslim-majority lands. Tariq Aziz, an Iraqi Christian who was deputy prime minister during the 1991 Gulf War, became a familiar face on American television as the primary spokesman for Saddam Hussein's regime. Only a secular government like the Baathist regime in Iraq would allow someone from a Christian background to rise to such a top post.

Saddam Hussein made little pretense about being a devout or pious Muslim, but as we shall see he was not above exploiting Islam for political ends. Religion figured prominently during his tenure in some unusual and ultimately explosive ways. Most of Iraq's massive oil reserves are situated in the Kurdish north and in the Shi'ite-dominated south. But the Sunni Arab Muslims, who are a smaller group than the Shi'ites and distinguish themselves from the mostly Sunni Kurds, benefited disproportionately from extensive oil revenues. This was particularly true for Sunnis from Saddam's home city of Tikrit who had family connections or mutually beneficial business dealings. By contrast, the Shi'ites and the Kurds both suffered enormously during the 10-year Iran-Iraq war. Close historical ties between Iraqi Shi'ites and the Shi'ites in Iran fueled mistrust in Saddam's government. The most egregious assault within Iraq occurred on March 16, 1988. On that dark day, Saddam's forces attacked the Kurdish town of Halabja and unleashed chemical weapons on the civilian population. More than 5,000 people were killed, and twice that many were seriously injured.

Amnesty International, Middle East Watch, and the annual U.S. State Department's country reports on human rights all published numerous case studies that cited Saddam Hussein's regime as one of the world's worst. So it was no surprise when Shi'ites and Kurds celebrated Saddam's demise. Nor was it surprising that many Sunnis who had clearly benefited during Saddam's rule feared reprisals after the regime fell in 2003.

Like many other political leaders in the Middle East, the United States, and elsewhere, Saddam Hussein was more than willing to use religion cynically if he saw an advantage. When the world denounced him for invading Kuwait in 1990, for instance, he did several things designed to play to religious sentiments. Saddam declared the invasion of Kuwait a great *jihad* or holy war. Most non-Muslims would not know that he had no authority to make such a declaration, but Muslims knew that only certain recognized religious authorities could render nonbinding legal opinions or sanction holy war. So Saddam assembled more than 200 religious scholars and authorities and asked them collectively to issue a fatwa declaring his war in Kuwait a true jihad. They were effectively locked in a room where they all understood that Saddam's request was clearly an order. Because anyone who wished to see the sun shine the next morning would have to comply, they dutifully issued the desired fatwa under considerable duress.

Clarifying the meaning of these two Islamic terms—fatwa and jihad—helps demystify important words often used in media coverage. A fatwa is a legal opinion rendered by a recognized religious authority. Many Americans first heard this term in 1989 when Ayatollah Khomeini issued a fatwa endorsing the death penalty for Salman Rushdie for publishing *The Satanic Verses,* which was considered a slanderous crime against the prophet Muhammad. When a recognized scholar of Islamic jurisprudence pronounces a ruling, he normally furnishes evidence from Islamic sources in support of the opinion. In many settings, the rulings are not technically binding since scholars often come to different conclusions on the same issue. Historically, Muslims would consult the local authority or the regional leader—such as the mufti (the top legal jurist in an area) of Lebanon or the mufti of Jerusalem or the grand mufti of Egypt—for a legal ruling. Individually and collectively, many of the top Muslim legal authorities have strongly condemned violent extremism in the name of Islam since September 11. But the potential of abuse of authority is ever present, as the example from Saddam's Iraq above makes clear. In the age of the Internet, another kind of abuse is taking place. Now, a Muslim can pose a question and search online until he or she finds a religious "authority" to supply the desired answer or sanction.

The term *jihad* has now become part of the common lexicon in the West. Employed by various Muslim individuals and groups, often harshly and provocatively, it is almost universally translated in the media as "holy war," which is in fact one of its meanings. But there are many restrictions and qualifications in Islamic law covering what respected religious authorities can and cannot determine to be a valid basis for taking up arms in defense of Islam. The literal meaning of the term is "striving" or "struggling in the way of God." The greatest jihad, according to the Prophet Muhammad, is the struggle within oneself to do what is right. On the way back to Medina after a battle with Meccan opponents, Muhammad told the Muslims that they were returning from the lesser jihad to the greater jihad. The outward struggle in defense of Islam is not the greatest challenge. That is the inner struggle to overcome selfish and sinful desires keeping human beings from doing what they know is right.

Saddam Hussein, like many other Muslim individuals and groups, sought to exploit the narrow meaning of jihad to offer religious justification for his predatory behavior. He also ordered that *Allahu Akbar* (God is the greatest) be sewn onto the Iraqi flag at that time. This particularly odd move for a secular government was calculated to bolster his Islamic credentials beyond the borders of Iraq. He began talking a great deal about the Islamic duty to liberate Jerusalem from the infidels. In other words, once Saddam felt strong international pressure after his invasion of Kuwait, he suddenly got religion.[17] Measuring the effectiveness of such tactics is difficult. Clearly, some people respond positively to positions of great concern. From the outside, however, it can be very misleading to people who don't know a great deal about Islam. Just because someone like Saddam Hussein uses the structures and language of Islam doesn't mean his actions are affirmed by most Muslims.

## The Postwar Iraqi Government

In the two years after removing Saddam Hussein from power in 2003, U.S. forces and civilian leaders deployed to Iraq began working with a provisional government to develop a process that would lead to national elections. The majority of Iraqis supported the plan. The idea of participating in free elections was especially appealing to people who had lived for decades under tyrannical rule in a police state. In addition, elections and forms of representative government were already in place in many Muslim lands. And the Shi'ite majority knew their superior numbers would give them an opportunity to shift the balance of power toward themselves.

Close observers of political and religious dynamics in Iraq will likely recognize the name of the most influential Shi'ite religious leader, Grand Ayatollah Ali al-Sistani. Born in Iran and educated in Qom, the city with the largest concentration of Shi'ite theological schools, Ayatollah Sistani's influence within Iraq surfaced when he embraced the election process and intervened to stop clashes among Shi'ites provoked in large part by militant rhetoric, political maneuvering, and militia activities orchestrated by Shi'ite leader Muqtada al-Sadr. Ayatollah Sistani regularly consults with Iranian leaders and plays a pivotal role in post-Saddam Iraq. In the seven years between the 2003 U.S. invasion and the 2010 formal end to combat operations in Iraq, however, he never once met with any U.S. representative or official. Despite massive media attention on Iraq since 2003, the paucity of information about Ayatollah Ali al-Sistani's central role is telling. It reflects the fact that a great deal of what shapes thinking and events at the intersection of religion and politics in Iraq has been poorly understood. Al-Sistani turned 80 in 2009, and there has been no indication that this powerful leader at the center of Iraqi religious and political life will change his pattern of consultation with colleagues in Iran and lend guidance for the majority Shi'ite community in Iraq.[18]

The process of drafting a new constitution in Iraq has been a specific way to infuse the Iraqi nation-state with elements of Islamic law that the Baathist regime had explicitly avoided. Western enthusiasm for the new Iraqi Constitution was dampened considerably when some of the details began to emerge. A major story in the New York Times announced "Iraqi Constitution May Curb Women's Rights." The news story detailed how Shi'ite interpretations of Islamic law were being woven into the draft constitution. Of particular concern were articles that replaced relatively liberal personal-status laws for women—laws that were enacted in 1959 when secular military leaders toppled the monarchy—with laws that would throw cases dealing with marriage, divorce, and inheritance into religious courts. Under some interpretations of shariah, men can divorce a wife simply by stating their intention three times in the wife's presence. Women in Baathist Iraq did not need to have their family's permission to marry and could require divorce cases to be handled by a judge.[19] Drafting the new constitution exposed some of the local dynamics that are shaping the political structures in the context of Shi'ite interpretations of what Islam requires.

There are many ways religion is woven into the politics of contemporary Iraq that defy simplistic analytical frameworks of clash of civilizations or Islam versus the West. Consider, for example, the particular history of the 20 million Kurds. They are largely Sunni Muslims (more than 90%; fewer than 10% are Shi'ites) with their own language and culture. They have been in a constant state of revolt since the British created the artificial borders of Iraq. With their people divided among Iraq, Iran, Turkey, Syria, Armenia, and Azerbaijan, the Kurds are the largest non-state nation in the world. Their conflicts are primarily with the governments of the ruling countries, not the West. In fact, the Kurds in Iraq have worked closely and cooperatively with U.S. forces and business interests since 2003. The close ties go back to 1991, when the United States implemented "no-fly zones" in Iraq to protect the Kurds in the north and the Shi'ites in the south from further atrocities by Saddam Hussein's government. Although strong political pressures inside Iraq and in neighboring countries continue to prevent establishment of an independent state, Iraqi Kurds have effectively carved out a largely autonomous region in the northern portion of Iraq.

Other obvious ways in which religion has become lethal in Iraq have received a great deal of media attention. In addition to Shi'ite leader Muqtada al-Sadr's provoking conflict within Iraq and with the U.S. military forces, the group called al-Qaeda in Iraq has been a formidable factor in the deadly conflict. Claiming inspiration from Osama bin Laden's al-Qaeda movement, these Iraqis (and some zealots from other lands who have enlisted in their cause) have terrorized civilians and wreaked havoc on U.S. and Iraqi forces. Although it is not easy to determine the degree to which Islam inspires these politically active violent extremists, their despicable behavior has fueled stereotypical images of Islam as violent and menacing in the West.

Soon after taking office in 2009, President Obama determined to wind down most U.S. military operations and the presence in Iraq by the end of 2011. Analysts and historians will be busy for many years trying to sort out what happened in Iraq during the first decade of the 21st century and why. There will be no easy answers or simple explanations, but we can learn much from the combination of factors converging in contemporary Iraq and the distinct yet related dynamics swirling in neighboring Iran.

## A Framework for Understanding

Islam is the world's second-largest (and possibly the fastest-growing) religion. More than 50 countries in the 21st century world of nation-states have clear Muslim majorities. In a large percentage of these lands, Muslims are hopeful that Islam can offer a constructive basis for political, economic, social, and other structures in their respective countries. A small minority would like to extend this hope to a larger vision where the world community is under Islamic rule. Even though history informs the hope that Islam can help lead the way, there is no consensus on what precisely this should mean in a particular country.

This overview has emphasized that multiple factors contributed to unfolding developments in various lands, including many that consider violence as a necessary component for achieving a particular goal. In a number of settings, religion has become a lethal force. There are no simple solutions to such violence that can be universally applied (or, for that matter, applied in any particular setting). It is no small task to develop an adequate framework for understanding that can inform the most constructive ways to move forward in these divergent countries. In my experience, there is substantial hope; the vast majority of people of faith and goodwill support nonviolent processes of change and desire constructive cooperation among nations and diverse religious communities.

Although easy answers are inaccurate and misleading, a better framework for understanding is possible that does not require a Ph.D. in Islamic studies or Middle East politics. It does require, however, willingness to spend some time in the complex particulars relevant to a given situation. Historical events, both old and more recent, clearly influence contemporary events, whether it is the history of divisions within and between communities, perceived injustices, external domination, and so forth. Our overview reveals how Iran and Iraq have much in common but also differ significantly. Shi'ite majorities now have a major stake in shaping the national government, but very different dynamics preceded what is happening politically in these two countries today and what will happen tomorrow. Iranians ousted a dictator in an overwhelming, popular revolution; Iraqi Sh'ites moved to center stage after an external army toppled Saddam's Baathist regime and then stayed to occupy Iraq for years. The dramatic changes in Iraq increased the regional power and presence of Iran and also led to a semiautonomous Kurdish state in the northern part of the country. The growing strength of the Shi'ite-led governments in Iran and Iraq has contributed substantially to the fears of regional Sunni-led governments and transnational groups. We have said repeatedly that Islam is not monolithic, and the dynamic relationships between religion and politics are always a work in progress. A brief look at these two countries highlights some of the factors required for developing a more accurate framework for understanding than simplistic stereotypes or a clash-of-civilizations theory can offer.

Intertwined with the distinctive and nuanced differences, Iran and Iraq also share elements of history and experience with other predominantly Muslim lands. For example, the legacy of colonial rule frequently presents serious and multilayered problems that defy easy solutions. Unrepresentative, sometimes ruthless indigenous leaders, human rights abuses, and various types of economic exploitation exacerbated by lucrative oil revenues are frequently major sources of anger and frustration. Some of the frustration gets channeled—fairly or unfairly—toward perceived external foes such as Israel and the United States. Many Muslims could well argue that Israeli and U.S. policies are provocative or hostile, but close examination often suggests that a large portion of their anger relates directly to internal issues.

In Saddam Hussein's Iraq, however, there was no way to express frustration over brutality and abuse without putting one's life and the well-being of one's family in serious jeopardy. In different ways at different times, Iranian dissent has also manifested publicly toward the "Great Satan" (the United States) and Israel. As with Iraq, Israel and the United States were sometimes the only legitimate outlets toward which to channel political anger and religious frustration. At the same time, the large protests following the 2009 presidential election in Iran may well foreshadow a new day because the deep frustrations were directed at the ruling regime. In both Iran and Iraq, we have seen a clear desire for fair elections and affirmation of democracy. In both countries, the forms of democracy are tinted by dissimilar interpretations of Islam. Even so, these are harbingers of hope for participatory democracy in the predominantly Shi'ite countries.

Although some frustration and anger directed toward the United States and Israel is understandable, much of it is displaced. Over time, however, the hostile religious and political rhetoric takes on a life of its own. Perception becomes more important than reality. When perceptions fuel extremist groups within Islam, Christianity, and Judaism, religion can quickly become a lethal force. Explicit examples of the deadliest manifestations of fundamentalist religion are the subject of the next chapter.

# A ROAD TO DISASTER

## THE FALLACY OF FUNDAMENTALISM

THE WORLD CHANGED ON SEPTEMBER 11, 2001, WHEN 19 MEN simultaneously hijacked four U.S. commercial passenger planes and turned them into weapons of mass destruction. Forever etched into the memory of Americans and many around the world are horrific images of two airplanes flying directly into the twin towers of New York's World Trade Center and scenes from the aftermath of planes crashing into the Pentagon in Washington, DC, and into a field in Pennsylvania. In fact, the world did not change on that fateful day. On that day, the United States of America simply joined the rest of the world, in a disturbing way.

There had been many other public terrorizing attacks in the United States in recent years: exploding packages mailed by Ted Kaczynski, the Unabomber; nearly two decades of shooting sprees in public schools and post offices; the failed attempt to bomb the World Trade Center in 1993; Timothy McVeigh's fertilizer-filled truck bomb at Oklahoma City's Murrah Federal Building in 1995; and a bomb detonated at Centennial Park during the 1996 Atlanta Olympics, to name only the most prominent. These and other deadly attacks were largely seen as isolated events perpetrated by unstable or disgruntled individuals or small groups. On September 11, a well-organized and seemingly well-financed al-Qaeda[1] international network with operatives hidden inside America was able to strike a massive blow at the symbolic centers of American financial and military power. The lethal threat posed by violent extremists claiming inspiration from their religion and prepared to die in suicidal self-sacrifice was just as real in the United States as it had been in Beirut or Jerusalem.

The ringleader of the September 11 terrorists, Muhammad Atta, left behind a five-page letter detailing the meticulous planning and preparation for the hijackings and attacks. It also revealed the particular understanding of Islam that supplied the framework and motivation for Atta and others who were eagerly preparing "to meet God."[2] Atta's documents and numerous materials and proclamations by Osama bin Laden, coupled with a series of brazen attacks in London, Madrid, Bali, and elsewhere, solidified the threat. A network of militant Muslims—sometimes well organized and sometimes acting independently—shared a religious and political worldview that spurred them toward violent action. The stunning "success" of the attacks on September 11, 2001, in the United States and July 7, 2005, on London's public transportation system, forced everyone to think about far worse scenarios. What if the people perpetrating future suicidal attacks had access to chemical, biological, or nuclear weapons?

In the decade since September 11, media attention has focused primarily on violence connected to Islam. But, as we have seen in earlier chapters, Muslims are by no means unique. Many devout believers within each of the Abrahamic communities are actively working to bring about their respective version of a theocratic state. Numerous cocksure Christians, militant Muslims, and extremist Jews openly proclaim they know exactly what God wants, for them and for everyone else. These unwavering believers readily justify violence as a redemptive or required component necessary to accomplish God's plan. In the interdependent and heavily armed world of the 21st century, the thought and actions of these fundamentalists offer little more than a recipe for disaster.

As we have seen repeatedly in this book, none of these religions offers a permanent template that firmly establishes the proper interplay between religion and politics. Rather, the structures defining and regulating this dynamic relationship have always been shaped in particular settings. Drawing on their principles and teachings, the religions that have stood the test of time can and do adapt to changing circumstances. Fundamentalists, however, believe they have a fixed template that dictates the way forward. Their roadmaps may appropriate a version of God's truth that benefits their communities, but it is not a viable approach to our shared future on this planet. Frequently, they offer detailed directions leading to apocalypse. They long for the end of the world as we know it and are happy to facilitate the conflagration envisioned as part of God's plan.

In this chapter, we take up examples of the most blatant and overtly violent fundamentalists. Although their numbers are relatively small, the threat they pose is both imminent and widespread. The events of September 11 remind us that a small number of people can wreak havoc on a global scale. Such actors lead us to acknowledge the next level of fundamentalists, the many millions of devout believers who embrace a rigid theological framework and take direction from leaders whose theology is tied explicitly to a political agenda. These leaders deliberately engender fear and dehumanize others as they prepare the way for the theocracy they presume God requires. These fundamentalists are not yet among the small fringe of suicidal extremists, but many are only one small step removed. They represent a ticking time bomb in the contemporary world. Understanding the dangers that fundamentalists pose and exposing and challenging their worldviews are critical steps if we hope to fashion a healthier path forward in the 21st century.

## Fundamentalism and Fundamentalisms

The term *fundamentalism* originated in the context of late-19th and early-20th-century Christianity. As many Christians endeavored to adapt traditional beliefs to the new academic and scientific understandings of the world, others recoiled in the face of modernism and sought to defend Christian doctrines against such heresies. This segment of the Christian community focused on what they described as "the fundamentals," including belief in the inerrancy of the Bible. For fundamentalists, the Bible offers an accurate description of science and history as well as clear guidance on morality and religious life. Their belief in the perfection of the Bible led them to reject a good deal of modern scientific thinking, most notably the theory of evolution. They maintained that a literal reading of Genesis meant the world was less than 10,000 years old. The clash between "fundamentalists" and "modernists" was dramatically played out during the famous 1925 Scopes trial in Tennessee,[3] but it continues to live on today in places such as the Creation Museum in Kentucky.[4]

Most fundamentalists in the 19th century and today embrace the doctrines of premillennial dispensationalism, an interpretive framework that dissects the Bible and history into seven great time periods or dispensations. While claiming to take the Bible literally, premillennialists find all kinds of hidden meanings, hints, clues, and messages that unlock prophetic secrets not readily obvious to the uninitiated. This framework is constructed by selecting verses from various parts of the Bible—Isaiah, Jeremiah, Daniel, Ezekiel, the Gospels, Paul's letters, and the book of Revelation, most notably—and patching the verses together for a detailed map of the end times. According to this view, we are now very close to the end of history as we know it. Soon, Jesus will return and "rapture" the faithful up into the heavens. The Tribulation, a nightmarish period of seven years, will follow the Rapture. During this time, Satan's agent, the Antichrist, will reign supreme and large segments of the population will be decimated. At the end of seven years, Jesus will return to defeat the Antichrist at the Battle of Armageddon in northern Israel. Jesus will then establish a thousand-year reign of peace on the earth, where Isaiah's vision of swords made into ploughshares and the lion lying down with the lamb become reality.

In the late 1970s and 1980s, when multiple religiously inspired and powerful political movements emerged globally, journalists and some academics referred to them as "fundamentalists," even though the specifically Christian context that defines the term poses problems when it is applied loosely in a cross-cultural way. What does it mean to talk of Islamic or Jewish fundamentalists? Is a belief in scriptural inerrancy a defining component for Jews and Muslims as it is for Christian fundamentalists? The pieces don't fit neatly. In one sense, virtually every practicing Muslim affirms the Qur'an as the literal, inerrant Word of God. As is true with Jews and Christians, the diversity of interpretations of sacred scriptures within Islam is enormous. Various theological, legal, and mystical schools share this affirmation about the Qur'an but come to radically different conclusions about what it teaches and what their faith requires. Further, all Muslims acknowledge that passages in the Qur'an can convey both a straightforward literal meaning and a mystical, hidden meaning, simultaneously.

In the late 1980s, a team of international scholars began a multiyear, cross-cultural study of various types of "fundamentalisms" that were increasingly powerful forces all over the world. The editors, Martin Marty and R. Scott Appleby, and numerous contributors wrestled with the problem of terminology. In the end, they concluded both that the term *fundamentalism* was valid and that there was no other serviceable alternative to categorize somewhat similar phenomena in various religions.[5] The various scholars and editors of this extensive study speak in terms of fundamentalisms and endeavor continuously to clarify common threads as well as distinctive features so that casual generalizations can be avoided.

This is a helpful caveat for our study as well. There are many differences between and among Jewish, Christian, and Muslim fundamentalist groups today. There are also several factors that connect them. This chapter centers on those fundamentalists who distinguish themselves from traditionalists or conservatives within their communities of faith precisely because they have organized to fight back against a perceived threat to their core identity. This is a key point. Fundamentalists feel besieged by scientific and societal assumptions that contradict their worldview. They rally their supporters around political action based on fear of whatever or whoever is besieging them. Such fundamentalists are engaged in a militant struggle on behalf of a worldview they believe God has ordained. In political terms, their visions include a return to an imagined "ideal" time in the past or an endeavor to facilitate the ideal time just about to break into human history. They perceive themselves to be God's chosen instruments to realize the divine purpose in creation. Jewish, Christian, and Muslim fundamentalists who have embarked on a sacred mission from God have been and are capable of justifying any type of violent behavior. They represent Exhibit A in the contemporary manifestations of religion becoming lethal.

## Jewish Fundamentalists

Jewish fundamentalism takes a variety of forms. Ultra-orthodox Jews are at one end of the religious spectrum. They visibly distinguish themselves from other Jews by their attire, worldview, and religious practices. These adherents assume the fundamental truths about their religion began with Abraham, were codified by Moses, and have been preserved through a continuous chain linking them to God and their origins. Samuel Heilman and Menachem Friedman succinctly describe the ultra-orthodox Jews who reject modern secular culture: "To these Jews the past is the great teacher: today is never as great as yesterday, and the best that tomorrow can promise is a return to the great days of yesteryear."[6] A large percentage of these Jewish fundamentalists actually reject the legitimacy of the state of Israel; in their view, reestablishment of the true Israel will not occur until the Messiah comes. Even so, many ultra-orthodox Jews returned to Israel because they sought refuge in a place where they could be protected and practice their faith while insulated from the corruptions of modern secular society.

During the past six decades, many of the ultra-orthodox have entered into the Israeli political system, often at the direction of their rabbis, to protect and preserve what they believe Jewish law requires, although not all agree on what that means. Within their ranks and in numerous disputes with various other Orthodox Jews, the ultra-orthodox clash over interpretations of Jewish law and with Zionists over who and what is a Jew.[7] Politically, some ultra-orthodox are closely related to the self-described Orthodox Jews who form the core of groups such as Meir Kahane's Kach movement and the "Block of the Faithful," the Gush Emunim. I have spent many days in conversation with Jewish leaders and

West Bank settlers in these groups and can attest to the diversity of their views, as well as their political clout.

Some Jewish fundamentalists pray for the coming of the Messiah; others have decided to give God a hand in order to facilitate the process. In Chapters 2 and 3 we identified several such individuals—Baruch Goldstein, Yigal Amir, and Ami Popper—and the groups who condone or celebrate their murderous actions. The line separating these violent extremists and the hard-core West Bank settlers within Gush Emunim is increasingly hard to discern. The settler movement that began following the Yom Kippur War of 1973 has become a dominant force shaping Israeli politics. Gideon Aran vividly describes the origins of Jewish Zionist fundamentalists and the clear intention of settlements in the Occupied Territories:

> During the mid-1970s, public attention in Israel turned to a band of skull capped and bearded young men, assault rifles on their shoulders and rabbinical texts in their hands. They spent their nights in the territories conquered and administered by the Israel Defense Forces since the 1967 war. . . . In the mornings, they marched through Arab towns, waving Israeli flags, breaking windows and puncturing tires. . . . Initially, the phenomenon was described as lunatic, esoteric, episodic, and marginal. Observers expressed their amazement or disdain. . . . These several hundred true believers constituted the future leaders and cadres of the central religiopolitical movement in Israel, the Gush Emunim. . . . The chief public manifestation of the Gush Emunim is its settlements, the earliest of which were founded contrary to government decision and against the will of significant segments of the Israel public. The proliferation of settlements surrounding and penetrating hostile Palestinian population centers has transformed the status, landscape, and atmosphere of the Territories. The settlements represent a planned effort to force the inclusion of this area within the boundaries of legitimate Israeli control.[8]

What began as a radical fringe movement has grown over four decades into an exceedingly powerful force within Israel. As various Labor, Likud, and coalition Israeli administrations have compromised or collaborated with Gush Emunim and other Orthodox and ultra-orthodox groups for four decades, many "facts on the ground" have been created in the Occupied Territories.[9] As we noted in Chapter 3, any effort to negotiate a peace settlement involving the return of land to the Palestinians has been opposed vehemently by those who are certain that God gave them all of this land. The two most right-wing Israeli prime ministers who negotiated for the return of land and dismantling of settlements in the Sinai peninsula and Gaza Strip—Menachem Begin and Ariel Sharon, respectively—were demonized by Gush Emunim. Yitzhak Rabin, who signed the Oslo Peace Accords, was assassinated.

Most Americans assume the Israeli-Palestinian peace process gets stuck because of intransigence on the part of Palestinians or because ongoing violent confrontations pose insurmountable threats to Israel's security. These are clearly significant factors in the mix. Jewish fundamentalists, however, represent the elephant in the room. Any Israeli government that truly seeks to negotiate a viable peace based on the internationally agreed pre-1967 boundaries and UN resolutions 242 and 338 risks civil war. The Jewish Zionist fundamentalist settlers are heavily armed and deadly certain that God gave them the land.

Many books have been written (and more could be) tracing the evolution of Israeli political decisions over the decades. As is true in other lands where voters can oust political leaders, short-term political pragmatism in Israel often triumphs over policies facilitating long-term goals. This helps explain how the more liberal and secularist Labor governments have been just as complicit as their conservative Likud counterparts in facilitating the illegal and insidious process of settlements.

Political pragmatism also clarifies the close relationships between various Israeli leaders and American Christian fundamentalists such as Jerry Falwell and John Hagee. This relationship is stronger today than ever. I have been in three churches in the past year where piles of glossy publications from the International Christian Embassy highlight the close connections with the Israeli government and invite American Christians to support their work.

The political pragmatism undergirding the long-standing ties with Christian fundamentalists was first spelled out to me clearly by a top aide to then Prime Minister Yitzhak Shamir. In April 1984 we met in the prime minister's offices. After a couple of minutes of pleasantries, I zeroed in on a burning issue. I said that I had spent three hours that morning with the head of the Christian Embassy in Jerusalem. I reported how this man had explained in detail how biblical events were unfolding and Jesus would be returning very soon. I shared several unsettling details from the morning conversation, including the man's remarks about Lebanon. (At the time, Israel was embroiled in a major internal debate about what to do in Lebanon. Their invasion in 1982 to decimate the PLO and provide "peace for Galilee" had turned into a quagmire. Shi'ites in Southern Lebanon had formed into an organized fighting force, Hizbullah ["Party of God"] and were inflicting heavy losses on the Israel Defense Forces.) I reported how the Christian Embassy representative was dismayed that Israel would even consider withdrawing from Lebanon. At one point, he leaned toward me and whispered, "The Jews here don't really understand what God is doing in Israel!"

I shared elements of the morning conversation and then moved on to talk about the end-of-the-world scenario embraced by millions of other premillennial dispensationalist Christians. In this scheme, all the Jews will be killed, except for a remnant of 144,000. At the end of the seven-year period of Tribulation, these Jews will convert and become followers of Jesus. I put the point bluntly: "Your government collaborates with and cajoles these Christian fundamentalists at great peril. They claim to love Israel and the Jewish people, but in fact they long for the day when there are no Jews! You are the object of their theology. I think you are in bed with a snake."

The advisor to the prime minister smiled. After the previous formality of calling me Reverend Kimball, he shifted to a more personal style and explained his government's stance. After the meeting, I recorded the details of the conversation.

> Charles, I very much appreciate you and your concern for Jews and Israel. As you know, we in Israel have a very sophisticated intelligence service. I know everything about you. I have a thick file on you detailing your Jewish family background, speeches you have given, people you meet in Israel and in the U.S. While I personally disagree with your views on the prospects for peace with the PLO, I consider you a friend of Israel. I say this behind closed doors. We know who our friends are and who support us because of their theology. When we go outside these doors, we enter the world of political reality. I will publicly disagree with you and the policies adopted by the National Council of Churches. Israel has few friends in the world. We will take support from wherever we can get it—from the Christian Embassy, American evangelists who bring groups here, from South Africa, wherever. . . . When it comes to people like those you've been discussing, you should know that we watch them carefully and have them on a very short leash. If it becomes necessary, we will pull in that leash.

Our conversation continued for another hour during which time I returned to the leash analogy and questioned whether they might instead have a tiger by the tail. Short-term political pragmatism can be a very dangerous path, especially when it yokes one to fundamentalists who long for the end of the world and may be prepared to facilitate the final conflagration.

Yitzhak Rabin, Ezer Weizman, Rabbi Arthur Hertzberg, and many other Jewish leaders have come to the conclusion that heavily armed Jewish

Zionist fundamentalists and their Christian supporters are propelling Israel down a dead-end road to oblivion. The status quo is untenable for Israel. Although the nation has an exceedingly effective military and nuclear weapons at its disposal, Israel's self-interest requires peaceful co-existence. It is probably only a matter of time until adversaries of the Jewish state gain access to nuclear, chemical, or biological weapons. In the absence of a negotiated peace, the Holy Land may well become the scene for the most horrific manifestation of religion becoming lethal.

## Cocksure Christians

The United States of America today includes large numbers of vocal, self-described "conservative" and "fundamentalist" Christians. Some are armed and clearly dangerous. Various Christian militia groups have become increasingly more visible as their members clash with police and government authorities in several states. They are tied in varying degrees to the Christian Identity movement, a confederation of groups with deep connections to the Ku Klux Klan and Aryan Nations.[10] Others are woven into the Sovereign Citizen movement, a right-wing anarchist collection of individuals and groups who consider almost all forms of government authority to be illegitimate intrusions into their lives. The crusade to restore a minimalist government takes many forms, including homicidal violence.[11] Others who have used deadly force rally around issues of abortion as the "Army of God."[12]

American church historian Richard Hughes offers an eloquent critique of such fringe groups and others who distort the Christian call to work for peace and social justice. Hughes sharply contrasts contemporary interpretations of Christianity that support a narrow political agenda against broader understandings of biblical terms such as "chosen people" and "Kingdom of God." He observes the "devastatingly ironic truth" that some of the most visible voices reflect the polar opposite of the "Christian" behavior identified in the New Testament. He cites best-selling author Ann Coulter as a prime example:

> While the apostle Paul argued that "the fruit of the Spirit is love, joy, peace, patience, kindness, generosity, faithfulness, gentleness, and self-control," Coulter has specialized in sarcasm, ridicule, mud-slinging, and hate-mongering. She scorned grieving widows in the aftermath of the September 11 disaster. She identifies the biblical vision of the kingdom of God with American nationalism. . . . She slanders those with whom she disagrees . . . and publicly consigns her political opponents to the fires of hell.[13]

Although Coulter is not a recognized religious leader, she frequently emphasizes the centrality of true Christianity in her life and as the motivating force in her relentless battle against Godless liberalism (including Christian "liberals" who believe in evolution or think Jesus wanted his followers to be nice to other people).

Hughes's research and writing challenges the frequently promoted idea of America as a Christian nation. Chris Hedges goes further. Hedges believes that, far more than misguided or offensive, a deeply rooted sinister movement is at work. He presents a case that the orientation and behavior of the politically active religious right in America is nothing less than contemporary fascism. Hedges, an award-winning author and former journalist for the *New York Times,* details the ideology and tactics of the Christian militia and other groups in *American Fascists: The Christian Right and the War on America.* He traces the powerful and seductive growth of fascism in the 20th century to illustrate how those who believe "it can't happen here" may easily be overtaken by religious and political ideologies—as similar people were in Germany and Italy.

The growing influence of the religious right within the government became more visible in the years following September 11.[14] The pervasive influence of evangelical and fundamentalist Christianity within the military began to be explored following news accounts about Lt. General William "Jerry" Boykin. In June 2003, Gen. Boykin was appointed deputy undersecretary of defense intelligence. At the time, U.S. wars in Afghanistan and Iraq were focal points in the larger "war on terrorism" declared by the administration of the second President Bush. Boykin soon garnered extensive media attention as he frequently spoke in Baptist and Pentecostal churches about what he believed was the true nature of the conflicts. In 2002 and 2003, Boykin spoke in 23 religiously oriented events and worship services. In all but two, he was dressed in his formal military uniform. The general presented his views unambiguously: "Islamic extremists hate the United States because we are a Christian nation . . . and the enemy is a guy named Satan." Journalists dug deeper and found much more. Nearly a decade before his top-level appointment in defense intelligence, Boykin's theological worldview was on the record. In published statements to a Muslim warlord in Somalia who had declared "Allah will protect me!" Boykin proudly proclaimed: "I knew my God was bigger than his. I knew that my God was a real God and his was an idol."[15]

Boykin has every right to his beliefs, of course. But how he acted on them given his position and wearing his uniform in churches conflated his professional role with his personal views. This is highly problematic both within the U.S. government and in the image conveyed to the rest of the world. Boykin's views, however, reflect the widespread influence of evangelical and fundamentalist leaders throughout the land. Much has been written and reported on the theological and political agendas of the late Jerry Falwell, the late James Kennedy, and Pat Robertson. As these dominant figures with their extensive influence through national television ministries pass from the scene, others now assume powerful leadership roles. Pastor John Hagee in Texas and the Rev. Rod Parsley of Ohio have emerged as two of the most prominent fundamentalist leaders in the early 21st century. Their respective religious and political worldviews influence many millions of Americans today. Their prominence drew national attention in 2008 when Republican presidential candidate John McCain publicly sought and received endorsements from both men. Less than a month after the media events staged for the endorsements, the McCain campaign visibly disassociated with both religious leaders. Why? What do these men believe, preach, and teach that made their political association with John McCain so toxic to most Americans?

Hagee, pastor of Cornerstone Church in San Antonio, is the epitome of a "cocksure Christian." Hagee's certainty about his understanding of biblical prophecy, the impending Rapture, and second coming of Christ is absolute. He preaches weekly and frequently publishes books in which he accounts for virtually every major event in the Middle East, Russia, China, the United States, and the Muslim world. In his theological worldview, every development of consequence can be connected to and interpreted by biblical prophecy. He and others claim to have the ability to discern the true meaning and interpret 2,500-year-old utterances from Ezekiel or 1,900-year-old symbolic language from the book of Revelation, as though the Bible were a big collection of coded messages and puzzles.

Tune in Hagee's weekly television program and you will get the picture. He often preaches and teaches in front of a gigantic pictorial schematic of God's prophetic timeline. Viewers are informed that all the biblical prophecies have been fulfilled and the culmination of history as we know it could occur at any moment. His 2006 book *Jerusalem Countdown: A Warning to the World,* and a modified 2010 version of the same material, *Can America Survive? 10 Prophetic Signs That We Are the Terminal Generation,* present Hagee's religious and political worldview in detail. Israel, God's chosen people, is the key. God's harsh judgment will fall on anyone or any nation that challenges Israel's absolute God-given authority to rule over all the land from the eastern end of the Mediterranean Sea to the Tigris and Euphrates rivers. Any talk of an Israeli-Palestinian peace process that involves one inch of land for Arabs is anathema. Reading Hagee's books or listening to his television program

is highly instructive. He is as extreme and unwavering as the most fundamentalist settlers in the occupied West Bank.[16]

> There is a clear and inconvenient truth about Israel that America and
> Europe need to remember. That truth is: Israel is a sovereign nation
> and not a vassal state of the United States. It does not need the
> approval of the White House or the U.S. State Department to build in
> its capital city. This land was given to Israel by covenant from God
> Almighty to Abraham 3,500 years ago and that covenant stands
> *today*![17]

True, Israel is a sovereign state. It has also been by far the largest
recipient of U.S. financial and military aid for half a century. In addition,
Israel's settlement policies in the occupied West Bank are widely seen as
both illegal and a monumental obstacle to any potential peace settlement both
inside and outside of Israel. Hagee may be wrong, but he is never in
doubt. Like the previously mentioned "ambassador" at the Christian
Embassy in Jerusalem, he is sure he knows more about God's activity
in contemporary Israel than many Israeli leaders do. In an hour-long
interview on the National Public Radio program *Fresh Air*, Hagee
proudly reported on his personal letter to then Israeli Prime Minister
Ehud Olmert. He was particularly upset and scolded Olmert for yielding
to internal pressures to end the July 2006 war in Lebanon against the
military forces of Hizbullah. Hagee believed that God wanted Israel to
crush the Muslims in Lebanon.[18]

Islam is a focus of evil in Hagee's worldview. He repeatedly and selectively quotes Muslim extremists to present a stereotypical, dehumanized
picture of Islam. Muslims apparently wake up each day with thoughts of
suicide bombings and world domination. Hagee repeatedly contrasts
Americans who "love life" with Muslims who seemingly think only of
death and sensual delights of paradise. He presents no distinctions
between or among Sunnis and Shi'ites; nor does he acknowledge the common humanity of Muslims as parents, grandparents, siblings, or friends.
We hear only of passionate fanatics who love death, perceive Christians
and Jews as infidels, and seek world domination.

According to Hagee, Iran will play a pivotal role in the final stages of
human history. The first part of *Can America Survive?* is titled "A Nuclear
Iran." In this section and at four other parts of the book, Hagee forcefully
assures readers that Iran is ready for war, is capable of attacking Israel
with a nuclear weapon, and is engineering plans to neutralize the United
States with an electromagnetic pulse (EMP) explosion that will eliminate
all types of electricity for months. The specificity and certainty with which

Hagee proffers his predictions is crystal clear. Iranian president Mahmoud Ahmadinejad, whom Hagee compares in a point-by-point way to Hitler, is cited as the authentic voice for what Muslims worldwide believe and desire. This is a particularly striking generalization in view of the massive media coverage of turmoil and protests in Iran following the 2009 presidential elections. Hagee highlights and magnifies deep-seated and long-standing fears about Islam as somehow inherently violent and menacing.

The main thrust of Hagee's books and preaching ministry, however, is that all the events that are happening are precisely what God intends, even though he sharply chides U.S. policy makers (most especially President Obama) for blatant mistakes on foreign policy, economic policies, health care policies, and so forth that are leading America to the point of disaster. But then he also claims everything is going according to the biblical script. God is in total control of every event. Therefore even natural disasters, such as Hurricane Katrina in 2005, are orchestrated by the God of Abraham, Isaac, and Jacob.[19] He repeatedly mocks Iran's Ahmadinejad and others for believing that nuclear war or some other conflagration will hasten the coming of the Islamic savior figure, the *mahdi*, even as he presents his stunningly similar Christian "end of days" scenario. It is a strange brew indeed.

Hagee is one of the most visible advocates for premillennial dispensational theology today. The pervasive influence of this approach to the Bible and theology in American Protestantism is reflected in the majority of national television ministries and the widely popular "Left Behind" books and movies.[20] As a Baptist, I readily affirm both the right and the responsibility of Christians to work out their theology. This particular theological worldview, however, intersects with and shapes powerful political agendas. For Hagee and millions of other Americans, it translates into uncritical support for the most extremist zealots in Israel, as well as overt hostility toward Islam in general and toward Iran, Saudi Arabia, and other countries in particular. Hagee and those who embrace his worldview bring intense political pressure on any political leader who is not in lockstep with this orientation.

Rod Parsley, senior pastor at the World Harvest Church in Columbus, Ohio, is another fundamentalist leader seeking to influence the political course of America. His book *Silent No More: Bringing Moral Clarity to America . . . While Freedom Still Rings* leaves little doubt about his religious and political worldview.[21] The cover of the book speaks volumes: a serious Parsley looks you in the eye with the nation's Capitol building framed over his right shoulder. Chapters on "Judicial Tyranny," "Homosexuality," "Life," and "The Media: The Enemy in Our Midst" convey precisely what

God demands on issues converging at the intersection of religion and politics today. Why is Parsley so important? The 2004 presidential election between incumbent George W. Bush and Senator John Kerry was decided in Ohio. Parsley's positions mirror those designed to bring out large numbers of conservative and fundamentalist Christians in this critical swing state. Parsley's "Silent No More" tour of the state was effective in persuading voters that Bush was all that stood between them and un-Christian policies on homosexuality, abortion, and liberal judges on the U.S. Supreme Court. Political pundits were intrigued but not surprised when 2008 presidential candidate McCain actively sought the public endorsement of Parsley.

Parsley's diatribes against Islam are particularly egregious. I can say without equivocation that his chapter on "Islam: The Deception of Allah" is among the most inaccurate and confused presentations I've seen in print since I began specializing in Islamic studies four decades ago. Parsley retells the story of Islam and declares repeatedly that Allah is a "demon spirit." He takes various key elements within Islam, ridicules people who embrace the faith, and pronounces the "truth" as the opposite. In his view, Queen Noor, the American-born wife of the late King Hussein of Jordan, tells "an astonishing lie" when she speaks of a Muslim's direct relationship with God, honesty, and moderation, and how Islam honors women. Parsley mocks the Five Pillars of Islam and emphasizes that the real goal Muslims seek is nothing less than world domination. He claims to offer a course in Islam 101 but instead inflames passions and spreads ignorance to millions already fearful and confused about the world's second-largest religion.

Christian fundamentalist leaders such as Hagee and Parsley propagate destructive doctrines and political policies. If American leaders follow their guidance, we may well become the terminal generation. Their uncritical support for the most extremist positions in Israel and their overt hostility toward Islam and Muslims are potent, explosive elements in the already volatile mix evident in our world today. Follow their lead, and their longed-for end-of-the-world conflagration may become a self-fulfilling prophecy.

Clearly, Muslims have their counterparts to the radical fringe and to cocksure Christian fundamentalists. Although some Muslims anticipate the imminent end of history as we know it, there are many millions of Muslims who are not yet in the camp of the most violent extremists who claim inspiration from Islam. They are fearful and susceptible to outspoken religious leaders with political agendas. We turn now to a closer look at this pivotal segment of global Islam.

## Militant Muslims

Reza Aslan, author of *No god but God,* a popular introduction to Islam, cogently describes the religious ideology embodied by a small minority of Muslims who believe they are fighting a cosmic war today. With God on their side, these warriors are certain that the forces of good will prevail over the forces of evil. As the world has seen repeatedly for more than a decade, Osama bin Laden and those who embrace a similar worldview will use any and all means at their disposal to achieve their goal of establishing their vision of the Islamic state, both in particular countries and in a global ummah ("Islamic community"). Israel (and infidel Jews) and the United States (and infidel Christians) are seen as orchestrating events and collaborating with corrupt governments in Egypt, Saudi Arabia, and elsewhere to thwart implementation of true Islamic rule. For these cosmic warriors, there is no room for negotiation or compromise. They are on a mission from God and will use chemical, biological, electronic, nuclear, and any other type of weapons available. If the men who hijacked the four planes on September 11 had been able to procure a nuclear device, they most certainly would have used it.

Aslan's book *How to Win a Cosmic War* offers a prescription: refuse to fight a cosmic war. Framing the contemporary conflict with a loosely connected network of Islamic extremists as a "war on terror" or a clash between "good and evil" simply plays into their script. This is precisely what religious leaders such as Robertson, Hagee, and Parsley do. The post–September 11 administration of President Bush also employed this terminology. Terrorism is not an enemy or a nation-state; it is a powerful and often successful tactic, particularly when employed by people who are prepared to sacrifice their life. It is exceedingly difficult to prevent such militants from striking a deadly blow against unsuspecting civilians because the target could be a marketplace, a bus, or an apartment building.

The most violent and extreme Muslim militants represented by al-Qaeda present an insidious and massively destabilizing threat in particular nations as well as the wider world community. No one knows how many people fit into this category of militant Muslims. It may be 10,000, 25,000, or 100,000. Although even at 100,000 these people represent a tiny fraction of the 1.5 billion Muslims worldwide, recent history illustrates the deadly havoc they can cause. Targeted international electronic, economic, and military efforts to thwart their efforts will remain a high priority for many years to come.

A second type of Muslim militant group is represented by the Hizbul-lah (Party of God) in Lebanon and HAMAS (Islamic Resistance Move-ment) in Palestine. Although many Americans—including many political leaders—lump these groups together with al-Qaeda as "terrorist organi-zations," they are quite different. Both Hizbullah and HAMAS were born in the 1980s. Both groups developed as unofficial governments in settings where no effective government was functional or delivering health care and education in their respective Shi'ite and Sunni communities in Leba-non and the Gaza Strip.

In the United States, these groups are associated primarily with their military activities. In addition to traditional forms of combat, both groups have resorted to kidnappings, suicide bombings, and firing rockets into civilian towns. Organizations such as Hizbullah and HAMAS have been supported militarily and financially—precisely because of their frontline combat with Israel—both by governments such as Iran and by transna-tional, nongovernmental groups such as al-Qaeda. But these kinds of mili-tant Muslim groups have more focused religious and political agendas. They put forth a vision for an Islamic state in Lebanon and Palestine. Some in their ranks may have even more grandiose global aspirations, but they recognize and seek to create their version of an Islamic state within the nation-state system as we know it. These organizations enjoy strong support within their communities, in large part because they have pro-vided structure and services where existing governments failed repeatedly. If given free rein, each group would implement a modified version of the Taliban's Islamic state in Afghanistan. They operate on the assumption that there is a template for the ideal Islamic state. In the end, this form of fundamentalism offers a false promise; both Lebanon and Palestine include religiously diverse communities with a significant recent history of participatory government. A sectarian Islamic state in such a setting would surely exacerbate tensions and fracture, not unify, the society.

It is important to underscore the point that most Muslims do not read-ily embrace the reality of a contemporary Islamic state as constructed by the Taliban. Recall that only three countries—Pakistan, Saudi Arabia, and the United Arab Emirates—officially recognized the Taliban as legiti-mate, while more than 50 other predominantly Muslim nations joined the rest of the world in rejecting the Taliban and their sectarian rule.

In my experience lecturing across America, most people are surprised by this information. Heavily influenced as they are by media coverage of violence and perpetual fearmongering by political and religious leaders, most Americans have no idea what 1.5 billion Muslims actually think about religion and the state, or about violence in the name of Islam.

Fortunately, we now have substantial data to replace anecdotes and media images.

In Chapter 7 we noted the Gallup Organization's 2007 publication of results from the most extensive and carefully crafted polling ever conducted among Muslims. The study revealed that the majority of Muslims do not see democracy and self-determination as inconsistent with Islam. Although a small minority of Muslims (7%) believe the September 11 attacks were justified, the overwhelming majority (74% in Indonesia, 86% in Pakistan, and 80% in Iran) say that terrorist attacks against civilians are never justifiable. Interestingly, in a similar poll only 46% of Americans believe that "bombing and other attacks intentionally aimed at civilians" were never justified, while 24% reported that such attacks are "often or sometimes justified."[22]

Gallup's remarkable study illustrates a point we have made repeatedly: Islam is not monolithic. Distinct histories, economic circumstances, political structures, and religious diversity are readily evident between and within countries as dissimilar as Iran and Indonesia, Algeria and Afghanistan. As we noted in Chapters 7 and 8, however, there are some elements on which Muslims find common ground. The legacies of colonial rule and subsequent corrupt, indigenous governments produce great disparity between the haves and have-nots. Lack of economic opportunity and oppressive human rights abuses contribute to frustration and anger in many settings. The Gallup study confirms attitudes toward the U.S. government that various analysts have identified in recent years in response to the question, "Why do they hate us?" Perceptions of one-sided U.S. policies on the Israeli-Palestinian conflict and support for repressive regimes are major sources that fuel anger among Arab and Muslim people, yet they extol the virtues of democracy and self-determination.

Rami Khouri, longtime editor of the *Jordan Times* and a frequently quoted Middle East analyst, articulated the widely held perception of U.S. government hypocrisy following a major conference in 2005 in the United Arab Emirates. Khouri was one of some 200 representatives from various Arab and Muslim countries invited to hear then Secretary of State Condoleezza Rice and Karen Hughes, President Bush's special envoy to the Arab world. Khouri reported that the morning session consisted of speeches by Rice and Hughes explaining and promoting democracy and free enterprise as the keys to a "new Middle East." Iraq could help lead the way forward, they argued. Then these same speakers spent the afternoon session scolding the Arab and Muslim countries for "electing" the wrong people! When free elections resulted in victories for HAMAS, Hizbullah, and Islamist parties in Egypt, Jordan, and other lands, Rice and Hughes left no doubt that economic and other forms of punishment would be the result. Khouri and others concluded that the United States is for democracy so long as the correct people are elected.[23]

Many millions of disenfranchised and deeply frustrated Muslims are not people who openly support or are prepared to join the ranks of al-Qaeda. They are not Lebanese Shi'ites within Hizbullah or Palestinian Sunnis in Gaza who populate HAMAS. A large segment within various Muslim lands—no one knows with precision how many millions or what percentage of the populations would fit—are frustrated on several levels and long for a better day for their children and grandchildren. Many believe Islam can help find the way forward for their country. But as we've seen, there is no consensus on what precisely this should mean in terms of an Islamic state in a given setting. Many are sympathetic with the defiant rhetoric of Osama bin Laden and leaders of Hizbullah. Some will cheer when militant Muslims strike a blow against the United States or Israel, but they have not crossed over into the ranks of those who believe violent confrontation is the only way forward. They are at the heart of the struggle for the soul of Islam.

The next two decades will be decisive. The war of ideas and ideology is raging. In the final chapter, we explore signs of hope and paths to a healthier future (even though a better future is far from certain). The options will depend in large part on the attitudes and actions of this third group of militant Muslims. How many will become irrevocably radicalized by systemic injustice in their countries, by the deaths or permanent injury inflicted on family members and friends, by pictures of suffering Palestinians or the still-circulating photos of sexually abused prisoners at the Abu Ghraib prison in Iraq or civilians killed in collateral damage when a U.S. missile hits a school or family home in Afghanistan? These powerful images are shown and discussed in the Western media; they appear daily in madrasas ("Islamic schools") and the media in Muslim lands. The constant drumbeat by highly visible Christian leaders attacking Islam—not only TV preachers such as Robertson, Hagee, and Parsley, but Franklin Graham and even Pope Benedict XVI[24]—is highlighted daily. Will these be the images that drive more and more Muslims toward violence? Or can the United States be seen as a consistent supporter of human rights and democratic rule? How many Muslim leaders will emerge to chart constructive options appropriate to particular communities and nations in the 21st century?

## Confronting Fundamentalism

Narrowly defined fundamentalist sectarianism coupled with a political agenda pose clear and present dangers in the interdependent world

community of the 21st century. We have seen strikingly similar movements actively at work today among Jews, Christians, and Muslims in
highly charged settings. In my view, it is imperative that these religious
and political positions being promoted be discussed and debated. In the
process, I believe most people will see the dead-end road down which the
false promises of fundamentalism lead. Others do not share my conviction. On several occasions in recent years, I have been challenged for
speaking directly about prominent Christian fundamentalists. During the
question-and-answer session following some public lectures, I have been
admonished that it is not polite to speak about people like Hagee,
Parsley, and Pat Robertson specifically, to name names. My response
is threefold.

First, many Americans routinely criticize Muslims for not being more
vocal in challenging and repudiating the theological and political rhetoric
and actions of Muslim extremists. Ask anyone who speaks regularly on
issues related to Islam, and she or he will tell you the most frequent questions posed are: Where are the "peaceful Muslims"? Why don't Americans
hear more from Muslims who oppose violence and extremism? These are
fair questions from those who haven't heard or been made aware of the
many ways in which Muslim leaders and individuals have been quite vocal,
especially since September 11. We will return to this important matter in
the final chapter. The question here is this: Why is it impolite to challenge
and disagree publicly with Hagee, Parsley, or Robertson and at the same
time be sharply critical of Muslims who are not publicly opposing the
theological worldviews and the calls to action by Muslim extremists?

Second, several fundamentalist leaders are extremely influential in
shaping the religious and political landscape. When self-appointed leaders
take to the public airways seeking to shape public opinion, their views
should be scrutinized. They have become public figures, and as such they
are open to discussion of the ramifications of theological and political
positions they are already propagating on television and in books.

Finally, the ignorance, fear, and hostility they promote certainly
encourage and sometimes embody hate speech. Hate speech easily leads
to hate crimes. The social and political impact of fundamentalists such as
Hagee and Parsley has serious consequences. We have already identified
international ramifications for the Israeli-Palestinian conflict, relationships with various Muslim countries, and the "war on terror." Within the
United States, there are numerous disconcerting manifestations of hostility toward Islam. This should be as alarming as a fire bell in the night, in
a country with a long and deep tradition of religious freedom.

Muslims may already be or soon will constitute the second-largest religious community in the United States. Demographic information is less

reliable when a number of Muslims choose not to identify themselves as such out of fear of discrimination. There is no doubt that the growing Islamic community is rapidly outpacing the American Jewish community. Public displays against Islam are visible all over the land. During the course of a July 2010 summer vacation, I was struck by three examples that illustrate this point.

Passing through Nashville, I picked up a copy of the *Tennessean* on July 15. A front-page story with accompanying photo reported on a heated debate over the proposed building of a mosque just south of Murfreesboro, the home of Middle Tennessee State University. More than 500 people marched to deliver petitions (which they claimed had 20,000 signatures) opposing the building of the mosque. Some protesters wore T-shirts bearing the word "infidel"; a prominent placard read, "Stop TN Homegrown Terrorism."

Later that same afternoon, the National Public Radio program *All Things Considered* reported at length on the vigorous protest being mounted against the building of an Islamic Center within blocks of the site of the World Trade Center in New York. The vision behind "Cordoba House" originated with Imam Feisal Abdul Rauf and his spouse, Daisy Khan. Rauf is the imam or leader of the mosque just blocks away from "Ground Zero." Cordoba House is to be a place for the arts, culture, performances, weddings, lecture series, and prayer. As we have noted previously, Rauf and Khan are well-known leaders in interfaith education and cooperation. Their dream for Cordoba House had the support of New York Mayor Michael Bloomberg and most other local political leaders. The NPR report stressed how strong opposition was mounting and various national political and religious leaders were beating the drum against the project.[25]

Returning to Oklahoma on July 31, I discovered an ongoing story about a woman in Edmond who had placed a big sign in her front yard that read "Muslims are Dangerous." The sign went up when Muslim neighbors moved in next door. An article on the religion page of Oklahoma City's paper, the *Oklahoman*, sparked strong letters to the editor and public comments from people who celebrated the Edmond woman's courage to proclaim the truth and stand up for the Bible.[26] The obvious problem in all three instances is that those who were enacting anti-Muslim sentiment were conflating the most extreme of extremists with Muslims seeking to express their faith—or to simply live peacefully in a neighborhood. This is like assuming that all Christians are members of violent separatist militias simply by virtue of being Christians. But Islamophobia is pervasive in America. Listen to such influential ministers as Hagee or Parsley or any number of radio and television pundits, and you can understand how so many Americans see Islam and Muslims monolithically and stereotypically. In the November 2, 2010, elections, my home state of Oklahoma passed a ballot initiative (State Question No. 755) that required the courts to rely exclusively on state or federal laws and prohibited "shariah and international law" from being used when making rulings. The measure, which immediately drew national and international attention, passed overwhelmingly with 70% of the vote. The generic way in which shariah law is presumed to be clearly defined and the inclusion of all international law raised a dozen legal and constitutional problems as soon as the measure passed.

All of these stories expose a hostile anti-Islamic undercurrent within America, but there are also hopeful, positive elements in evidence. All of these stories included thoughtful and measured views from Muslims, Christians, and Jews who were ashamed of hateful bigotry or the uniformed presumptions in evidence. Many identified how First Amendment guarantees were in play and articulated the importance of modeling constructive interfaith relationships in the United States. The *Tennessean* article also reported on those who turned out in support of the mosque project. When the story continued on page 6, the paper presented a good deal of helpful information in a sidebar. The section explained the basics about mosques, clarified the private local funding for the project, and highlighted main tenets and major branches of Islam.

Exposing the theological worldview and political goals of various types of fundamentalists is neither easy nor painless. People of faith and goodwill often come to differing conclusions about proper approaches to religion and politics. It is essential, however, to have clear, open, and frank debate. Silence for fear of being criticized or appearing to be impolite is unacceptable when the stakes are so exceedingly high.

In the final chapter, we discover how some Muslims are responding to the challenges with courage and clarity. Accurate information and open debate are crucial components in the quest to secure a healthier future for our planet. There are no easy answers, but there are good reasons for hope in the 21st century.

# HOPE FOR THE PERILOUS
# JOURNEY AHEAD

A BEAUTIFUL HAND-PAINTED TILE IN MY OFFICE IS INSCRIBED with the words "Pray for the Peace of Jerusalem." It is a constant reminder to me of the central importance of Jerusalem for nearly half the world's population, and the urgent need for peace in that Holy Land. Jerusalem is a powerful symbol of how religion and politics converge, with the potential for both conflagration and peaceful coexistence. The New Testament articulates this sentiment with its description of Jesus approaching Jerusalem: "As he came near and saw the city, he wept over it, saying 'If you, even you, had only recognized on this day the things that make for peace! But now they are hidden from your eyes'" (Luke 19:41–42). The lovely tile crafted by Armenian Christian artisans in the old city of Jerusalem reminds me daily that Jews, Christians, Muslims, and others can and should pray for the peace of Jerusalem.

A second reminder in my office is a plaque displaying a well-known Arabic proverb that some people attribute to the Prophet Muhammad: "Trust God but tie up your camel first." The proverb underscores that having faith does not eliminate human responsibility. God gave us brains and expects us to use them. As a person of faith, I am also a person of hope. My hope for a healthier future is not simply wishful thinking. Hope calls us to act in pursuit of that future. The central stories at the beginning of Judaism, Christianity, and Islam are stories of faith in God and hope for the future connected to action. Against all odds, Moses confronts the pharaoh and calls on him to let the children of Israel go from their bonds of slavery. The Exodus and 40-year sojourn in the wilderness of Sinai is a compelling story of faith and hope in action. So too are the narratives about the early Christian community that perseveres and triumphs without resorting to violence in the face of horrific persecution. Similarly, Muhammad and the small band of converts to Islam endured economic, social, and physical persecution in Mecca before their faith and hope informed constructive steps toward a better future. After 12 years in Mecca, the 70 or so Muslims left their homes to build their ummah (community of faith) in Medina, a more secure and welcoming setting some 200 miles to the north.

## A Hopeful Way Forward

The history and contemporary case studies we have explored in this book have much to teach us about Jews, Christians, and Muslims engaging challenges of religion and politics, constructively and destructively. We have seen how religion and politics are always connected in multiple ways within every religious tradition. We can identify some key principles in the sacred texts and early history of the religions, but neither Judaism nor Christianity nor Islam presents a template for precisely how faithful believers are to structure the relationship between religion and political rule. These religious communities are not monolithic now, nor have they ever been, in governmental structures or vastly different doctrinal and theological positions, all of which are enmeshed in particular cultural contexts. The dynamic relationship between religion and politics is always a work in progress. There are heartening examples of mutuality and cooperation as well as horrific episodes of religious intolerance. Some of the most destructive situations occur when religion is used to justify mistreatment of people in minority communities, often as part of an attempt to impose some perceived divinely inspired template. And there have always been and probably always will be powerful and highly motivated fundamentalist groups and movements within each religion that are certain they possess the template for the religious state God intends.

This final chapter highlights specific initiatives and actions we can advocate for and use to fashion a more workable framework for the interactions of religion and politics. There are many positive initiatives and encouraging programs where Jews, Christians, and Muslims are working within their communities and across religious traditions today. Learning about, becoming involved with, and helping to publicize news of these good efforts is ever more important at a time when media attention gravitates toward the violent extremes, ignorant punditry, and sound-bite explanations. Being better informed and taking personal responsibility in our circles of influence—from friends, neighbors, and family members to religious and civic organizations and elected government officials—is an invaluable way to counter the partial and often misleading information that engenders fear among otherwise fair-minded people. Silence or acquiescence is an unacceptable response to the widely propagated bombastic rhetoric of some politicians, pundits, religious leaders, bloggers, and Internet enthusiasts. The place to start, the foundation on which the framework for a healthier future will be built, can be summed up in three words: education, education, education.

## Overcoming Religious Illiteracy

There is considerable evidence that significant numbers of Jews, Christians, and Muslims operate and view the "other" on the basis of "detailed ignorance." Boston University professor Stephen Prothero's provocative book *Religious Literacy: What Every American Needs to Know—and Doesn't* documents how little most Americans know about the most rudimentary teachings and practices in the world's major religions. Even more surprising, however, is his research on how little many self-identified Christians know about basic components of their own religion. Although more than 80% of the American public describe themselves as Christians, most adults cannot name the first book of the Bible, and only half can name even one of the four Gospels. Prothero underscores what many national surveys have revealed.[1] The Pew Forum on Religion and Public Life, for example, released findings from their "U.S. Religious Knowledge Survey" in September 2010. On average, Americans could correctly answer just 16 of the 32 questions on the survey; Jews, Mormons, and atheists were the most knowledgeable, with an average of more than 20 correct answers. Even though the survey confirmed that nearly 60% of U.S. adults declared that religion is "very important" in their lives and 40% reported they attend worship services at least once a week, only a small percentage were well informed about the tenets, practices, history, and leading figures of the major world religions—including their own.[2]

Data from the survey indicate that the single best predictor of religious knowledge is one's level of education, with college graduates averaging eight more correct answers than those with a high school education or less. The first and critically important step on the road to a better future involves concerted effort—individual and collective—to educate ourselves about religion. There are hopeful signs that intentional efforts to do so, at least in the United States, are taking root and growing.

In the decade since September 11, 2001, the number of religious studies courses (especially dealing with Islam and world religions) and enrollments have grown significantly in many colleges and universities.[3] Many religious studies departments report a significant rise in majors, minors, and students who double-major or double-minor with political science, psychology, sociology, or history. Similarly, thousands of churches in the United States have pursued substantial adult study programs focused on understanding the world's religions as well as their non-Christian neighbors. I am among many who teach and preach in a variety of churches and are heartened by the serious and concerted efforts to address the problem of religious illiteracy head-on.

If you want to do something to contribute to this educational effort, a good place to begin is with the human resources in your city. With more than 1,600 mosques in the United States, it is not too difficult to locate an American Muslim nearby who could speak and answer questions in a local church or for a civic organization. This is happening all over the United States today, so much so that many Muslim leaders I know have a hard time keeping up with the requests.[4] In my experience over the past three decades, and especially since September 11, the large majority of Jewish and Muslim leaders are happy to speak about their religious traditions and engage challenging questions about their communities and the often explosive mix of religion and politics in the United States and internationally.

Of the many valuable electronic resources on the major religions and contemporary events, two stand out. *Religion and Ethics News Weekly* on PBS and *Speaking of Faith*[5] on NPR are particularly helpful in presenting and exploring a variety of issues with depth and insight. Many other resources, such as DVD and CD-ROM courses published by the Teaching Company[6] and broadcasts such as NPR's weekday *Fresh Air* program, frequently probe many of the topics woven throughout this book. One great benefit of the Internet age is that we can easily locate and access archived programs. Similarly, anyone who wishes to know what is being published today in the *New York Times, Jerusalem Post,* or *Tehran Times* or one of the English language newspapers in Iraq is only two mouse clicks away from the websites of these publications. One of the most helpful online resources is called "The Pluralism Project." Under the leadership of Diana Eck at Harvard University, this 20-year-old and ongoing research project offers excellent materials on all religions and up-to-date information on the changing religious landscape in America.[7]

Books, of course—both fiction and nonfiction—are also invaluable educational tools. The Selected Bibliography at the end of this book identifies several of the many contemporary nonfiction books offering valuable insights on a range of related topics. Some popular fiction books are also of considerable educational value. For example, Khaled Hosseini's award-winning novels *The Kite Runner* and *A Thousand Splendid Suns*[8] paint vivid pictures of life—of children, friends, merchants, mullahs, business and political leaders, bullies, thugs, opportunists, and others—during the recent turbulent decades in Afghanistan. His gripping novels illuminate issues such as the divisions between Sunni and Shi'ite Muslims, cultural and religious practices, and the broader dynamics of tribalism and national identity both in Afghanistan and for Muslim immigrant communities in the United States. In the process, Hosseini helps put a human face on Islam.

Greg Mortenson and David Relin's compelling nonfiction book *Three Cups of Tea: One Man's Mission to Promote Peace . . . One School at a Time* tells the story of Mortenson's determination to repay people who saved his life by providing educational opportunities for underprivileged Pakistani children—especially girls—in remote villages. As with Hosseini's novels, this narrative does not sidestep real problems or gloss over deeply disturbing behavior on the part of some Muslims. It does, however, open the reader to a more balanced and accurate perspective by revealing the everyday world of good, hard-working people, which offers a context for the dramatic events that dominate media attention about Pakistan or Afghanistan. In 2009, Admiral Mike Mullen, chairman of the Joint Chiefs of Staff, reinforced this book's educational value when he made *Three Cups of Tea* required reading for all U.S. troops deployed to Afghanistan.[9]

*Three Cups of Tea* goes further in other important ways. As Mortenson and his well-intentioned friends in a number of villages labor to build schools and supply materials and teachers for children in remote areas, they encounter stiff resistance from narrow-minded Muslim leaders who oppose education for girls. Readers learn a great deal about the closed system and incendiary indoctrination that occurs in many strict Islamic schools (madrasas), which are funded by Saudi Arabia and which represent the kind of "education" that reinforces biases and thus dehumanizes the "other." Mortenson addresses squarely the urgent educational challenges facing people in Pakistan and Afghanistan and reveals specific ways in which many Muslims in those lands and supporters around the world are seeking constructive solutions.

Mortenson's story is a vivid example of education that informs constructive action. As his book has remained atop the best-seller list for more than three years, hundreds of thousands of Americans have been touched and empowered to support this worthy project. Between 2006 and 2010, Mortenson's Central Asia Institute financed and helped local villagers build more than 150 schools. Mortenson's efforts ran headlong into many formidable obstacles along the way. The positive outgrowth of his hard work and perseverance represent a concrete response to a question that is often used to justify inaction: "What can I as just one person really do?"[10]

In fact there are many things individuals, and civic and religious groups, can do to promote fair-minded education and constructive action on both the local and global levels. The well-known bumper sticker that encourages citizens to "think globally, act locally" needs to be expanded; we must also be more intentional in how we think locally and act globally. None of us can do most or all the things we might like to do, but almost everyone can do something constructive.

## Reaching Out in Good Will

How, then, can people of different faiths reach out to one another? How can people of faith and goodwill transcend the confines of our own perspectives, our own language, and our ideas of God, in order to encounter and work cooperatively with people of other faiths and worldviews? How can we build on educational opportunities and develop bonds of real relationships—even friendships—with others in our communities and around the world? One answer comes through intentional interreligious dialogue. Dialogue programs take many forms, from structured meetings to explore theological differences to simple engagement with others through dialogue in everyday life. Many churches, councils of churches, and other ecumenical organizations have been organizing dialogue programs for several decades. A prominent Muslim organization, the Institute for Interfaith Dialogue (IID), is active in many American cities as well. The group is an outgrowth of the visionary work of Fethullah Gulen, the Turkish-born Muslim thinker whose large following combines a commitment to education and combating social ills with nonviolence and interfaith engagement. Information on programs, educational materials, and helpful guidelines are readily available on the websites of the IID as well as many Jewish and Christian denominations.[11]

With minimal effort, people in most cities can locate religious congregations or civic groups that organize interreligious dialogue programs and intercultural events designed to celebrate diverse traditions. The Interfaith Alliance, a national organization with offices and programs in many cities, can assist making these connections. Jewish Americans and many Jewish congregations invite non-Jews to celebrate Passover Seders every year. Similarly, a growing number of American Muslims and Islamic centers include non-Muslims in *iftar* meals (breaking the fast after sundown each day during the month of Ramadan). These kinds of interfaith encounters are effective ways to learn more about other traditions and deepen appreciation for the rich diversity in our communities. Oklahoma City, for example, has several organizations that sponsor dialogue through programs around meals. "Open Table" brings together people from diverse religious traditions for a series of six monthly dinners. Another initiative, "Amazing Faiths," organizes dinner gatherings among Christians, Muslims, Hindus, Jews, and Buddhists all across the city. Such modest efforts are enormously important in fostering community and dismantling stereotypes and misconceptions.

My former pastor and friend, the late William Sloane Coffin Jr., spoke eloquently and succinctly in support of this kind of personal engagement with people different from ourselves:

> Human beings are fully human only when they find the universal in the particular, when they recognize that all people have more in common than they have in conflict, and that it is precisely when what they have in conflict seems overriding that what they have in common needs most to be affirmed. Human rights are more important than a politics of identity, and religious people should be notorious boundary crossers.[12]

In the last 50 years, and especially under Pope John Paul II, the Roman Catholic Church has encouraged its members to seek out opportunities to engage our neighbors daily across religious and cultural traditions. John Paul embodied and modeled this intentional spirit of interfaith dialogue and cooperation; he was the first pope in history to visit a synagogue or a mosque and met frequently with leaders of other religious communities.[13] In 1985, the pontiff articulated a forward-looking message and a challenge to Christians and Muslims when he spoke to an audience of 80,000 Muslim youths at a football stadium in Casablanca. His words from over a quarter century ago are even more timely and urgent today:

> We believe in the same God, the one God, the Living God who created the world. . . . In a world which desires unity and peace, but experiences a thousand tensions and conflicts, should not believers come together? Dialogue between Christians and Muslims is today more urgent than ever. It flows from fidelity to God. Too often in the past, we have opposed each other in polemics and wars. I believe that today God invites us to change old practices. We must respect each other and we must stimulate each other in good works on the path to righteousness.

Although the Roman Catholic Church has been at the forefront of interreligious dialogue, not all Catholics have the same theological perspective on religious diversity. The official teaching of the Catholic

Church is an inclusive theology,[14] but John Paul II and his successor, Benedict XVI, interpret the meaning of inclusivity somewhat differently. When Benedict delivered a speech in Regensburg, Germany, in September 2006, he cited a 14th-century Byzantine emperor's comments about Muhammad: "Show me just what Muhammad brought that was new, and there you will find things only evil and inhuman, such as his command to spread by the sword the faith he preached."[15]

The response from Muslim leaders (and many Christians as well) around the world was swift and vocal. A month after Regensburg, 38 prominent Muslim leaders sent the pope an open letter about the speech. On the one-year anniversary of the speech, 138 prominent Muslim leaders (muftis, academics, intellectuals, and government officials) issued an open letter, called "A Common Word Between Us and You," to the leaders of the major Christian church communities. The heart of the message is this:

> Muslims and Christians together make up well over half the world's population. Without peace and justice between these two religious communities, there can be no meaningful peace in the world. The future of the world depends on peace between Muslims and Christians. . . . The basis for this peace and understanding already exists. It is part of the very foundational principles of both faiths: love of the One God, and love of the neighbour. These principles are found over and over again in the sacred texts of Islam and Christianity. The Unity of God, the necessity of love for Him, and the necessity of love of the neighbour is thus the common ground between Islam and Christianity. . . . With the terrible weaponry of the modern world, with Muslims and Christians intertwined everywhere as never before, no side can unilaterally win a conflict between more than half the world's inhabitants. Thus our common future is at stake. The very survival of the world itself is perhaps at stake.[16]

A large number of very diverse Christian leaders and scholars all over the world responded quickly and positively to this Muslim initiative. In the United States, more than 300 Christian leaders (including many evangelicals) signed on to an open letter response ("Loving God and Neighbor Together") published in the *New York Times* and elsewhere. In subsequent months, the original 138 Muslim leaders who issued "A Common Word" grew to more than 300, while more than 460 Islamic organizations also publicly endorsed the statement.[17]

The questions I (and others I know who speak regularly about Islam, the Middle East, and Jewish-Christian-Muslim relations) am asked most frequently are: Where are the peaceful Muslims? Why don't we ever hear

Muslims denouncing violent extremists? If Islam is a religion of peace, why is there such silence about terrorism? These are fair questions, given the predictable media focus expressed in the dictum "If it bleeds, it leads!" In fact, many prominent Muslims all over the United States and the world have been vocal and consistent in their opposition to violent Islamic extremists. In July 2005, 200 Muslim scholars from 50 countries came together in Amman, Jordan, to address the abuses of Islam by Muslims who were declaring others to be apostates and issuing fatwas without the requisite qualifications or authority. The Amman Message—which was formulated on the basis of input from both the Sunni Shaykh al-Azhar in Egypt and the Shi'ite Grand Ayatollah Ali al-Sistani of Iraq—was subsequently endorsed by a range of international Islamic organizations and recognized religious leaders and jurisprudents.

In the decade following the attacks on September 11, in university events I have hosted or attended where a Muslim leader was also speaking or serving on a panel, audience members have asked some version of the where-are-the-peaceful-Muslims question. To a person, all of the Muslim speakers rejected those who believe that the violence and terrorism are justified or endorsed by Islam. Non-Muslims who have participated in dialogue programs and "open table" events or shared a Ramadan iftar dinner with Muslims discover firsthand that the vast majority of Muslims understand and practice Islam as a peaceful religion.

Dialogical encounter does not anticipate or require that participants agree, but it does require civility and respectful listening and speaking. People do not need to have political or theological agreement in order to cooperate on issues of common concern. In fact, cooperating on important projects in one's community is an extremely valuable form of interfaith engagement. In many U.S. cities, for instance, churches, mosques, and synagogues join together to build Habitat for Humanity homes. Many religious professionals working as military chaplains or in hospital or prison ministries already work cooperatively with colleagues from various religious traditions.

All of us can make an effort to learn more about how interfaith programs are being pursued successfully in our neighborhood or country, or in the service of peaceful coexistence in the Middle East. For example, learn about and share information with others, or support organizations such as the Interfaith Youth Core (IFYC), the Chicago-based international nonprofit organization that brings together young people from various religions for cooperative service and dialogue about shared values. Eboo Patel, the founder and executive director of IFYC, is a Muslim American Rhodes Scholar whose visionary leadership looks beyond mere toleration and affirms religious pluralism, an orientation that respects one another's religious identity and develops mutually enriching relationships.[18]

Many Jewish organizations have active interfaith programs in the United States; some also pursue interfaith approaches to peace in the Middle East. The American Jewish Committee and the Union of American Hebrew Congregations have long histories of cooperative interfaith programs. Americans for Peace Now and J Street are Jewish-based organizations working to facilitate a just, durable, and secure peace in the Israeli-Palestinian conflict. Rabbi Michael Lerner produces *Tikkun* (taken from the Hebrew *tikkun olam* meaning "repairing the world") and is co-chair of a network of spiritual progressives along with Princeton professor and author Cornel West and Catholic activist Sister Joan Chittister. Each of these organizations has websites and educational materials to guide those who share their vision. Not surprisingly, these groups—and many others that could be named—have differing understandings and approaches to the vexing challenges they engage. But they share a commitment to programs that foster peaceful and cooperative coexistence.[19]

These examples don't begin to exhaust the possibilities. They do illustrate, however, that there are many ways for people to learn more and lend support to people and groups whose vision for the future is symbolized by building bridges to connect, rather than barriers to further isolate the "other." This sampling also reminds us that you don't have to have a Ph.D. to know enough to contribute constructively. Few of us have an advanced degree in economics, but this does not keep us from learning enough about economics to make reasonably good decisions (or at least avoid harmful decisions) about our resources. At a minimum, we need to adopt a similar level of commitment to interfaith understanding and cooperation.

The more we engage the "other" personally, the more we find how much we have in common. When Jews, Christians, or Muslims engage one another intentionally in dialogue or while working on a Habitat for Humanity home, they inevitably discover fellow human beings with families, people who want good educational opportunities and a better future for their children, people who grieve the loss of a loved one and are concerned about affordable and high-quality health care, and so forth. Putting a human face on the "other" dismantles the stereotypical and monolithic images and defuses fear. When I meet and become friends with a Muslim of Indonesian descent, I learn more about what most of the 200 million Muslims are doing right now in Indonesia. They are not building bombs or planning attacks on infidels. They are working to put food on the table, getting children ready to go to school, figuring out how to fix a flat tire, and making plans for grandmother's birthday party tomorrow night. They are human beings living their lives very much as we are living ours.

We live in a dangerous world in which many people—including many religious people—think and talk in terms of "us" and "them." In our religiously diverse and interdependent neighborhoods, nations, and world community, education and intentional dialogue facilitate the much-needed final step in the engagement where "we all" are talking *with* each other about "all of us."[20] Understanding our communities, nations, and world less in terms of *we* and *they* and more in terms of *us* converges with the urgently needed paradigm for the communities and planet we all share: we must endeavor consistently to think and act both locally and globally.

## 21st-Century Paradigms for Religion and Politics

In this book I, have often said that religion and politics are always connected, that there is no fixed template for their interaction, and that the dynamic relationship has always been a work in progress set in its time and place. The question today, then, is this: What are the models or paradigms that are connected to the religious traditions and that can work in today's world?

In my view, the United States offers the most helpful and constructive model for negotiating the explosive mix of politics and religion today. The founders of the nation laboriously hammered out a structure for their vision of a new type of participatory democracy. The particular framework and judicious approach to religion and politics they fashioned was and is exceptional. In addition, the fundamental ways in which America has affirmed freedom *of* religion and freedom *from* religion in a religiously diverse society presents a principled approach to the vexing challenges now confronting nations all over the world.

There is much to celebrate and to affirm about the ongoing American experiment. But, as we observed in Chapter 5, the lived reality has often fallen far short of the ideal. The heartening story of America includes continuing efforts by its citizens to keep the government accountable to the principles and standards in the Constitution and established law. Coffin embodied this ongoing struggle to hold the country to the principles and high standards that all Americans should embrace:

> There are three kinds of patriots, two bad, one good. The bad are the uncritical lovers and the loveless critics. Good patriots carry on a lover's quarrel with their country, a reflection of God's lover's quarrel with all the world.[21]

What does this mean for Americans today? It means that we have a responsibility to take citizenship seriously, educate ourselves, and participate actively in the democratic processes. The success of the system depends on an informed citizenry. Clearly, the principles and openness to religious diversity captured in the 18th century by America's founders have stood the test of time. Nevertheless, the specific application of those principles requires flexibility as circumstances evolve and change. History and contemporary debate make it abundantly clear that Americans are far from united on where and how to draw the lines when issues of religion and politics converge. Even where there are serious points of contention and disagreement—on prayer in public schools, faith-based programs receiving public funding, the limits of tax-exempt status for religious groups promoting partisan politics, and so on—the debate should be civil. In a world where some religious partisans are prepared to inflict violence or death on those who don't share their vision of what God wants, Americans can present a very different and positive model, one where honest disagreement on religiously based views can be expressed with civility.

Many overtly religious communities live out this commitment precisely as a manifestation of their faith. The Sojourners community, based in Washington, DC, illustrates the point. Founded in the late 1970s, Sojourners is an evangelical Christian group whose ministries include a monthly magazine that addresses domestic and international issues such as religious response to poverty and social injustice, public education, beginning- and end-of-life issues, and peacemaking. Jim Wallis, the founder and leader of the community, is a highly visible activist at the intersection of religion and politics. The author of the best seller *God's Politics: A New Vision for Faith and Politics in America*, he spearheaded a campaign encouraging people of faith to be engaged in the 2008 presidential elections, using a clever bumper sticker: "God is not a Republican . . . or a Democrat." Wallis and others in Sojourners model a commitment to faith in action that is focused on ministries of reconciliation, and on nonviolent conflict resolution that includes respectful engagement across religious lines.[22]

Standing up for the religious rights of minority communities is one of the most important ways to manifest American core principles. This is especially true for those of us who are part of the majority Christian community. Christians have been and should be at the forefront of those who insist on freedom *of* religion and freedom *from* religion for everyone in the land. Numerous groups (including the U.S. State Department) constantly monitor how other countries discriminate against or persecute religious minorities. Having spent a good deal of my professional life working in the Middle East, I know how much it means to the minority Christian communities there when leaders of the Muslim majority protect and defend freedom of worship for Christians. The United States can and should model for the world how freedom of religion can work. The history of anti-Semitism and anti-Islamic attitudes and actions reminds us that rights guaranteed by the U.S. Constitution and established law still need principled local support.

This is not to say everyone will agree on where and how some lines are to be drawn. One of the challenging issues is raised by religious groups whose worldviews strongly oppose the pluralist society that freedom of religion invites and protects. Some wish, therefore, to separate themselves from the larger society. Freedom of religion includes the freedom to segregate one's community from settings or influences deemed harmful. The United States once again has a history on which to draw as the Amish, some Mormons, some Orthodox Jews, some Muslim sects, and other small groups have exercised their right to live apart. The challenge becomes more acute when the separatist group in question is armed and pursues a mission to make over the government to fit its image, or aims hate speech at groups deemed unwelcome in their country. Vigilance regarding those who would use their freedom to overturn the system allowing freedom for everyone is necessary. Yet another danger is what the sociologist of religion Mark Juergensmeyer calls "anti fundamentalism." In his contribution to the five-volume study of fundamentalism, Juergensmeyer cites examples where the "fear of fundamentalism" may lead to human rights violations against fundamentalists.[23]

Although I believe the United States offers the best model for negotiating these kinds of converging points between religion and politics, there are still devils in the details. This will be true during the course of the next decade, as we see further developments in countries where citizenship is somehow linked to religion. In nations such as Israel and Iran, those who are not within the official state religion are relegated to second- or third-class citizenship. Until fairly recently, Israeli leaders managed to maintain the tension between being a self-defined Jewish state and a democracy in which civil rights are guaranteed to everyone. In recent years, however, the problems and points of disconnect for the Israeli Arab Christians and Muslims have become more visible alongside the even more troublesome dilemmas presented by the Palestinian Arabs living as stateless people under military occupation in the West Bank (or Judea and Samaria). The continuing process of settlement in occupied territories has created facts on the ground that make the status quo increasingly difficult to change. The majority of people on all sides agree that the status quo is untenable.

Iran faces its own set of challenges as an Islamic theocracy, with visible growing pains, nuclear ambitions, and serious challenges from within and outside its borders. This ancient land is steeped in more than a thousand years of Islamic history and in a century's worth of desire for participatory democracy. In this sense, Iran is an exceedingly important experiment in what will likely be a series of experiments with versions of Islamic states in the years to come. In *The Fall and Rise of the Islamic State,* Harvard law professor and Middle East expert Noah Feldman summarizes the dynamics that will define the next decade or more:

> This movement [in many Muslim-majority countries] toward the Islamic state is riding a wave of nostalgia, but it is also looking forward. The designers and advocates of the new Islamic state want to recapture the core of what made the traditional Islamic state great. They declare their allegiance to the *shari'a,* while simultaneously announcing an affinity for democracy. This means the new Islamic state will be different from the old one. There is no turning back the clock of history, no matter what anyone says. . . . Can the new Islamic state succeed? This question has enormous implications for the residents of Muslim countries and for the rest of the world that must engage with Islamic states and movements that promote Islam as a political solution.[24]

As American citizens—of any faith or religious tradition or none at all—who recognize the importance of thinking and acting both locally and globally, we are connected to what happens next in countries like Israel, Iraq, and Iran. We are connected first by virtue of whatever our government does in those places, regardless of whether or not we personally agree with or support particular actions. At the very least, then, responsible citizenship requires that we know what our government is doing and why, and that we try to educate policy makers and other citizens who see Israel and the Jews, Christians, and Muslims living there as objects of their theology. We must substantially raise the level of informed discourse among policy makers and other citizens who think of Islam in monolithic terms, or who believe everything can be defined by a clash-of-civilizations theory, or who think it doesn't matter if decision makers don't know the difference between Sunnis and Shi'ites in Iraq. At times, it means helping others to discover the human face of Muslims, Jews, Christians, and others who don't look like us or talk as we do. When we take a moment to think, we realize that there are many ways we can educate ourselves and participate meaningfully in our society and democracy. Holding elected officials, religious leaders, and political pundits accountable is one important way to take citizenship seriously and model for the world the best of what participatory democracy can look like in a very diverse society.

On another level, we are all connected as human beings who should care about the well-being—the civil rights, human rights, access to health care, economic and educational opportunities—of all who share our planet. We will not all agree on what our faith or conscience requires when we encounter violations of basic human rights or systemic poverty linked to economic exploitation, but people of faith and goodwill do not stop caring about those who live on the other side of a national border. In the 21st century, it should be obvious to everyone that we are inextricably bound together. What happens to the world economically, ecologically, and militarily is of central concern to us all.

## The Next 10 Years

Some years ago, after September 11, I was attending a meeting of religious leaders who had spent three days wrestling with the most challenging issues in Jewish-Christian-Muslim relations and the treacherous intersections where religion and politics converge. As we neared the end of the meeting, a rabbi rose, cleared his throat, looked around the room at all of us, and spoke: "Friends, the *next ten years* will be the most difficult." After a short pause to allow the words to sink in, he continued, "The next ten years will be *the most difficult* . . . they always have been!"

With insight, humor, and a subtle inflection, the wise rabbi articulated a profound truth. We are not the first generation to confront serious and deadly challenges. Even though we are not unique in human history, we are keenly aware of the exceedingly dangerous dynamics in our interconnected, interdependent world, where even a small number of people can wreak havoc on a wide scale. We all live with the reality of nuclear, chemical, biological, and other weapons of mass destruction, including commercial airplanes and computer viruses. We know well that some people are prepared to use whatever means they can to achieve the religious or political goals they believe firmly that God and their religion require.

There are indeed good reasons for our anxiety about the future, but it need not immobilize us or engender strong and sometimes counterproductive responses from those who feel their worldview or way of life is under siege. The real and threatening dangers can also motivate us to constructive action. The lessons of history show how people of different faiths have responded positively and productively to even the most dire circumstances. I have witnessed numerous examples in which individuals and minority communities in the Middle East faced deadly threats squarely and took thoughtful steps to avoid disaster. There are alternative ways forward for people of faith and goodwill who recognize we must ceaselessly seek productive opportunities to talk with one another about "us." That is the key to navigating the next difficult decade—and all those that follow.

# NOTES

## CHAPTER 1: CHRISTMAS WITH THE AYATOLLAH

1. Our group included three prominent religious leaders (the Rev. Dr. Jimmy Allen, the immediate past president of the Southern Baptist Convention; Bishop Dale White, United Methodist Bishop of New York and New Jersey; and the Rev. Charles Caesaretti, assistant to the presiding bishop of the Episcopal Church), Baptist (the Rev. John Walsh) and Methodist (the Rev. William Kirby) chaplains at Princeton University, and a Georgetown University professor of Middle East studies (Dr. Thomas Ricks) who had been a Peace Corps worker in Iran. I was the youngest member of the delegation, a 29-year-old Baptist minister in the final stages of a doctoral program in comparative religion. Apart from a select few in the media and one Iranian-born American scholar, we were the only Americans invited to meet personally with the Ayatollah Khomeini during the 444-day hostage ordeal.

2. The return of Ayatollah Khomeini from Paris to Tehran on February 1, 1979, marked the end of the shah's regime and the success of the Iranian revolution. Although this was the most far-reaching event that year, other major developments also proved to be of great regional and global consequence. On March 26, 1979, President Jimmy Carter presided over the signing of the peace treaty between Egypt and Israel. This event had profound consequences—positive and negative—for almost everyone in the Middle East. And in December 1979, the Soviet military moved decisively into Afghanistan, marking the beginning of what would become a decade-long quagmire for the USSR. For an in-depth analysis of the momentous events of 1979, see David W. Lesch, *1979: The Year That Shaped the Modern Middle East* (Boulder, CO: Westview Press, 2001).

3. In addition to numerous radio and newspaper interviews, a variety of local and national television media were eager to discuss developments in Iran with the small number of people who were able both to travel there and have access to government and religious leaders. The major networks—NBC, CBS, ABC, and PBS—were particularly interested in

covering the hostage crisis from any and all angles. The high point of the media frenzy on Iran occurred on January 20, 1981, the day the hostages were released and Ronald Reagan was inaugurated as president. John Walsh and I appeared live from Frankfurt on the first half hour of *Good Morning America* that memorable day, interviewed by Peter Jennings in Frankfurt and David Hartman in New York. Because we were the only Americans who had been in direct communication through personal meetings with Iran's president (Abolhasan Bani Sadr), foreign minister (Sadeq Ghopzadeh), speaker of the parliament (Hashami Rafsanjani), various ayatollahs, and the student militants, ABC News led off that morning with our interview. On a subsequent appearance on *Good Morning America*, ABC officials reported that the convergence of those historic events made January 20, 1981, "the most watched" edition in the history of the program.

4. See Malcolm Gladwell, *The Tipping Point: How Little Things Can Make a Big Difference* (New York: Little, Brown, 2000); Gladwell, *Blink: The Power of Thinking Without Thinking* (New York: Little, Brown, 2005); Gladwell, *Outliers: The Story of Success* (New York: Little, Brown, 2008); Steven D. Levitt and Stephen J. Dubner, *Freakonomics: A Rogue Economist Explores the Hidden Side of Everything* (New York: William Morris, 2005); and Robert A. Pape, *Dying to Win: The Strategic Logic of Suicide Terrorism* (New York: Random House, 2005).

5. *Wahhabism* is a term denoting an extremely conservative movement within Sunni Islam. The name derives from the 18th-century Arabian Muhammad ibn Abd al-Wahhab. He followed the Hanbali school of Islamic law, the most conservative of the four major Sunni legal schools. He taught strict adherence to what he understood to be the beliefs and practices of the earliest Muslims. This uncompromising, puritanical approach to Islam took root in Saudi Arabia. During the second half of the 20th century, this version of Islamic law spread widely by virtue of the massive resources available to the government of Saudi Arabia from its oil revenues.

6. Randall Balmer has chronicled the rise of the religious right and the various ways in which evangelical and fundamentalist Christians have plunged deeply into U.S. political life since the 1980s. See, for instance, *Mine Eyes Have Seen the Glory: A Journey into the Evangelical Subculture in America* (New York: Oxford University Press, 1989) and Balmer, *Thy Kingdom Come: An Evangelical's Lament* (New York: Basic Books, 2006).

7. Although President Obama wrote extensively about his Christian faith and was a member of a Christian congregation in Chicago for two decades, efforts to link him to his father's religion took root in some quarters. The

Pew poll revealed how 34% of conservative Republicans believed Obama
was a Muslim and 43% of the general population was not sure about his
religious affiliation. See http://pewresearch.org/pubs/1701/poll-obama
-muslim-christian-church-out-of-politics-political-leaders-religious.

8. See Michelle Goldberg, *Kingdom Coming: The Rise of Christian
Nationalism* (New York: Norton, 2006); Chris Hedges, *American Fascists:
The Christian Right and the War on America* (New York: Free Press,
2006); and Kevin Phillips, *American Theocracy: The Peril and Politics of
Radical Religion, Oil, and Borrowed Money in the 21st Century* (New
York: Viking, 2006).

9. Lawrence Wright, *The Looming Tower: Al-Qaeda and the Road to 9/11*
(New York: Knopf, 2006), p. 166.

10. Jonathan Sacks, *The Dignity of Difference: How to Avoid the Clash of
Civilizations* (London: Continuum, 2002), p. 11.

11. For those who wish to go deeper into this exploration, a number of references are found throughout the notes.

## CHAPTER 2: GOD GAVE US THIS LAND

1. *Al-khalil* means "the friend." It refers to Abraham as the friend of God.

2. "Graveside Party Celebrates Hebron Massacre" (BBC News, March 21,
2000).

3. A selective approach to the Hebrew Bible can offer support for the harsh
position of Goldstein and others who share his worldview. Stories about
the "conquest of Canaan" under the leadership of Joshua, the successor to
Moses, include examples of a take-no-prisoners, scorched-earth policy. See,
for instance, the stories of three Canaanite cities that were destroyed and
put to the torch: Jericho (Josh. 6:21–24), Ai (Josh. 8:18–19), and Hazor
(Josh. 11:10–11).

4. The most dramatic episode about Abraham centers on God's command
that he sacrifice his son. Genesis 22 records the compelling narrative in
which the aged Abraham's faith in God is tested in the extreme. As he
raises the knife to slay Isaac, the heir of God's promise to Abraham, an
angel intervenes to stop the sacrifice. The Qur'an also records the story
of Abraham's near sacrifice of his son (37:102–113), though the son is
not named. Some early Muslim commentators suggest it was Isaac. The
large majority of subsequent commentators believe, and the standard view
among virtually all Muslims today is, that Ishmael was the son who was
nearly sacrificed.

5. See Bruce Feiler, *Abraham: A Journey to the Heart of Three Faiths* (New York: Harper Perennial, 2005) and Joan Chittister, Murshid Saadi Shakur Chishti, and Arthur Waskow, *The Tent of Abraham: Stories of Hope and Peace for Jews, Christians, and Muslims* (Boston: Beacon Press, 2006).

6. See I Samuel 15. Saul is told to utterly destroy every living thing—men, women, children, infants, sheep, camels, oxen, and so on. Saul decides to spare the king and the best of the sheep and cattle.

7. The Ark of the Covenant was an ornate box or carrying case in which the stone tablets containing the Ten Commandments were kept. For the ancient Israelites it was the most sacred object, a symbol of God's law and presence. There are many stories in the Bible about the power associated with this sacred object. The Ark was lost or destroyed in 70 CE when the Romans sacked the Temple. Popular stories about the lost Ark and its power abound, including the 1981 film *Indiana Jones and the Raiders of the Lost Ark*.

8. *The Late Great Planet Earth* still enjoys a large audience more than 35 years after its publication. More than 16 million copies of the book have been printed.

9. Abraham J. Heschel, *The Prophets* (New York: Harper & Row, 1962) was an instant classic. Reissued in paperback in 2001, Rabbi Heschel's study remains a compelling, scholarly exploration that is accessible for a wide audience.

10. The comparative study of religion reveals many commonalities among various religions. Every religion, for instance, includes one or more types of "sacred" people. These people are perceived to have particular insight and wisdom to guide the community. Prophets, sages, saviors, priests, and shamans are primary examples. Sages—such as Siddartha Gautama (the Buddha) and Confucius—somehow apprehend a body of wisdom. They teach others the way to live as individuals and in community. Savior figures—such as Jesus, Krishna, and Amida Buddha—are uniquely connected to and even embody the divine. Like sages, savior figures reveal paths to the ultimate goal(s). They also assist or even accomplish salvation for followers who respond in faith, devotion, or disciplined action. Priests are those who are set apart or "ordained" to carry out the ritual functions for religious communities. They often help interpret the traditions to the faithful and are frequently perceived to be particularly close to the deity or deities. Shamans, also called witch doctors or medicine men (and women), are found in tribal societies all over the world. They perform a variety of functions, including connecting the physical world with the spiritual realm. The medium whom King Saul implored to "bring up" the spirit of Samuel was a shaman.

11. The sycamore tree produces a figlike fruit that is bitter unless it is cut open at an early stage and exposed to the air. Amos described his pre-prophetic, humble background as a shepherd and one who tended to the fruit of these trees.

12. There is some debate about the precise dates for the reign of Jereboam II. His reign overlaps not only with Amos but also with Hosea, Jonah, and Joel. The prophets condemn the materialism and selfishness of the elite in his kingdom.

13. The Islamic tradition identifies two types of intermediaries between God and humankind: prophets (*nabi*) and messengers (*rasul*). Prophets are those whose message is directed to a particular people or nation. Messengers have a wider audience; they deliver the message to a particular people, but the revelation has universal application. Jesus and Muhammad are both considered messengers by Muslims.

14. The book of Lamentations offers a window into this time for the Jews left in Jerusalem. The prophet Ezekiel and the Psalmist reflect the traumatic experience of those in exile:

    By the waters of Babylon—
    There we sat down and there we wept
    When we remembered Zion.
    On the willows there we hung up our harps.
    For there our captors asked us for songs,
    and our tormentors asked for mirth, saying,
    "Sing us one of the songs of Zion!"
    How could we sing the Lord's song in a foreign land?
    If I forget you, O Jerusalem, let my right hand wither!
    Let my tongue cling to the roof of my mouth if I do not
        remember you,
    if I do not set Jerusalem above my highest joy [Psalm 137:1–6].

15. Historical information about this period can be found in the apocryphal books of I and II Maccabees and in *The Wars of the Jews* by Josephus (who lived from ca. 37 to 100 CE).

16. Milton Viorst, *What Shall I Do with This People? Jews and the Fractious Politics of Judaism* (New York: Free Press, 2002), p. 52.

17. The history of Judaism between 70 CE and the creation of the modern state of Israel, a history that is not well known to most Christians and Muslims, goes beyond the scope of this study. See Viorst for an accessible overview of Jewish political history. An older but far more detailed study is found in a collection of articles by leading scholars at Hebrew University

in Jerusalem. See H. H. Ben Sasson, *A History of the Jewish People* (Cambridge, MA: Harvard University Press, 1976). For a comprehensive resource, see Norman A. Stillman, ed., *Encyclopedia of Jews in the Islamic World,* 4 vols. (Leiden: Brill Academic, 2010).

18. Arthur Hertzberg writes eloquently about the "saving remnant," a term introduced by the prophet Isaiah (Isa. 10:21). In 1998, he calculated that there would be 100 million Jews in the world—rather than the estimated 13 million—if all the Jews by birth had remained within their tradition. See Hertzberg, *Jews: The Essence and Character of a People* (New York: HarperCollins, 1998), pp. 50–51.

19. See James Carroll, *Constantine's Sword: The Church and the Jews* (Boston: Houghton Mifflin, 2001) for an extensive study detailing the history of Christian domination and persecution of Jews.

20. My great-grandfather, Harris Skelskie, was the Orthodox Jewish cantor who brought his family to the United States in the late 19th century. Although I am a direct male descendent in the Skelskie family, my grandfather legally changed his name (and the names of my father and his three brothers) to Kimball in 1942. My grandfather and one of his brothers were a successful song and dance/comedy team for many years on the vaudeville circuit; their stage name was "The Kimball Brothers." My father told me that the name change was something of a formality because he and his brothers had always used Kimball as their last name. My grandfather met and married my grandmother, who was in the chorus line, in vaudeville. She was Presbyterian; he remained Jewish. Their children—my father and his three brothers—were exposed to both religions and allowed to choose. It turned out that my grandmother has the most influence in things religious: the children all embraced Christianity.

21. See Arthur Hertzberg, ed., *The Zionist Idea: A Historical Analysis and Reader* (New York: Jewish Publication Society of America, 1959, reissued in paperback in 1997) for an excellent overview of the intellectual history of Zionism together with numerous primary sources.


CHAPTER 3: ISRAEL

1. For an extensive study of *Gush Emunim* as the leading manifestation of Jewish fundamentalism in Israel, see Ian S. Lustick, *For the Land and the Lord: Jewish Fundamentalism in Israel,* rev. ed. (New York: Council on Foreign Relations, 1994).

2. An intense meeting with Ezer Weizman on October 6, 1985, illustrates the point. Weizman, who was serving as minister-without-portfolio in the

Labor-Likud coalition Israeli cabinet at the time, was a lead story in headlines all over the world. Five days earlier, on October 1, Israeli fighter jets
had conducted a long-range mission designed to destroy the PLO headquarters in Tunisia. The attack, ostensibly in response to the PLO-orchestrated
murder of three Israeli civilians in Cyprus a week before, was a remarkable military success. Although seemingly all of Israel celebrated, Weizman
stood alone in the cabinet in opposition to this action. As a well-known
fighter pilot and former minister of defense, his opposition was a big story.
His view was that this action did not help the necessary process that could
lead to Israeli-Palestinian peace. It was counterproductive. I was leading a
group of prominent U.S. religious leaders through the Middle East at the
time. Since I knew Weizman and had met with him several times before,
he honored the scheduled two-hour meeting despite being a controversial
figure at the center of the news, both in Israel and internationally. At one
point I asked him why Israel would seek to kill Yasser Arafat at this time.
All the news reports indicated that Arafat's headquarters and home had
been leveled but also that he was not there, as expected, when the attack
occurred. It didn't make sense to me that Israel would eliminate Arafat.
Weizman smiled at my question, leaned over, putting his hand on my knee,
and said, "Charles, my friend, Yasser Arafat is alive today because we want
him alive. Don't believe the news reports. We knew where he was. We
always know where he is. If we wanted to put a missile through his bath-
room window while he was seated on the toilet, we could do so . . . and we
know when he's on the toilet!" He then proceeded to describe the sophisti-
cation and precision that was involved in the undetected attack on Tunisia.
There was a gleam in the corner of the old fighter pilot's eye as he spoke
with pride about the prowess of the Israeli air force. But he concluded by
saying the rest of the cabinet was dead wrong in approving this action. This
was not the way toward peace and stability for Israel, in his view.

3. The Foundation for Middle East Peace tracks and publishes detailed
   information on settlement activities in the West Bank, East Jerusalem,
   and the Golan Heights. In 1972 there were 10,608 settlers (1,182 in the
   West Bank, 700 in Gaza, 8,649 in East Jerusalem, and 77 in the Golan
   Heights). In 2007, approximately 1 of every 11 Israeli Jews was living in
   the Occupied Territories (276,462 in the West Bank, 0 in Gaza, 189,708
   in East Jerusalem, and 18,692 in the Golan Heights). See Foundation for
   Middle East Peace, 1761 N Street NW, Washington, DC, 20036 (http://
   www.fmep.org).

4. There are many helpful books dealing with the Israeli/Palestinian conflict.
   For a resource used in many colleges, see Charles D. Smith, *Palestine and*

*the Arab-Israeli Conflict: A History with Documents*, 7th ed. (New York: Bedford/St. Martin's, 2010). For a dated but still useful overview, see also Thomas J. Friedman, *From Beirut to Jerusalem*, rev. ed. (New York: Farrar Straus Giroux, 1991).

5. Viorst, p. 169.

6. A *Kibbutz* is a collective community in Israel that centered primarily on agriculture. The Kibbutz movement during the decades prior to statehood brought together Jews who shared values of socialism and Zionism. Working together in farming, these collective efforts were able both to make a living and to redeem what were previously swamp and desert lands in Israel.

7. This system has been modified in the past 20 years; citizens now vote directly for candidates to serve as prime minister and for parties to fill out the Knesset.

8. The problems and tensions within Israel and among Jews are significant. I've known several Reform and Conservative rabbis from the United States who were not at all amused that their standing was not recognized in Israel. On a more personal level, one of my cousins married a woman who was raised as a Christian. She converted to Judaism many years ago and has been a devout, practicing person of faith for decades. When one of her daughters wanted to marry an Israeli-born man (a *sabra*), the state did not recognize her as a Jew. Why? Although her mother had converted long before she was born, her parents were Reform Jews in the United States. From a legal standpoint in Israel, my cousin's Judaism was not considered valid.

9. During numerous visits to the Holocaust museums in Jerusalem and Washington, DC, I have been horrified by sight of the first edicts by Adolf Hitler. As you enter the museum, a replica of the prominently displayed edict defines clearly who was considered "tainted" by Jewish blood; any-one with at least one Jewish grandparent was Jewish and subject to all the edicts and imprisonment in a concentration camp. As a Christian with a Jewish grandparent, I could have been subjected to the strictures of these edicts.

10. The Druze are a monotheistic religious community located primarily in Lebanon, Israel, Syria, and Jordan. Historically, the group is most closely related to the Ismaili branch of Shi'ite Islam. Their teachings and practices have been highly secretive for more than a thousand years.

11. In 2006, Chacour became the Greek Catholic Archbishop of Northern Galilee. The compelling story of his family is relayed in his first book, Elias Chacour, *Blood Brothers* (Waco, TX: Word Books, 1985). See also

Chacour, *We Belong to the Land: The Story of a Palestinian Christian Who Lives for Peace and Reconciliation* (San Francisco: HarperSanFrancisco, 1990) and Laurence Louer, *To Be an Arab in Israel* (New York: Columbia University Press, 2007) for more about the daily challenges of Israeli Arabs.

12. Haim Cohen is a superb example. I spent the evening of my 34th birthday in his Jerusalem home. He had retired three years earlier after serving for 21 years as a justice on Israel's Supreme Court. His illustrious career also included service as Israel's UN representative for human rights and as a member of the World Court at the Hague. I had come to know him as the first president of the Association of Civil Rights in Israel. On this particular evening, Cohen discussed a number of problems that he believed Israel must and would rectify. He spoke at length about many successes and some disappointments in judicial rulings. Cohen cited and discussed the significance of the extensive Kahan Commission report as a powerful illustration of Israel's deep commitment to justice. The report was prepared at the direction of the Israeli cabinet in order to investigate all the facts and factors connected with the atrocity carried out in 1982 by Lebanese forces against the civilian population in the Sabra and Shatila refugee camps in Beirut. The Kahan Commission report found Prime Minister Begin, Defense Minister Sharon, and other top Israeli leaders to be indirectly responsible for the massacre of hundreds of Palestinians (possibly as many as 3,000) in these refugee camps. The extensive report recommended that the defense minister resign, the director of military intelligence not continue in his post, and other senior officials be removed from their positions. The full report is available at http://www.jewishvirtuallibrary.org.

13. The archived reports are available at http://www.state.gov.

14. Israeli Prime Minister Benjamin Netanyahu underscored Israel's position in his highly publicized statement at the beginning of direct negotiations with the Palestinians, Jordanians, and Egyptians in Washington, DC, on September 2, 2010: "There are more than one million non-Jews living in Israel, the nation-state of the Jewish people, who have full civil rights. There is no contradiction between a nation-state that guarantees the national rights of the majority and guaranteeing the civil rights, a full civil equality of the minority." See http://www.nytimes.com/2010/09/03/world/middleeast/03diplo.html?ref=israel.

15. June 5, 1967, marked the start of the Six-Day War. Israeli military forces won decisive victories over enemy forces in the neighboring states of Egypt, Jordan, and Syria. Israel seized lands that had been under the control or guardianship of Egypt (the Sinai Peninsula and the Gaza Strip) and Jordan

(from the West Bank of the Jordan River up to the border of Israel, including the old city and Arab East Jerusalem). The UN-sponsored agreement to end the armed conflict produced Resolution 242. The centerpiece of this resolution calls for a return of the occupied territories in exchange for a permanent peace between Israel and its Arab neighbors.

16. Lustick, p. 40.

17. Lustick, pp. 9–10.

18. The Foundation for Middle East Peace keeps up-to-date data on the settlements. See note 3 above.

19. Gershom Gorenberg, *The End of Days: Fundamentalism and the Struggle for the Temple Mount* (New York: Oxford University Press, 2002).

20. For a moving account of daily life growing up in the West Bank, see Raja Shehadeh, *Samed: Journal of a West Bank Palestinian* (New York: Adama Books, 1984). Shehadeh is a lawyer whose work on human rights and nonviolent conflict resolution is well known in Israel/Palestine. Twenty years after the military occupation began, David Grossman's book *The Yellow Wind* presented a gripping account of his journey into Palestinian refugee camps, Jewish settlements, courtrooms, and classrooms. It was the best-selling book in Israel in 1987–88. Almost 20 years later, in June 2005 Haim Yavin, Israel's leading news anchor for 30 years, known affectionately as "Mr. Television," produced an unvarnished five-part series in which he concluded that Israel had behaved as brutal conquerors and occupiers in suppressing the Palestinian Arabs since 1967. Grossman, Yavin, and many others have decried how the occupation humiliated and harmed both the occupier and the occupied. See Grossman, *The Yellow Wind*, trans. by Haim Watzman (New York: Farrar Straus Giroux, 1988).

21. On May 20, 1990, Ami Popper put on an army uniform and asked men waiting at a bus stop for their identity cards. When he determined they were Arabs, he lined them up, opened fire, and killed seven Palestinians in a southern Israeli town. He was found to be sane before he was tried and given a long prison sentence. He later married an adopted daughter of Meir Kahane, and his compatriots continue to appeal for his release every year on the grounds that he is a "political prisoner."

22. The defeat of three-term senator Charles Percy sent a strong message in 1984. At his home in Georgetown two years later, he spoke at length about how he was targeted, along with several Middle Eastern church leaders and me. As a visible and vocal advocate for peace in the Middle East, he first evoked the wrath of the pro-Israel lobby in the mid-1970s when he suggested that Israel was being intransigent and should deal with Arafat.

He was consistent in what he considered an even-handed approach to the Middle East and discovered this was political suicide. See Paul Findley, *They Dare to Speak Out: People and Institutions Confront Israel's Lobby* (Westport, CT: Lawrence Hill) for a detailed account of how the American-Israeli Public Affairs Committee (AIPAC) effectively targeted numerous political leaders, editors, journalists, and educators.

23. Jimmy Carter, *Palestine: Peace Not Apartheid* (New York: Simon & Schuster, 2006).

24. John J. Mearsheimer and Stephen M. Walt, *The Israel Lobby and U.S. Foreign Policy* (New York: Farrar Straus Giroux, 2007).

25. Although President Bill Clinton was the host for the White House ceremony with Rabin and Arafat in 1993, the hard work leading to the Oslo Accords was done primarily by the previous administration of President George H. W. Bush under the guidance of Secretary of State James Baker. Baker personally made more than a dozen trips to the Middle East to facilitate key steps along the way toward Oslo.

26. Stephen Sizer, *Christian Zionism: Road Map to Armageddon?* (Leicester, England: Inter-Varsity Press, 2004), p. 255.

27. Churches for Middle East Peace (CMEP) has been a constructive education and advocacy group supporting a negotiated settlement between Israel and the Palestinians for more than a quarter century. As one of the founders of the group, I continue to serve on the advisory board along with other Middle East specialists and former U.S. diplomats with extensive service in that region. For information about the organization, see http://www.cmep.org.

28. See, for instance, Ted A. Smith and Amy-Jill Levine, "Habits of Anti-Judaism: Critiquing the PCUSA Report on Israel/Palestine," *Christian Century* (June 29, 2010); and the website for the Jewish Council for Public Affairs (http://engage.jewishpublicaffairs.org). The Middle East Study Committee and various resolutions from the 2010 Presbyterian General Assembly can be found at http://www.pcusa.org.

29. The seven dispensations or time periods begin with creation and end with Jesus' thousand-year reign of peace on earth. The period from creation until the sin of Adam and Eve in Genesis 3 is the first dispensation. The flood during Noah's time marks the end of the second dispensation. Other definitive blocks of time are fixed around the changing religious circumstances with the appearance of Abraham, Moses, and Jesus. The sixth dispensation is the time of "grace," from the resurrection of Jesus until the Battle of Armageddon.

30. Tim LaHaye and Jerry Jenkins have co-authored 16 books in the "Left Behind" series. Their total sales top 60 million.

31. President Obama's position was laid out succinctly in his first two addresses to the UN General Assembly on September 24, 2009, and September 23, 2010. These excerpts from the 2009 speech express his position:

    I will also continue to seek a just and lasting peace between Israel, Palestine, and the Arab world. . . . We have made some progress . . . We continue to call on Palestinians to end incitement against Israel, and we continue to emphasize that America does not accept the legitimacy of continued Israeli settlements. . . . The time has come to re-launch negotiations without pre-conditions that address the permanent status issues: security for Israelis and Palestinians, borders, refugees, and Jerusalem. And the goal is clear: Two states living side by side in peace and security—a Jewish state of Israel, with true security for all Israelis; and a viable, independent Palestinian state with contiguous territory that ends the occupation that began in 1967, and real-izes the potential of the Palestinian people. [The full texts of the UN General Assembly speeches can be found at http://www.whitehouse.gov.]

32. The Geneva Accord peace proposal was unveiled in mid-October and pro-mulgated officially on December 1, 2003, in Switzerland. Fifty-eight former presidents, prime ministers, and foreign ministers—including Carter, British Prime Minister Tony Blair, and Morocco's King Hassan II—strongly sup-ported the plan. Detailed coverage related to this initiative and a text of the Geneva Accord is available at the website of the leading newspaper in Israel (http://www.haaretz.com). In fact, Israeli governments of various composi-tions have been in quiet dialogue and negotiations with leaders of neighbor-ing states for a long while. As King Hussein of Jordan neared the end of his life in 1999, it was revealed that he had been meeting secretly with Israeli leaders for 30 years. In addition, Israel has a long history of quiet dealings with Iran. See Trita Parsi, *Treacherous Alliance: The Secret Dealings of Israel, Iran, and the U.S.* (New Haven: Yale University Press, 2007).

33. In 2005, the Rand Corporation addressed this growing concern head-on. Rand published a comprehensive document based on analysis of their three-year study focused on the requirements for a successful Palestinian state. The study, entitled *The Arc: A Formal Structure for a Palestinian State*, examined a variety of approaches to developing the kind of infrastructure all states require in the context of a large and growing Palestinian population. Their research team designed plans for a modern, high-speed transportation infrastructure—called the Arc—connecting current Palestinian urban centers with new commercial and residential development. Those who follow events in the Middle East closely may be

familiar with this detailed work by Rand. For most Americans, however, media coverage of the latest explosion or hostile threat obscures the fact that a range of individuals and organizations have been actively working on specific components that could facilitate a viable peace process.

34. See Meron Benvenisti, *Son of the Cypresses: Memories, Reflections, and Regrets from a Political Life* (Berkeley: University of California Press, 2007); Benvenisti, *Intimate Enemies: Jews and Arabs in a Shared Land* (Berkeley: University of California Press, 1995); and Benvenisti, *Sacred Landscape: The Buried History of the Holy Land Since 1948* (Berkeley: University of California Press, 2000).

35. Nuseibeh's views are included in a study produced in 2004 by an International Quaker Working Party on Israel and Palestine: *When the Rain Returns: Toward Justice and Reconciliation in Palestine and Israel.* This exceptionally helpful book gives voice to a variety of people, explores the major dimensions of the conflict (occupation, settlements, peace talks, views of Jerusalem, Palestinian refugees, Palestinian-Jewish relations inside Israel), and offers a nuanced assessment of how to move toward a just resolution of the crisis. See Kathy Bergen et al., *When the Rain Returns: Toward Justice and Reconciliation in Palestine and Israel* (Philadelphia: American Friends Service Committee, 2004). This resource not only gives a nuanced overview of the multiple issues converging in this conflict and helpful guidance on steps toward nonviolent reconciliation but also includes numerous key documents, an extensive bibliography, and contact information on a variety of Jewish, Christian, Muslim, and nonreligious organizations committed to reconciliation. The Quakers have a long history of constructive, nonviolent work in Israel/Palestine. The American Friends Service Committee produced three other superb studies related to the Israeli-Palestinian conflict: *Search for Peace in the Middle East* (1970); *A Compassionate Peace: A Future for Israel, Palestine and the Middle East* (1982); and *Principles for a Just and Lasting Peace Between Palestinians and Israelis* (1999).

36. See Arthur Hertzberg, ed., *The Zionist Idea: A Historical Atlas and Reader* (New York: Harper & Row, 1959). The Jewish Publication Society in America published a revised edition in 1997.

37. Despite, or perhaps because of, his willingness to address controversial issues directly, Hertzberg was elected to many leadership positions, among them president of the American Jewish Congress (1972–1978) and vice-president of the World Jewish Congress (1975–1991). I had the good fortune of working with, learning from, and sometimes vigorously debating Rabbi Hertzberg over the course of a 25-year friendship.

38. Arthur Hertzberg, *The Fate of Zionism: A Secular Future for Israel & Palestine* (San Francisco: HarperSanFrancisco, 2003), pp. 121, 155, 170, and 172.

CHAPTER 4: "RENDER UNTO CAESAR"

1. "Interview with Jimmy Carter," *Playboy* (November, 1976). The full quotation reads: "Because I'm just human and I'm tempted and Christ set some almost impossible standards for us. The Bible says, 'Thou shalt not commit adultery.' Christ said, 'I tell you that anyone who looks on a woman with lust has in his heart already committed adultery.' I've looked on a lot of women with lust. I've committed adultery in my heart many times. . . . This is something that God recognizes, that I will do and have done, and God forgives me for it."

2. Warren Harding and Harry Truman were Baptists; Abraham Lincoln was raised as a Baptist, though he did not affiliate with any denomination later in life.

3. See Randall Balmer, *God in the White House: How Faith Shaped the Presidency from John F. Kennedy to George W. Bush* (San Francisco: HarperOne, 2008) for an accessible yet comprehensive overview of the prominent role of religion in presidential politics during the past 50 years.

4. The ambiguities are readily evident when people cite distinctly different issues, from prayer in public schools or posting the Ten Commandments in public buildings to highly emotional issues such as abortion.

5. See Luke 23:1–4.

6. See John Howard Yoder, *The Politics of Jesus* (Grand Rapids, MI: Eerdmans, 1972).

7. See Acts 4:32–6:7.

8. The extent to which the gospel of Jesus was to be understood apart from the religion of the Jews is most visibly manifest in Acts 15. Paul, Peter, Barnabas, and other leaders gather in Jerusalem to debate whether non-Jewish men who become believers must be circumcised and follow the law of Moses.

9. See I Thessalonians 5:1–11.

10. See Hebrews 6:4–6 and 10:32–36.

11. Hans Conzelman, *History of Primitive Christianity,* trans. by John E. Steely (Nashville, TN: Abingdon Press, 1973), pp. 128–129, summarizes how Paul's career as a missionary was threatened in multiple ways: "He was conscious of being threatened constantly. He was imprisoned

repeatedly. Five times he was scourged in the synagogues; he does not say when or where, but the number of times shows that the intra-Jewish punishments accompanied him on his mission. In addition there was scourging three times by authorities as official punishment. Once he was stoned; this suggests a riot. In Ephesus he hovered in immediate danger of death (II Cor. 1:8). Paul's sufferings were climaxed finally in his arrest, transport to Rome, and death. Why he was condemned is not told in the tradition. In any case, the reason lies in his activity as a missionary."

12. In addition to letters and manuscripts associated with early Christian leaders and studies of well-known noncanonical gospels, previously unknown materials have been discovered during the past 60 to 70 years. The most extensive such collection was unearthed in 1945 at Nag Hamadi, Egypt, when 52 mostly Gnostic documents were discovered buried in an earthen jar.

13. Helena is particularly famous in Christian history for her pilgrimage to the Holy Land in 326, when she was approximately 70 years old. She had churches built on the Mount of Olives and at the presumed site of Jesus' birth in Bethlehem.

14. The Council of Chalcedon confirmed the two natures of Christ—fully God and fully human simultaneously—in distinction from those bishops who were thought to diminish the humanity of Jesus in favor of his divinity.

15. The Maronites are a quite distinctive church with roots in the Orthodox tradition. They have been in full communion with Rome since 1182 CE. Because of Lebanon's mountainous terrain, it has always been a difficult place to conquer and hold militarily. Consequently, many minority communities—Christians, Muslims, Jews, and Druze—sought refuge in Lebanon through the centuries. By the time of Lebanon's independence in 1943, it was by far the most religiously diverse country in the Middle East. Although no census was taken, the departing French colonial rulers determined that Christians made up the majority, and the Maronites were the largest Christian community. They then devised a unique system of proportional representation based on religion. The system guaranteed that the president of Lebanon and the largest delegation in the parliament would be Maronite Christians. The prime minister would be a Sunni Muslim, and the speaker of the parliament would be a Shi'ite Muslim. The system worked reasonably well until the mid-1970s, when several factors converged (a substantial demographic change resulting in Shi'ite Muslims being the largest community, while political and economic power remained disproportionately with the Maronites; the intense conflict between Israel and the Palestinians began to be played out primarily in Lebanon after the

PLO set up headquarters there in 1970; and so on) and sparked a 15-year, multisided civil war.

16. Richard P. McBrien, *Lives of the Popes: The Pontiffs from St. Peter to John Paul II* (San Francisco: HarperSanFrancisco, 1997), pp. 73–77, 96–97. Pope Gregory the Great was one of the most influential popes in history. McBrien reports that Gregory I's *Pastoral Care* became a textbook for medieval bishops. St. Thomas Aquinas quotes Gregory's homilies on Ezekiel, the gospels, and exposition on the book of Job some 347 times in the second part of *Summa Theologiae*. A former monk, Gregory the Great was particularly noted for his love of monasticism, the liturgy, and liturgical music. McBrien points out how "his name is so closely identified with plainsong that it came to be known as Gregorian chant."

17. Henry Mayr-Harting, "The West: The Age of Conversion (700–1050)," in *The Oxford History of Christianity*, ed. by John McManners (Oxford, UK: Oxford University Press, 1993), pp. 111–112.

18. McBrien, p. 127.

19. Ibid., p. 181–182.

20. Raymond of Agiles, quoted in Roland H. Bainton, *Christian Attitudes Toward War and Peace*, 2nd ed. (New York: Seabury Press, 1982), pp. 112–113. For an overview of the Crusades and Holy War as one of the three primary Christian responses to war—"pacifism" and "just war" being the other two—see Charles Kimball, *When Religion Becomes Evil* (San Francisco: HarperOne, rev. ed., 2008), pp. 166–177.

21. Much more detail about the thousands of cases recorded in the Vatican archives will become known in coming years. Soon after the files were partially opened by Pope John Paul II, a documentary filmmaker began research for a four-part program scheduled for broadcast on the Canadian Broadcasting Network in 2007. I reviewed the programs in the fall of 2006. Many of the details about the Inquisition confirm the worst images already documented by church historians.

22. See Philip Benedict, *Christ's Churches Purely Reformed: A Social History of Calvinism* (New Haven, CT: Yale University Press, 2002), pp. 77–120, for a detailed study of the various reform movements. A comprehensive exposition of Calvin's work in Geneva is found in William Naphy, *Calvin and the Consolidation of the Genevan Reformation* (Louisville, KY: Westminster John Knox Press, 2003).

23. Calvin speaks of the event in the preface to his *Commentary on the Psalms*, acknowledging how God "subdued and made teachable a heart . . . [that] was far too hardened in such matters." See François Wendel, *Calvin*

(London: Collins, 1963) for an analysis of Calvin's early years and his embrace of reform movements.

24. The original version contained some 85,000 words. The final edition has more than 450,000 words, organized around "four broad themes: the knowledge of God, the process of salvation, the character and consequences of the faith, and the institutions and sacraments of the church." See Benedict, p. 84.

25. Owen Chadwick, *The Reformation,* rev. ed. (New York: Penguin Books, 1977), p. 86.

26. See Robert C. McCune, *Adultery and Divorce in Calvin's Geneva* (Cambridge, MA: Harvard University Press, 1995) for a fascinating and sometimes chilling study of numerous cases adjudicated by the Geneva Consistory.

27. Benedict, p. 89.

28. Wendel, p. 97.

29. David Sorkin, *The Religious Enlightenment: Protestants, Jews, and Catholics from London to Vienna* (Princeton, NJ: Princeton University Press, 2008), pp. 12–13.

30. Deism is a type of natural religion. Deists believe in the existence of God on the basis of a rational approach to the universe rather than an authoritative scripture that adherents (such as Jews, Christians, or Muslims) believe was revealed or inspired by God.

31. Nathan is a wealthy merchant in Jerusalem. A monk leaves a baby girl in his care, but only Nathan and his Christian servant know the infant's identity. The girl grows up and is rescued by a Crusader knight, who then falls in love with her. The knight is disgusted by Jews but is comforted to learn from the servant that the girl was brought to Jerusalem by a monk. In the process of seeking advice, the self-righteous knight speaks with the patriarch of Jerusalem and later the legendary Muslim leader Saladin. It turns out the girl is an offspring of Saladin. So she has experiences as a Jew, Christian, and Muslim. In a pivotal scene, Saladin calls in Nathan and asks him which of the three religions is superior. Nathan responds, cleverly, with a parable of the "three rings." For each of three people, his "ring" is shown to be genuine and true.

## CHAPTER 5: AMERICA

1. D. James Kennedy, *What If America Were a Christian Nation Again?* (Nashville, TN: Thomas Nelson, 2003), pp. 4–5.

2. John McCain interview with Beliefnet (http://www.beliefnet.com) on September 28, 2007. When asked the question, McCain said, "I would probably have to say yes, that the Constitution established the United States of America as a Christian nation."

3. My daughter, a high school math teacher, has pointed out that neither God nor prayer can be "kicked out" of the schools: "As long as you have math tests, you will have students praying in public schools!"

4. Jon Meacham, *American Gospel: God, the Founding Fathers, and the Making of a Nation* (New York: Random House, 2006), p. 232.

5. One particular exhibit set up near Faneuil Hall was designed to determine how you would have aligned yourself as a resident of Boston in 1776. The exhibit had you go from station to station, where you would read about a particular issue and respond to questions. The process took 30 minutes, and in the end your responses were tabulated to determine where you would have landed on a scale from revolutionary soldier on one end to Tory on the other. My father and two of his brothers visited this exhibit with me and took the test. We all came out in different places. One uncle, who was ostensibly the most patriotic, flag-waving American among us, was deeply distressed when the test revealed he would have been a Tory, 100% in support of the status quo provided by the king of England and the Anglican Church.

6. One is reminded here of late-20th-century "three strikes and you're out" laws passed in some states, where even relatively minor offenses result in mandatory, harsh sentences.

7. See Ed Southern, ed., *The Jamestown Adventure: Accounts of the Virginia Colony, 1605–1614* (Winston-Salem, NC: John F. Blair, 2004), pp. 178–194.

8. In addition to Meacham's *American Gospel,* see Forrest Church, *So Help Me God: The Founding Fathers and the First Great Battle over Church and State* (Orlando, FL: Harcourt, 2007) and Jacob Needleman, *The American Soul: Rediscovering the Wisdom of the Founders* (New York: Penguin Books, 2002).

9. For an extensive compendium organized around 70 topics, see James H. Hutson, ed., *The Founders on Religion: A Book of Quotations* (Princeton, NJ: Princeton University Press, 2005).

10. Hutson, p. 29.

11. Jefferson removed, for instance, all references to angels, miracles, and the resurrection, along with what he deemed the "dross . . . the stupidity of some, and roguery of others of His disciples." See Christopher Hitchens,

*Thomas Jefferson: Author of America* (New York: HarperCollins, 2005), pp. 177–184, for a thoughtful presentation on Jefferson's lifelong effort to distill the essence of Jesus' teachings.

12. Meacham, p. 89.

13. Although the Jewish population gathered in six congregations (in Newport, New York, Philadelphia, Richmond, Charleston, and Savannah) numbered fewer than 200 during Washington's presidency, five of his 19 letters on the rights and obligations of religious groups were addressed to Jewish congregations. See Church, pp. 64–65.

14. See Hutson, pp. 116–129.

15. Donald W. Shriver Jr., *Honest Patriots: Loving a Country Enough to Remember Its Misdeeds* (New York: Oxford University Press, 2005).

16. There are passages that regulate some behavior. For example, the 21st chapter of Exodus outlines some rights of slaves and responsibilities of slave owners, including the right to beat a slave: "When a slave owner strikes a male or female slave with a rod and the slave dies immediately, the owner shall be punished. But if the slave survives a day or two, there is no punishment; for the slave is the owner's property" (Exod. 21:20–21).

17. This appeal to biblical images is deeply rooted in the arguments against the crime of slavery. Frederick Douglass was born into slavery in 1818. He escaped to the north at age 20 and became a powerful and widely respected voice for eradicating slavery. In a famous speech in Rochester, New York, on July 5, 1852, Douglass used the language and vision of the Declaration of Independence to illustrate the injustice of slavery. He also appealed to the compelling language of Psalm 137, reflecting Israel's experience during the Babylonian Captivity: "By the Rivers of Babylon, there we sat down and there we wept when we remembered Zion. On the willows there we hung up our harps. For our captors asked us for songs and our tormentors asked for mirth, saying, 'Sing us one of the songs of Zion!' How could we sing the Lord's song in a foreign land?" Frederick Douglass, "What to the Slave Is the Fourth of July?" in John W. Blassingame and John R. McKivigan, eds., *The Frederick Douglass Papers,* series 1, vol. 2 (New Haven, CT: Yale University Press, 1982), p. 368.

18. One measure of the changing interpretation is seen in leadership roles for women. The Episcopal Church began regularly ordaining women priests only in 1976, the first female bishop was consecrated in 1989, and the Most Rev. Katherine Jefferts Schori became the first female to serve as presiding bishop of the Episcopal Church in 2006. Although the Roman Catholic Church, various Orthodox Churches, and some Protestants

continue to interpret the Bible to prohibit women from being ordained as clergy, most Protestants—Methodists, Lutherans, Presbyterians, Episcopalians, and so on—have changed dramatically. By 2010, women made up more than half the students preparing for ministerial vocations in many Protestant seminaries and divinity schools.

19. One of the most famous episodes occurred in Tennessee during the 1925 Scopes trial. The trial centered on the teaching of evolution in public schools. Despite losing in court, biblical literalists have continued to insist on teaching the creation story in public schools for nearly a century. Courts have ruled repeatedly in favor of scientific approaches to teaching about the origin of the earth, the solar system, and the cosmos as we know it. Every year or two, however, a school board in Texas, Kansas, Pennsylvania, or some other state grabs national attention when it endorses teaching the biblical creation story or "creation science" in its schools, sometimes alongside scientific theories about the origin and evolution of life forms. These debates are always heated.

20. Alabama's Chief Justice, Roy Moore, grabbed national attention when he refused to remove a monument displaying the Ten Commandments from the State Supreme Court Building. In a unanimous 9–0 decision, the Alabama Judicial Ethics Panel voted to remove him from office on November 13, 2003. The case spurred many others to action, including some political opportunists. One of the more humorous episodes occurred on Comedy Central's *The Colbert Report*. On September 5, 2008, Georgia Congressman Lynn Westmoreland was being interviewed about his co-sponsorship for federal legislation requiring the posting of the Ten Commandments in Congress and courthouses. When the host, Stephen Colbert, commended him on this effort and then asked him to recite the Ten Commandments, Congressman Westmoreland was flummoxed. He could name only three of the ten.

21. See Diana L. Eck, *A New Religious America: How a "Christian Country" Has Become the World's Most Religiously Diverse Nation* (San Francisco: HarperSanFrancisco, 2001). This book brings together more than a decade of research conducted by Eck and dozens of Harvard graduate students in the Pluralism Project. The research, for which Eck received the National Humanities Medal in 1998, continues to document the changing religious landscape in America. See http://www.pluralism.org.

22. See Michelle Phillips, *Kingdom Coming: The Rise of Christian Nationalism* (New York: Norton, 2006); Chris Hedges, *American Fascists: The Christian Right and the War on America* (New York: Free Press, 2006); and Kevin Phillips, *American Theocracy: The Peril and Politics of Radical*

*Religion, Oil, and Borrowed Money in the 21st Century* (New York: Viking Press, 2006). Phillips's 480-page volume is particularly noteworthy as he details the explosive interplay among dependence on oil, the power of the religious right, and unmanageable debt. His 2006 book anticipated the global economic meltdown that occurred in 2008.

23. My first personal encounter with Falwell came in the spring of 1984, when we were two of six "experts" giving congressional testimony before the House Foreign Affairs Committee (the subcommittee on the Middle East was chaired by Indiana Congressman Lee Hamilton). The burning issue was whether or not Congress should require the United States to move its embassy from Tel Aviv to Jerusalem. The timing of the resolution was closely linked with the U.S. presidential primary season. The testimony lasted almost three hours. The Rev. Bryan Hehir (representing the U.S. Conference of Catholic Bishops) and I (representing the National Council of Churches) supported the Reagan Administration's position of not moving the embassy while the United States sought to broker a peace process between Israel and the Palestinians. Falwell (representing the Moral Majority), Thomas Dine (representing the America-Israel Public Affairs Committee), and others advocated in favor of moving the U.S. embassy to Jerusalem posthaste. Falwell's political interests were global in scope. He had recently returned from South Africa and publicly called Bishop Desmond Tutu a "nut," while urging Americans to buy gold Krugerrands in support of the South African regime.

24. See Rousas John Rushdoony, *The Institutes of Biblical Law* (Dallas: Craig Press, 1973).

25. Gary North, *The Theology of Christian Resistance* (Tyler, TX: Geneva Divinity School Press, 1983), p. 63.

26. Pat Robertson, *The Turning Tide* (Dallas, TX: Word Books, 1993), pp. 62–63.

27. Nancy Ammerman, "North American Protestant Fundamentalism," in *Fundamentalisms Observed,* ed. by Martin E. Marty and R. Scott Appleby (Chicago: University of Chicago Press), pp. 51, 53.

28. Pat Robertson on *The 700 Club* (November 14, 2006).

29. See "Pat Robertson Haiti Comments Spark Uproar" at http://www .cbsnews.com (January 14, 2010).

30. See Charlie Savage, "Scandal Puts Spotlight on Christian Law School: Grads Influential in Justice Department," *The Boston Globe* (April 8, 2007). The article focuses on infiltration of the Department of Justice by large numbers of graduates from a school ranked in the fourth (and lowest)

tier. In Monica Goodling's 1999 graduating class, more than 60% failed the bar exam on their first attempt.

31. The website for Patrick Henry College is clear about the theological orientation of the school and its intentional efforts to change the world through the Christian vocation of its students. Michael Farris, founder and president of the college, sees his work with mostly home-schooled students as preparation for "Generation Joshua," a reference to the leader who followed Moses and led the children of Israel in the conquest of the Promised Land. See http://www.phc.edu.

32. Jeff Sharlet, *The Family: The Secret Fundamentalism at the Heart of American Power* (New York: HarperCollins, 2008), p. 7.

33. When I returned to Washington a couple of weeks before the Presidential Prayer Breakfast, I was invited by leaders of the Fellowship to go to each member of the cabinet and hand-deliver the invitation to the secretaries of state, defense, commerce, the Treasury, and so forth. Such access in the corridors of power was very heady for a 21-year-old college senior.

34. Sharlet, p. 45.

35. See also the lengthy article by Peter J. Boyer, "Frat House for Jesus: The Entity Behind C Street," *New Yorker* (September 13, 2010).

## CHAPTER 6: THERE IS NO GOD BUT GOD

1. The proposed community center is not a mosque; nor is the location at "Ground Zero." Rather it is to function much like a YMCA or a Jewish community center. In addition to physical activities and meeting rooms, the organizers anticipate that interfaith dialogue and cooperation will be major components in a multifaceted program.

2. When Muslims refer to Allah, they are talking about the God of the Bible. The Qur'an is full of stories and references to Noah, Abraham, Moses, David, Jesus, John the Baptist, and other prominent biblical figures. Since *Allah* is the Arabic word for God, when the 15 to 17 million Arabic-speaking Christians living in the Middle East today worship God, they pray to Allah.

3. There are a few supernatural events linked to Muhammad's life. Here is a popular story, for instance, from boyhood. Muhammad was approached by two angelic figures when he was very young. They removed his heart, took out a dark spot, and washed the heart in a bowl of pristine white snow before putting it back into his body. As another example, the famous story of the *mi'raj* or "night journey," is perhaps the most widely known and affirmed supernatural event associated with Muhammad. According to

the tradition, he was taken miraculously from Mecca to Jerusalem, where he prayed with the great prophets at the site of the al-Aqsa mosque. From there he traveled a few hundred yards to the site of the Dome of the Rock, where he was taken up to heaven for a vision of paradise and an encounter with God. The five daily prayers are linked to this heavenly sojourn; during Muhammad's encounter with God, he promises that the faithful will pray five times per day.

4. As a Christian who has studied Arabic and the Qur'an, I believe this argument has merit. The lyrical beauty of the recited Qur'an is readily evident even to people who do not know any Arabic. For three decades, I have watched the reactions and discussed this point with more than a thousand American students and Christian religious leaders in classes and on study trips to the Middle East. People across the theological spectrum, as well as self-described nonbelievers in any organized religion, consistently attest to the artistic beauty and compelling power of skilled recitation of the Qur'an.

5. Ahmed Ali, trans., *The Qur'an: A Contemporary Translation* (Princeton, NJ: Princeton University Press, 1993), p. 522.

6. At a personal level, pious Muslims seek to know as much as possible about all aspects of Muhammad's life in order to emulate his example. He enjoyed breaking the fast of Ramadan with dates and milk or water. Whenever possible, most Muslims today will break their daily fast during Ramadan with the same food and drink.

7. Precisely because the sayings of Muhammad were authoritative, the body of material associated with him began to grow in the decades following his death. In the absence of a definitive word from the Qur'an, the words of Muhammad became paramount. For various reasons—ranging from preferences over religious practice to substantial theological disputes—devout Muslims "remembered" stories about Muhammad somewhat differently. This quickly began to pose problems as contradictory sayings might be invoked or slight nuances might make a substantial difference in a legal decision. During the first two centuries of Islam, a sophisticated system was developed whereby scholars could authenticate and evaluate the degree of certainty that could be assigned to the voluminous collections of hadith. During my doctoral studies, I took a semester course on hadith. In addition to reading the authoritative collections from the second and third centuries of Islam, we studied the various techniques employed by Muslims in the "science of hadith." The process of grading the validity, strength, or weakness of a saying required careful examination of the background and theological views of the earliest transmitters (who are listed with each hadith) and the variations in content of each passage.

8. There were many resources examining, and much global reaction to, *The Satanic Verses* in the months and years after the Ayatollah Khomeini issued a *fatwa* (legal opinion) on February 19, 1989, calling for Rushdie's death. For an in-depth study of the "Danish Cartoon crisis," see Jytte Klausen, *The Cartoons That Shook the World* (New Haven, CT: Yale University Press, 2009).

9. *Medina* is the Arabic word for "city." Yathrib was renamed "the city of the prophet" (*madinat an-nabi*). Medina is simply the abbreviated version of the name.

10. See Abdullahi Ahmed an-Na'im, *Islam and the Secular State: Negotiating the Future of Shari'a* (Cambridge, MA: Harvard University Press, 2008), pp. 48–55, for a detailed analysis of how traditional Muslim scholars used the example of the prophet to argue for distinctive approaches to religious and political functions within predominantly Muslim lands.

11. One of the most widely cited versions of the Constitution of Medina is found in Ibn Ishaq, *The Life of Muhammad (Sirat Rasul Allah)*, trans. by A. Guillaume (Lahore, Pakistan: Oxford University Press, 1974), pp. 231–233.

12. One of the well-known passages reads as follows:

Surely We sent down the Torah, wherein is guidance and light; thereby the Prophets who had surrendered themselves gave judgment for those of Jewry. . . . And We sent, following their footsteps, Jesus, son of Mary, confirming the Torah before him, as a guidance and an admonition to the god-fearing. And We have sent down to you the Book with the truth, confirming the book before it, and assuring it. So judge between them according to what God has sent down, and do not follow their caprices, to forsake the truth that has come to you. To every one of you We have appointed a right way and an open road. If God had so willed, He could have made all of you one community; but He has not done so that He may test you in what He has given you. So, compete with one another in good works. To God you shall all return and He will tell you (the truth) about that which you have been disputing [Qur'an 5:4–48].

13. In 2:62 and 5:69, the Qur'an emphasizes the promise of paradise for "people of the book": "Behold! Those who have faith, and those who are Jews, Christians, and Sabaeans—those who trust in God and the Last Day, and do what is righteous, they shall have their reward; no fear shall come upon them, neither shall they grieve." The religious diversity resulting from the various communities formed around God's prophets and messengers is part of God's plan: "If God had so willed, He would have made all of you one

community, but (He has not done so) that He may test you in what He has given you; so compete with one another in good works. To God you shall all return and He will tell you (the truth) about that which you have been disputing" (Qur'an 5:48).

14. In I Samuel 15, for example, Samuel delivers God's harsh directive to King Saul: "Now go and attack Amaelk, and utterly destroy all that they have; do not spare them, but kill both man and woman, child and infant, ox and sheep, camel and donkey" (I Sam. 15:3). Saul's failure to carry out this extreme action—he spared the king and the best of the sheep and oxen—was later cited as the reason God tore the kingdom out of Saul's hand and made David the new king of Israel.

15. Two versions recounting the treatment of Jews in Medina are found in Norman A. Stillman, *The Jews of Arab Lands: A History and Source Book* (Philadelphia: Jewish Publication Society of America, 1979), pp. 3–21; and W. M. Watt, *Muhammad at Medina* (Oxford, UK: Oxford University Press, 1956), pp. 193–220.

16. For a thorough and accessible overview of the early decades of Islam, see Asma Afsaruddin, *The First Muslims: History and Memory* (Oxford, UK: Oneworld Publications, 2008).

17. Afsaruddin, pp. 32–33.

18. Detailed accounts of the events surrounding the caliphate of Uthman and the other "successors of the messenger of God" can be found in many sources. In addition to Afsaruddin, pp. 19–58, see Patricia Crone, *God's Rule: Government and Islam—Six Centuries of Medieval Islamic Political Thought* (New York: Columbia University Press, 2004), pp. 3–32; and W. Montgomery Watt, *Islamic Political Thought* (Edinburgh, UK: Edinburgh University Press, 1968), pp. 31–45.

19. Depending on the source, Hasan accepted a handsome stipend and retired to Medina or he was poisoned at the direction of Mu'awiya.

20. See Hugh Kennedy, *The Great Arab Conquests: How the Spread of Islam Changed the World We Live In* (Philadelphia: Da Capo Press, 2007), pp. 344–362.

21. See Daniel J. Sahas, *John of Damascus on Islam* (Leiden, Netherlands: Brill, 1972).

22. See Howard R. Turner, *Science in Medieval Islam: An Illustrated Introduction* (Austin: University of Texas Press, 1995) for a helpful overview of the remarkable advances in mathematics, astronomy, medicine, optics, and natural sciences during the flowering of Islamic civilization.

23. Marshall G. S. Hodgson, *The Venture of Islam: Conscience and History in a World Civilization*, Vol. I (Chicago: University of Chicago Press, 1974), p. 294.

24. For a brief but very accessible and helpful overview, see David Vishanoff, "Islamic Law: A Long Work in Progress," *Army Chaplaincy* (Winter–Spring, 2009), pp. 65–68.

25. There are many helpful books that survey Islamic history. For those wanting to explore beyond short introductory texts, see Albert Hourani, *A History of the Arab Peoples* (Cambridge, MA: Harvard University Press, 1991). This book is also available in an audio format through http://www.audible.com. For the most ambitious student, Hodgson's three-volume work, *The Venture of Islam*, remains the most comprehensive study of Islamic history in English.

26. Maria Rosa Menocal, *The Ornament of the World: How Muslims, Jews, and Christians Created a Culture of Tolerance in Medieval Spain* (Boston: Little, Brown, 2002), p. 11.

27. Norman Stillman has done extensive work on Jews living under Arab and Muslim rule. See his book *The Jews of Arab Lands* and the *Encyclopedia of Jews in the Islamic World*.

28. There are many detailed studies exploring different aspects of the centuries of Ottoman rule. A helpful overview of major structures and developments is found in Hourani's *History of the Arab Peoples*, pp. 207–262.

## CHAPTER 7: MUSLIM VS. MUSLIM

1. See Samuel Huntington, "The Clash of Civilizations?" *Foreign Affairs* (Summer 1993); and Huntington, *The Clash of Civilizations and the Making of World Order* (New York: Simon and Schuster, 1996).

2. Bernard Lewis, "The Roots of Muslim Rage," *Atlantic Monthly* (September 1990), p. 59.

3. Bernard Lewis, *What Went Wrong? The Clash Between Islam and Modernity in the Middle East* (New York: Harper Perennial Books, 2003). The hardbound version of the book was first published in December 2001.

4. This hadith is cited in John O. Voll, "Renewal and Reform in Islamic History: *Tajdid* and *Islah*," in *Voices of Resurgent Islam*, John L. Esposito, ed. (New York: Oxford University Press, 1983), p. 33.

5. The Wahhabi movement in Saudi Arabia subscribes to the Sunni legal school of thought founded by Ahmad ibn Hanbal (780–855 CE).

6. For an excellent, detailed, and accessible introduction to modern Islamic reform movements, see John L. Esposito, *Islam: The Straight Path*, 4th ed. (New York: Oxford University Press, 2010), pp. 141–186.

7. Gallup's sample population included young and old, wealthy and poor, urban and rural dwellers, men and women, well educated and illiterate, and so forth. The results of the extensive study had a statistical error rate of plus or minus 3%.

8. John L. Esposito and Dalia Mogahed, *Who Speaks for Islam? What a Billion Muslims Really Think* (New York: Gallup Press, 2007), pp. xii, 80–84, and 140–142.

9. *Who Speaks for Islam?* pp. 93–94.

10. *Who Speaks for Islam?* pp. 66–98. The chapter on "What Makes a Radical?" includes some startling data on attitudes of American Christians, noting that a higher percentage justifies violence targeted at civilians than is the case among Muslims worldwide.

11. See John L. Esposito, *The Future of Islam* (New York: Oxford University Press, 2010), pp. 102–105.

12. Honor killings refer to the practice of men (a father, brother, or uncle, for instance) killing a female relative who has somehow besmirched the family's honor. Female circumcision is an African-based practice of female genital mutilation. It is practiced in one form or another among about 20% of the Muslim community worldwide. For more details on these practices, see Charles Kimball, *When Religion Becomes Evil* (San Francisco: HarperOne, rev. ed. 2008), pp. 149–153.

13. Greg Mortenson and David Oliver Relin, *Three Cups of Tea: One Man's Mission to Promote Peace ... One School at a Time* (New York: Penguin Books, 2006).

14. See Azizah Al-Hibri, "Legal Reform: Reviving Human Rights in the Muslim World," *Harvard International Review* (May 6, 2006). The website for Karamah (http://www.karamah.org) includes many useful articles, interviews, and other resources dealing with a range of women's human rights issues in Islam. Several Muslim women have written best-selling books on gender inequity and the need for reform within Islam. See, for instance, Ayaan Hirsi Ali, *Infidel* (New York: Free Press, 2006); and Irshad Manji, *The Trouble with Islam* (New York: St. Martin's Press, 2003).

15. See http://www.foreignpolicy.com/articles/2009/11/30/the_fp_top _100_global_thinkers?page=full.

16. Tariq Ramadan, "The Way of Islam," in *The New Voices of Islam*, ed. by Mehran Khamrava (London: Tauris, 2006), pp. 72–73.

17. http://www.tariqramadan.com/To-be-a-European-Muslim.html.

18. Tariq Ramadan, *Western Muslims and the Future of Islam* (New York: Oxford University Press, 2004).

19. Some of the families of September 11 victims and some New York City residents were also vocal opponents of the Park51 Islamic community center project. Although it had been in the works for several years and passed through the various steps necessary for such building projects, the Park51 controversy erupted when several national political figures with possible future presidential aspirations portrayed the community center as a symbolic victory for the terrorists who attacked on September 11.

20. See Imam Feisal Abdul Rauf, *What's Right with Islam: A New Vision for Muslims and the West* (San Francisco: HarperSanFrancisco, 2004).

21. See Khaled Abou El Fadl, *The Grand Theft: Wrestling Islam from the Extremists* (San Francisco: HarperSanFrancisco, 2005).

22. See Abdullahi Ahmed an-Na'im, *Islam and the Secular State: Negotiating the Future of Shari'a* (Cambridge, MA: Harvard University Press, 2008).

23. See George Packer, "The Moderate Martyr: A Radically Peaceful Vision of Islam," *New Yorker* (September 11, 2006).

CHAPTER 8: IRAN AND IRAQ

1. "Attacks Erupt During Iraqi Election," United Press International (UPI. com), March 7, 2010.

2. Vali Nasr, *The Shia Revival: How Conflicts Within Islam Will Shape the Future* (New York: Norton, 2006) offers an excellent primer on the history of Shi'ite Islam, sectarian politics among Iraqi Shi'ites, and often unpredictable political developments within Iran.

3. Jeff Stein, "Can You Tell a Sunni from a Shi'ite?" *New York Times* (October 17, 2006). See http://www.nytimes.com/2006/10/17/opinion/17stein.html.

4. Various sources furnishing recent demographic data are available on the Internet. Detailed information on every country is also published every year in an 800-page *CIA World Factbook*.

5. Ali Gheissari and Vali Nasr, *Democracy in Iran: History and the Quest for Liberty* (Oxford, UK: Oxford University Press, 2006), p. 23.

6. See Stephen Kinzer, *All the Shah's Men: An American Coup and the Roots of Middle East Terror* (Hoboken, NJ: Wiley, 2003). For a larger exploration that places the 1953 CIA-led coup in Iran in the context of

10 U.S.-engineered efforts precipitating regime change during the past century, see Kinzer, *Overthrow: American's Century of Regime Change from Hawaii to Iraq* (New York: Times Books, 2006).

7. Ray Takeyh, *Hidden Iran: Power and Paradox in the Islamic Republic* (New York: Times Books, 2006), pp. 23–25.

8. This framework is distinctively Shi'ite. It is consistent with the hierarchical structure for clergy in this branch of Islam. Shi'ite clergy are expected to provide leadership and guidance in all manner of human affairs. One's rank (and title) is determined, in part, by the number of people who look to a person as their spiritual leader and guide. The highest rank is ayatollah, which literally means "a sign or miracle from God." Although there are recognized religious leaders among Sunni Muslims, technically there are no clergy in the dominant form of Islam.

9. See Imam Khomeini, *Islamic Government: Governance of the Jurist,* trans. by Hamid Algar (Seattle: CreateSpace, 2004).

10. Everyone in Iran knows stories of the efforts to break Montazeri. In addition to physical torture, he did not relent even in the face of one of the most horrific episodes imaginable. At one point during his imprisonment, he was forced to witness the gang rape of his daughter. This and innumerable other stories of torture and murder by SAVAK operatives fueled widespread distain for the shah's dictatorial rule. I have personally met with more than 100 torture victims of secret police, the SAVAK. Beatings and electrical shocks to genitals were among the lesser horrors. One woman told her heartbreaking story as I held her five-year-old son on my lap. Her husband had been caught with a cassette tape of a Khomeini speech from Paris. In an effort to get the man to divulge the names of people with whom he shared such cassette tapes, the man and his three young sons were arrested and tortured. The two older boys were slowly tortured to death in front of their father. The youngest son's arms and legs were systematically dismembered. The father, most likely knowing they would all be killed in any case and not wanting to give up names of friends for whom a similar fate would be forthcoming, did not give in. He was killed, and the dismembered youngest son was returned to the mother.

11. "Top Dissident Cleric Attacks President," *USA Today*, January 22, 2007. See http://www.usatoday.com/news/world/2007-01-22-iran_x.htm.

12. The Iran-Contra Affair refers to a secret foreign policy operation directed by White House officials in the National Security Council under the direction of President Reagan. The secret initiative came to light in 1986, triggering a legal and political outcry. The operation had two differing goals.

First, by selling arms to Iran the United States hoped for Iranian assistance in gaining the release of American hostages being held in Lebanon. The second component of the secret operation involved diverting the off-the-books profits from the arms sales to the Contra rebels trying to overthrow the government of Nicaragua.

13. See Trita Parsi, *Treacherous Alliance: The Secret Dealings of Israel, Iran, and the United States* (New Haven, CT: Yale University Press, 2007) for a superb and fascinating analysis of the relationships and history beyond the headlines. See also Ray Takeyh's chapter on "Israel and the Politics of Terrorism" in his *Hidden Iran*.

14. The *Fresh Air* program can be accessed via the NPR archive at http://www.npr.org/templates/rundowns/rundown.php?prgId= 13&prgDate=05-May-2003.

15. The Sykes-Picot Agreement concluded on May 16, 1916, determined the national boundaries for Iraq. This secret agreement was worked out between by the British, French, and Russians in anticipating the end of the Ottoman Empire.

16. A detailed, yet reasonably succinct history of this region is found in William R. Polk, *Understanding Iraq: The Whole Sweep of Iraqi History— from Genghis Khan's Mongols to the Ottoman Turks to the British Mandate to the American Occupation* (New York: HarperCollins, 2005).

17. See Charles Kimball, *Religion, Politics, and Oil: The Volatile Mix in the Middle East* (Nashville, TN: Abingdon Press, 1992) for a detailed analysis of the converging roles of religion and politics during and immediately after the Gulf War of 1991.

18. For a helpful overview of Ayatollah Ali al-Sistani's role, decisions, influence, and relationships with Iranian leaders, see the excellent background article "Iraq: Grand Ayatollah Ali al-Sistani," published by the Council of Foreign Relations (http://www.cfr.org/publication/7636/iraq.html).

19. Edward Wong, "Iraqi Constitution May Curb Women's Rights" (*New York Times*, July 20, 2005). See http://www.nytimes.com/2005/07/20/inter national/middleeast/20women.html.

## CHAPTER 9: A ROAD TO DISASTER

1. Al-Qaeda is an international umbrella organization including numerous Sunni groups committed to expelling foreign powers from Muslim lands and constructing a new Islamic empire. The Arabic term literally means "the base." Founded in 1989 by Osama bin Laden in opposition to Soviet

domination in Afghanistan, al-Qaeda today is made up of largely autonomous groups—some in communication with bin Laden's group, some simply claiming inspiration from him—in Europe, Africa, Asia, and North America.

2. See the *Washington Post* (September 28, 2001) for a full transcript of Muhammad Atta's document published in English translation.

3. The trial received extensive press coverage at the time as the legendary political leader and lawyer William Jennings Bryan prosecuted the case against a science teacher for the "crime" of teaching evolution. Clarence Darrow was the lawyer for the defense. Bryan died just five days after winning the case, but the verdict was overturned later by a higher court. The event was later immortalized in the play and motion picture *Inherit the Wind*.

4. Rejection of modern scientific discoveries was not uniform, however. They acknowledged, for instance, that the earth is round and orbits the sun. In addition, some problematic biblical texts—such as passages condoning slavery or polygamy—have to be "interpreted." Even so, the premise remains firm: the Bible is understood as being without error in any sense.

5. See Martin E. Marty and R. Scott Appleby, eds., *The Fundamentalism Project*, 5 vols. (Chicago: University of Chicago Press, 1991–1995). The titles of the five volumes reveal the foci and scope of this mammoth project: *Fundamentalisms Observed; Fundamentalisms and Society; Fundamentalisms and the State; Accounting for Fundamentalisms;* and *Fundamentalisms Comprehended*.

6. Samuel C. Heilman and Menachem Friedman, "Religious Fundamentalism and Religious Jews: The Case of the Haredim," in *Fundamentalisms Observed*, p. 197.

7. See note 8 in Chapter 3 for a personal illustration of how approaches to the question "Who is a Jew?" can play out in unexpected ways.

8. Gideon Aran, "Jewish Zionist Fundamentalism: The Bloc of the Faithful (Gush Emunim)," in *Fundamentalisms Observed*, pp. 265–266.

9. The Foundation for Middle East Peace, a Washington, DC-based organization, produces a bimonthly newsletter ("Report on Israeli Settlement in the Occupied Territories") that details the debates, decisions, and building activities by Israel in the Occupied Territories.

10. The Christian Identity movement refers to an assortment of individuals and churches professing a Eurocentric interpretation of Christianity. See Chester L. Quarles, *Christian Identity: The Aryan American Bloodline Religion* (Jefferson, NC: Macfarland, 2004).

11. The Sovereign Citizen movement in the United States dates to the 1970s. With the advent of the Internet, the ability to connect with like-minded people, share tactics and strategies, and recruit others has grown significantly. Some leaders of the movement have surfaced periodically when a violent confrontation makes the news. For example, on May 20, 2010, Jerry Kane and his teenage son, Joseph, were recorded by a police car camera as Joseph opened fire and killed two policemen following a routine traffic stop in West Memphis, Arizona. *NBC Nightly News*, reporting on the gruesome episode on July 5, 2010, noted one prominent conspiracy theory advanced by Kane, namely that the U.S. government auctions off shares in the taxes on future earnings when a baby is born. Kane and others believe the Chinese government is buying up the future earnings of U.S. babies in collusion with the U.S. government.

12. On March 10, 1993, Michael Griffin shot and killed Dr. David Gunn outside an abortion clinic in Pensacola, Florida. Less than a week later, the Rev. Paul Hill defended Griffin's action on the *Donahue* television program. A little over a year later, on July 29, 1994, Hill shot and killed Dr. John Britton and a traveling companion in the parking lot of the same clinic. Other such attacks have occurred in various parts of the United States. The website http://www.armyofgod.com remains a focal point for those who share the view that such actions are justifiable homicide.

13. Richard T. Hughes, *Christian America and the Kingdom of God* (Urbana: University of Illinois Press, 2009), p. 5. Ann Coulter's shrill, acerbic voice has drawn a great deal of negative criticism for more than a decade. She clearly has many supporters as well. Since 2002, she has published five books that achieved best-seller status on the *New York Times* weekly list.

14. One disturbing manifestation surfaced following a series of complaints by cadets and several chaplains at the Air Force Academy in Colorado. More than 50 formal complaints about religious intimidation and discrimination prompted academy officials to impose mandatory religious sensitivity courses for the 9,000 cadets in 2005. The response was appropriate given the likelihood of abuse within the highly structured and authoritative nature of the military system. On the other hand, there is always a danger of overcompensation rooted in a fear of fostering discrimination. Numerous critics cited the possible role of "political correctness" and a desire not to be seen as anti-Islamic in the aftermath of the tragedy at Fort Hood in Texas on November 5, 2009. Major Nidal Hasan, a U.S. Army psychiatrist and practicing Muslim, killed 12 people and wounded 31 others during an assault within the military base. News reports and a subsequent congressional inquiry revealed various indications of deep distress

and emotional instability. How could so many people miss the warning signs? It is certainly fair to ask whether the fear of being labeled anti-Muslim prevented some military officials from reporting concerns about erratic or potentially threatening behavior exhibited by Dr. Hasan in the months prior to his murderous rampage.

15. "General Faulted for Satan Speeches" (http://www.cbsnews.com/stories/2003/10/16/terror/main578471.shtml).

16. See John Hagee, *Jerusalem Countdown: A Warning to the World* (Lake Mary, FL: Frontline, 2006); Hagee, *Can America Survive? 10 Prophetic Signs That We Are the Terminal Generation* (Brentwood, TN: Howard Books, 2010); and the website for John Hagee Ministries (http://www.jhm.org).

17. Hagee, *Can America Survive?* p. 11.

18. *Fresh Air*, National Public Radio broadcast (September 18, 2006).

19. Hagee drew national attention and a good deal of criticism for his proclamations following the tragic events following Hurricane Katrina in 2006. Hagee declared this was God's judgment on the city of New Orleans for licentious behavior. When questioned about his views on the *Fresh Air* program noted above, he held firm. He didn't clarify, however, how a gay pride parade or other behavior in a section of New Orleans related to the widespread devastation and suffering of people all across the states bordering on the Gulf of Mexico.

20. In 2010, more than 70 million copies of the "Left Behind" books were in print in various languages around he world.

21. See Rod Parsley, *Silent No More: Bring Moral Clarity to America . . . While Freedom Still Rings* (Lake Mary, FL: Charisma House, 2005). Having watched and studied Parsley's ministry for more than a decade, I find the title particularly striking. To my knowledge, he has never felt compelled to be silent about any of his views.

22. Esposito and Mogahed, *Who Speaks for Islam?* pp. 34–63 and 94–95.

23. Khouri made these points in a university lecture at Wake Forest University (March 5, 2005) and in several national interviews during a lecture tour in the United States at that time.

24. Franklin Graham, son of the Rev. Billy Graham, has declared publicly, "Islam is a wicked and evil religion." Muslims around the world know both of these statements and that Franklin Graham was the minister who prayed at the January 20, 2001, presidential inauguration ceremony. Pope Benedict XVI was criticized heavily—by Muslims and by many Christians—for statements regarding Islam. He ignited an international

firestorm, for example, with his September 2006 speech in Regensburg, Germany.

25. For the transcript of the report, see http://www.npr.org/templates/ transcript/transcript.php?storyId=128544392.

26. See Carla Hinton, "Yard Sign Prompts Readers to Speak Freely on Issue," *Oklahoman,* July 31, 2010, p. 2D.

## CHAPTER 10: HOPE FOR THE PERILOUS JOURNEY AHEAD

1. See Stephen Prothero, *Religious Literacy: What Every American Needs to Know—and Doesn't* (San Francisco: HarperSanFrancisco, 2007), pp. 21–38.

2. See http://pewforum.org/Other-Beliefs-and-Practices/U-S-Religious-Knowledge-Survey.aspx.

3. http://education.newsweek.com/2010/09/12/religious-studies-thrive-in-troubled-times.html.

4. Several Muslim leaders have had the same experience as Imam Sayid Hassan al-Qazwini, head of the Islamic Center of America in suburban Detroit: "I have been to over eighty-five churches, colleges, schools, public places, speaking about Islam (in the first seven months after 9/11)." See Gustav Niebuhr, *Beyond Tolerance: Searching for Interfaith Understanding in America* (New York: Viking, 2008), p. 19.

5. *Speaking of Faith* changed its name to *Being* in 2010. The newer website (http://being.publicradio.org/) includes all the previous archived programs, including more than a dozen on Islam in America, the changing face of Islam, women in Islam, religion in the Israeli-Palestinian conflict, the poetry of Rumi, and so forth. See also Krista Tippett, *Speaking of Faith: Why Religion Matters—and How to Talk About It* (New York: Penguin Books, 2008).

6. See http://www.teach12.org. The Teaching Company has several courses on the major world religions. My 24-lecture course "Comparative Religion" was published by the Teaching Company in 2008.

7. See http://pluralism.org.

8. See Khaled Hosseini, *The Kite Runner* (New York: Riverhead Books, 2003); and Hosseini, *A Thousand Splendid Suns* (New York: Riverhead Books, 2007).

9. See Greg Mortenson and David Relin, *Three Cups of Tea: One Man's Mission to Promote Peace . . . One School at a Time*; and Mortenson, *Stones into Schools* (New York: Viking, 2009). Similar observations could

be made about another best seller, Azar Nafisi, *Reading Lolita in Tehran: A Memoir in Books* (New York: Random House, 2003).

10. This initiative is growing in strength and influence. Mortenson gave a major lecture at the University of Oklahoma in the spring of 2010. Several hundred elementary and middle school children were among the 5,000 people who attended the event. These children had collected more than $75,000 in their schools and local churches in a "Pennies for Peace" campaign to support Mortenson's efforts to offer educational opportunities for children in Pakistan.

11. There are several national Christian, Islamic, and interfaith organizations offering helpful resources for interfaith work. The National Council of Churches has a website with many ecumenical resources and links for connecting with interfaith websites maintained by the Episcopal Church, the United Methodist Church, the Evangelical Lutheran Church in America, the Presbyterian Church (USA), and others; see http://www.ncccusa.org/interfaith/. The website and information on programs for the Muslim-based Institute for Interfaith Dialogue can be found at http://interfaithdialog.org. See also the website for the Interfaith Alliance at http://interfaithalliance.org.

12. William Sloane Coffin Jr., *A Passion for the Possible: A Message to the Churches* (Louisville, KY: Westminster/John Knox Press, 1993), pp. 7–8.

13. Perhaps the most celebrated interfaith event occurred in 1986, when Pope John Paul II invited leaders from all the world's religions to come to Assisi for a day of prayer.

14. An inclusive theology of religions is similar to the more traditional "exclusive" approach in affirming that Jesus is the way God reconciles the world to God's self, But inclusive theology goes much further by acknowledging that God may be working through other religions and beyond the visible walls of the Church. In other words, the reconciling ministry and work accomplished by Jesus may be understood to include people who do not even know his name or how his death and resurrection has reconciled them to God. For an overview of exclusive, inclusive, and pluralist theological approaches to world religions, see Kimball, *When Religion Becomes Evil*, pp. 215–224.

15. Pope Benedict XVI went on to say that the Qur'an's declaration "There is no compulsion in religion" (2:256) came from the early Meccan period and was superseded by later revelations about holy war. Many Muslims and many non-Muslim scholars of Islam pointed out that there is very little evidence to support what has become a popular view of Islamic expansion by the sword. Muslims conquered territory rapidly, but conquered people

were not systematically required to convert. The pontiff's assertion about the dating and applicability of the "no compulsion in religion" verse is incorrect.

16. See http://www.acommonword.com.

17. See Esposito, *The Future of Islam*, pp. 187–190, for an overview of this Muslim initiative and the Christian responses.

18. See Eboo Patel, *Acts of Faith: The Story of an American Muslim, the Struggle for the Soul of a Generation* (Boston: Beacon Press, 2007) and the website for Interfaith Youth Core (http://www.ifyc.org).

19. There are several Jewish organizations with a long history of constructive interfaith work, including the American Jewish Committee (http://www. ajc.org/site/c.ijITI2PHKoG/b.823789/k.7F9/Interfaith.htm), the Union of American Hebrew Congregations (http://urj.org/socialaction/issues/ muslimdialogue/), Tikkun (http://www.tikkun.org/), and J Street (http:// jstreet.org/).

20. In 1959, Wilfred Cantwell Smith summarized the trends in scholarly study about, and personal engagement between, people in different religions. More than half a century ago, he anticipated the progression as follows: the traditional form of Western scholarship in the study of other (religious traditions) was that of an impersonal presentation of an "it." The first great innovation in recent times has been personalization of the faiths observed, so that one finds a discussion of a "they." Presently the observer becomes personally involved, so that the situation is one of a "we" talking about a "they." The next step is a dialogue where "we" talk to "you." If there is listening and mutuality, this may become "we" talking *with* "you." The culmination of the process is when "we all" are talking *with* each other about "us." See Wilfred Cantwell Smith, "Comparative Religion— Whither and Why?" in *The History of Religions: Essays in Methodology*, M. Eliade and J. M. Kitagawa, eds. (Chicago: University of Chicago Press, 1959), p. 34.

21. William Sloane Coffin Jr., *Credo* (Louisville, KY: Westminster/John Knox Press, 2004), p. 84.

22. Jim Wallis, *God's Politics: A New Vision for Faith and Politics in America* (San Francisco: HarperSanFrancisco, 2005). The website for Sojourners is http://www.sojo.net.

23. See Mark Juergensmeyer, "Anti-Fundamentalism," in *Fundamentalisms Comprehended,* Vol. 5, pp. 353–356.

24. Noah Feldman, *The Fall and Rise of the Islamic State* (Princeton, NJ: Princeton University Press, 2008), p. 3.

# SELECTED BIBLIOGRAPHY

Abdul Rauf, Feisal. *What's Right with Islam: A New Vision for Muslims and the West.* San Francisco: HarperSanFrancisco, 2004.

Abou El Fadl, Khalid. *The Great Theft: Wrestling Islam from the Extremists.* San Francisco: HarperSanFrancisco, 2005.

Ahmed an-Na'im, Abdullahi. *Islam and the Secular State: Negotiating the Future of Shari'a.* Cambridge, MA: Harvard University Press, 2008.

Aslan, Reza. *No god but God: The Origins, Evolution, and Future of Islam.* New York: Random House, 2005.

Aslan, Reza. *How to Win a Cosmic War: God, Globalization, and the End of the War on Terror.* New York: Random House, 2009.

Balmer, Randall. *God in the White House: How Faith Shaped the Presidency from John F. Kennedy to George W. Bush.* San Francisco: HarperOne, 2008.

Bergen, Kathy, et al. *When the Rain Returns: Toward Justice and Reconciliation in Palestine and Israel.* Philadelphia: American Friends Service Committee, 2004.

Carroll, James. *Constantine's Sword: The Church and the Jews.* New York: Houghton Mifflin, 2001.

Carter, Jimmy. *Palestine: Peace Not Apartheid.* New York: Simon & Schuster, 2006.

Church, Forrest. *So Help Me God: The Founding Fathers and the First Battle over Church and State.* Orlando, FL: Harcourt, 2007.

Coffin, William Sloane, Jr. *A Passion for the Possible: Message to the Churches.* Louisville, KY: Westminster/John Knox Press, 1993.

Cox, Harvey. *Many Mansions: A Christian's Encounter with Other Faiths.* Boston: Beacon Press, 1988.

Eck, Diana L. *A New Religious America: How a "Christian Country" Has Become the World's Most Religiously Diverse Nation.* San Francisco: HarperSanFrancisco, 2001.

Esposito, John L. *Unholy War: Terror in the Name of Islam.* New York: Oxford University Press, 2002.

Esposito, John L. *The Future of Islam.* New York: Oxford University Press, 2010.

Esposito, John L. *Islam: The Straight Path,* 4th ed. New York: Oxford University Press, 2010.

Esposito, John L., and Dalia Mogahed. *Who Speaks for Islam? What a Billion Muslims Really Think.* New York: Gallup Press, 2007.

Feldman, Noah. *The Fall and Rise of the Islamic State.* Princeton, NJ: Princeton University Press, 2008.

Friedman, Thomas L. *From Beirut to Jerusalem.* New York: Farrar, Straus and Giroux, 1989.

Gheissari, Ali, and Vali Nasr. *Democracy in Iran: History and the Quest for Liberty.* Oxford, UK: Oxford University Press, 2007.

Goldberg, Michelle. *Kingdom Coming: The Rise of Christian Nationalism.* New York: Norton, 2006.

Gopin, Marc. *Holy War, Holy Peace: How Religion Can Bring Peace to the Middle East.* New York: Oxford University Press, 2002.

Gorenberg, Gershom. *The End of Days: Fundamentalism and the Struggle for the Temple Mount.* New York: Oxford University Press, 2002.

Hagee, John. *Jerusalem Countdown: A Warning to the World.* Frontline, 2006.

Hagee, John. *Can America Survive? 10 Prophetic Signs That We Are the Terminal Generation.* Brentwood, TN: Howard Books, 2010.

Hedges, Chris. *War Is a Force That Gives Us Meaning.* New York: Perseus Books, 2002.

Hedges, Chris. *American Fascists: The Christian Right and the War on America.* New York: Free Press, 2006.

Hertzberg, Arthur. *The Fate of Zionism: A Secular Future for Israel and Palestine.* San Francisco: HarperSanFrancisco, 2003.

Hughes, Richard T. *Christian America and the Kingdom of God.* Urbana: University of Illinois Press, 2009.

Hutson, James H. *The Founders on Religion: A Book of Quotations.* Princeton, NJ: Princeton University Press, 2005.

Juergensmeyer, Mark. *Terror in the Mind of God: The Global Rise of Religious Violence.* Berkeley: University of California Press, 2000.

Juergensmeyer, Mark. *Global Rebellion: Religious Challenges to the Secular State, From Christian Militias to Al-Qaeda.* Berkeley: University of California Press, 2008.

Kamali, Mohammad Hashim. *Shari'ah Law: An Introduction.* Oxford, UK: Oneworld, 2008.

Kennedy, D. James. *What If America Were a Christian Nation Again?* Nashville, TN: Thomas Nelson, 2003.

Kimball, Charles A. *Religion, Politics, and Oil: The Volatile Mix in the Middle East.* Nashville, TN: Abingdon Press, 1992.

Kimball, Charles. *When Religion Becomes Evil: Five Warning Signs,* rev. ed. San Francisco: HarperOne, 2008.

Kinzer, Stephen. *All the Shah's Men: An American Coup and the Roots of Middle East Terror.* Hoboken, NJ: Wiley, 2003.

Kurzman, Charles, ed. *Liberal Islam: A Sourcebook.* New York: Oxford University Press, 1998.

Kurzman, Charles, ed. *Modernist Islam: A Sourcebook.* New York: Oxford University Press, 2002.

Lerner, Michael. *The Left Hand of God: Taking Back Our Country from the Religious Right.* San Francisco: HarperSanFrancisco, 2006.

Lustick, Ian S. *For the Land and the Lord: Jewish Fundamentalism in Israel.* New York: Council on Foreign Relations Press, 1988.

Majd, Hooman. *The Ayatollah Begs to Differ: The Paradox of Modern Iran.* New York: Doubleday, 2008.

Majd, Hooman. *The Ayatollah's Democracy: An Iranian Challenge.* New York: Norton, 2010.

Marty, Martin E., and R. Scott Appleby, eds. *The Fundamentalism Project.* 5 vols. Chicago: University of Chicago Press, 1991–1995.

Meacham, Jon. *American Gospel: God, the Founding Fathers, and the Making of a Nation.* New York: Random House, 2006.

Mearsheimer, John J., and Stephen M. Walt. *The Israel Lobby and U.S. Foreign Policy.* New York: Farrar, Straus and Giroux, 2007.

Menocal, Maria Rosa. *The Ornament of the World: How Muslims, Jews and Christians Created a Culture of Tolerance in Medieval Spain.* Boston: Little, Brown, 2002.

Mortenson, Greg, and David Oliver Relin. *Three Cups of Tea: One Man's Mission to Promote Peace . . . One School at a Time.* New York: Penguin Books, 2006.

Nasr, Vali. *The Shia Revival: How Conflicts Within Islam Will Shape the Future.* New York: Norton, 2006.

Needleman, Jacob. *The American Soul: Rediscovering the Wisdom of the Founders.* New York: Penguin Books, 2002.

Pape, Robert A. *Dying to Win: The Strategic Logic of Suicide Terrorism.* New York: Random House, 2005.

Parsi, Trita. *Treacherous Alliance: The Secret Dealings of Israel, Iran and the United States.* New Haven, CT: Yale University Press, 2007.

Parsley, Rod. *Silent No More: Bring Moral Clarity to America . . . While Freedom Still Rings.* Lake Mary, FL: Charisma House, 2005.

Patel, Eboo. *Acts of Faith: The Story of an American Muslim, the Struggle for the Soul of a Generation.* Boston: Beacon Press 2007.

Phillips, Kevin. *American Theocracy: The Peril and Politics of Radical Religion, Oil, and Borrowed Money in the 21st Century*. New York: Viking Press, 2006.

Prothero, Stephen. *Religious Literacy: What Every American Needs to Know—and Doesn't*. San Francisco: HarperSanFrancisco, 2007.

Ramadan, Tariq. *Western Muslims and the Future of Islam*. New York: Oxford University Press, 2004.

Rogers, Jeffrey S. *Building a House for All God's Children*. Nashville: Abingdon Press, 2008.

Sacks, Jonathan. *The Dignity of Difference: How to Avoid the Clash of Civilizations*. London: Continuum, 2002.

Sharlet, Jeff. *The Family: The Secret Fundamentalism at the Heart of American Power*. New York: HarperCollins, 2008.

Sharlet, Jeff. *C Street: The Fundamentalist Threat to American Democracy*. New York: Little, Brown, and Co., 2010.

Shriver, Donald W., Jr. *Honest Patriots: Loving a Country Enough to Remember Its Misdeeds*. New York: Oxford University Press, 2005.

Sorkin, David. *The Religious Enlightenment: Protestants, Jews, and Catholics from London to Vienna*. Princeton, NJ: Princeton University Press, 2008.

Takeyh, Ray. *Hidden Iran: Paradox and Power in the Islamic Republic*. New York: Henry Holt and Co., 2006.

Takeyh, Ray. *Guardians of the Revolution: Iran and the World in the Age of the Ayatollahs*. Oxford, UK: Oxford University Press, 2009.

Viorst, Milton. *In the Shadow of the Prophet: The Struggle for the Soul of Islam*. Boulder, CO: Westview Press, 2001.

Viorst, Milton. *What Shall I Do with This People? Jews and the Fractious Politics of Judaism*. New York: Free Press, 2002.

Viorst, Milton. *Storm from the East: The Struggle Between the Arab World and the Christian West*. New York: Random House, 2006.

Wallis, Jim. *God's Politics: A New Vision for Faith and Politics in America*. San Francisco: HarperSanFrancisco, 2005.

Wallis, Jim. *The Great Awakening: Reviving Faith & Politics in a Post-Religious Right America*. San Francisco: HarperOne, 2008.

Wright, Lawrence. *The Looming Tower: Al-Qaeda and the Road to 9/11*. New York: Knopf, 2006.

Zogby, James. *Arab Voices: What They Are Saying to Us and Why It Matters*. New York: Palgrave MacMillan, 2010.

# THE AUTHOR

**Charles Kimball** is Presidential Professor and Director of Religious Studies at the University of Oklahoma. Between 1996 and 2008, he served as Professor and Chair of the Department of Religion and Professor of Comparative Religion in the Divinity School at Wake Forest University. He is the author of five books, including *When Religion Becomes Evil* (rev. ed. 2008), which was named one of the "Top 15 Books on Religion" by *Publishers Weekly* and one of the top 10 books of the year by the Association of Parish Clergy. His articles have appeared in a number of publications, among them *Sojourners,* the *Christian Century,* the *Los Angeles Times,* the *Atlanta Journal-Constitution,* the *Boston Globe,* and the *International Herald-Tribune.* He lived in Egypt in 1977–1978 and has made more than 40 trips to the Middle East during the past 35 years. Since the Sept. 11, 2001, terrorist attacks on the World Trade Center and Pentagon, he has been interviewed by more than 500 TV and radio programs, newspapers, and broadcast outlets throughout the United States, Canada, Great Britain, France, Sweden, Australia, and South Africa. A native of Tulsa, Oklahoma, he received his doctoral degree from Harvard University in comparative religion.

# NAME INDEX

## A

Abbas, Abu 'l, 112–113
Abbas, M., 52–53, 120
Abbas, Shah, 118
Abd al-Rahman, 113, 115, 116
Abd al-Wahhab, M. ibn, 124, 132, 194$n$. 5
Abduh, M., 125–126, 132
Abdullah II, King, 120
Abraham, 17–18, 195$n$. 1, 195$n$. 4
Abu Bakr, 102, 103, 108
Abu Talid, 98, 102
Abudullah II, King, 52–53
Adams, J., 81, 83
Afghani, J. al-Din al-, 125–126, 132
Afsaruddin, A., 108, 217$n$. 16
Agah, A., 2
Ahmadinejad, M., 145, 146, 147, 169
Aisha, 108, 110
Alexander II (Czar), 30
Alexander the Great, 28
Ali, 107–108, 109–110, 112
Allen, J., 193$n$. 1
Amaziah, 24
Amir, Y., 33–34, 162
Ammerman, N., 91, 93
Amos (the prophet), 24, 197$n$. 11, 197$n$. 12
An-Na'im, A. A., 135, 216$n$. 10
Appleby, R. S., 160, 223$n$. 5
Aquinas, T., St., 123, 208$n$. 16
Arafat, Y., 33, 48, 53, 199$n$. 2, 203$n$. 25
Aran, G., 161
Aslan, R., 171
Assad, H. al-, 149–150
Atta, M., 158
Attila the Hun, 66
Ayatollah Khomeini. See Khomeini, Ayatollah
Azhar, S. al-, 186
Aziz, T., 150

## B

Bahati, D., 95
Baker, J., 41, 203$n$. 25
Baker, S., 41
Balmer, R., 194$n$. 1, 206$n$. 3
Banna, H. al-, 126, 132
Baruch, 25
Bathsheba, 23, 24
Begin, M., 5, 8, 34, 43, 44, 45, 163, 201$n$. 12
Belin, Y., 53
Bellah, R., 83
Ben Gurion, D., 53
Ben Sasson, H. H., 198$n$. 17
Benedict, P., 208$n$. 22
Benedict XVI, Pope, 96, 174, 185, 225–226$n$. 24, 227–228$n$. 15
Benvenisti, M., 55
Bhutto, B., 131
Bilal, 102
Blair, T., 204$n$. 32
Bloomberg, M., 176
Boniface VIII, Pope, 67
Boykin, W. "J.", Gen., 166–167
Britton, J., 224$n$. 12
Bryan, W. J., 223$n$. 3
Buber, M., 53
Bush, G. W., 6, 52, 86, 89, 91, 138, 147–150, 166, 170, 171
Bush, G. H. W., 89, 203$n$. 25

## C

Caesaretti, C., 193$n$. 1
Calvin, J., 68–72, 90, 208–209$n$. 23, 208$n$. 22, 209$n$. 24
Canaan (son of Ham), 85
Carter, J., 48, 49, 58–59, 193$n$. 2, 204$n$. 32, 206$n$. 1
Chacour, E., 41–42, 200–201$n$. 11

Chadwick, O., 69–70
Charlemagne, 66
Chavez, H., 92
Chittister, J., 187
Clinton, B., 33, 48, 203n. 25
Clinton, H., 52, 96
Clovis, 66
Coe, D., 93, 94
Coffin, W. S., Jr., 2, 184, 188
Cohen, H., 201n. 12
Colson, C., 93
Columbus, 68
Constantine, 63–64, 66, 79
Conzelman, H., 206–207n. 11
Coulter, A., 165–166
Cyrus II, 28

## D

Darrow, C., 223n. 3
David, King, 19, 20, 23–24
Dine, T., 50, 213n. 23
Diocletian, 63, 64
Dole, B., 89
Douglass, F., 211n. 17
Dubner, S., 4

## E

Eck, D. L., 88, 181, 212n. 21
Eisenhower, D., 141
El Fadl, K. A., 134–135
Ensign, J., 94
Esposito, J. L., 219n. 6, 228n. 17

## F

Fadl, K. A. El, 134–135
Falwell, J., 6, 50, 59, 89, 163, 167, 213n. 23
Farris, M., 214n. 31
Fatima (daughter of Muhammed), 115
Feiler, B., 18
Feldman, N., 191
Ferdinand, King, 68
Findley, P., 48, 203n. 22
Fox, G., 80
Franklin, B., 81, 83, 86
Friedman, M., 161

## G

Gabriel, Angel, 22, 98
Ghazali, al-, 103, 124

Gheissari, A., 140, 141
Gladwell, M., 4
Goldberg, M., 6–7, 89
Goldstein, B., 15–16, 47, 106, 162, 195n. 3
Gonzales, A., 92
Goodling, M., 92, 214n. 30
Gorenberg, G., 45–47
Graham, B., 89, 93, 225n. 24
Graham, F., 174, 225n. 24
Gregory I (the Great), Pope, 66, 208n. 16
Gregory VI, Pope, 67
Griffin, M., 224n. 12
Gross, T., 148
Grossman, D., 202n. 20
Gulen, F., 183
Gunn, D., 224n. 12

## H

Hagar, 17
Hagee, J., 51, 163, 167–169, 171, 174, 175, 225n. 19
Halevi, J., 116
Hall, D., 94
Ham, 84–85
Harding, W., 206n. 2
Harun al-Rashid, 113–114
Harvard, J., 79
Hasan (grandson of Muhammad), 107, 111, 217n. 19
Hasan, N., 224–225n. 14
Hasdai ibn Sheprut, 116
Hassan II, King, 204n. 32
Hatfield, M., 93
Hedges, C., 6–7, 89, 166
Hehir, B., 50, 213n. 23
Heilman, S., 161
Helena, 63, 207n. 13
Hemmings, S., 84
Henry, P., 81
Herod, 28, 29
Hertzberg, A., 30, 55–56, 164, 198n. 18, 205n. 37
Hertzl, T., 30
Heschel, A. J., 22, 196n. 9
Hibri, A. al-, 131, 134, 219n. 14
Hill, P., 224n. 12
Hilliard, E., 48
Hitchens, C., 210–211n. 11
Hitler, A., 200n. 9
Hodgson, M. G. S., 114, 218n. 25

Hosseini, K., 181–182
Hourani, A., 218n. 25, 218n. 28
Hughes, H., 93, 94
Hughes, K., 173–174
Hughes, R., 165–166, 224n. 13
Huntington, S., 121–122
Hussein (grandson of Muhammad), 107, 111
Hussein, King, 204n. 32
Hussein, S., 2, 91–92, 118, 137, 139, 141–142, 146, 148, 149–152, 153, 155

**I**

Ibn Hanbal, A., 218n. 5
Ibn Ishaq, 216n. 11
Ibn Sa'ud, 124
Ibn Taymiyyah, 103, 124
Inhofe, J., 94–95
Innocent III, Pope, 67
Isaac, 17, 195n. 4
Isabella, Queen, 68
Ishmael (Isma'il), 17, 195n. 4
Islambuli, K. al-, 126
Ismail I, Shah, 118

**J**

Jackson, A., 87
Jacob, 18
James, King, 79
Jay, J., 81
Jefferson, T., 76, 80, 81–83, 84, 210–211n. 11
Jefferts Schori, K., 211n. 18
Jehoiakim, King, 25
Jenkins, J., 51, 204n. 30
Jereboam II, 24, 197n. 12
Jeremiah (the prophet), 22, 25–26
Jesus. See In Subject Index
John, the Apostle, 94
John of Damascus, 112
John Paul, Pope, 184–185
John Paul II, Pope, 68, 185, 208n. 21, 227n. 13
Jones, T., 96–97
Joseph, 18
Josephus, 197n. 15
Joshua, 195n. 3, 214n. 31
Josiah, 25, 66
Judas the Maccabee, 28
Juergensmeyer, M., 190

**K**

Kaczynski, T., 157
Kahane, M., 16, 44, 161, 202n. 21
Kane, J., 224n. 11
Karzai, H., 137
Kennedy, J. (James), 75, 88, 167
Kennedy, J. F., 58, 92
Kerry, J., 170
Khadija, 98, 102
Khalid ibn al-Walid, 103
Khamenei, A., Ayatolla, 144, 145
Khan, A., 125–126, 132
Khan, D., 133, 176
Khan, R., 140–141
Khatami, M., 145
Khomeini, Ayatollah, 1, 3, 14, 118, 140, 143–144, 145, 151, 193n. 2, 216n. 8
Khoury, R., 173–174, 225n. 23
Kimball, C., 198n. 20, 208n. 20, 214n. 33, 219n. 12, 222n. 17, 227n. 14
Kimball Brothers, The, 198
King, M. L. K., Jr., 55, 85–86
Kinzer, S., 141, 221n. 6
Kissinger, H., 2

**L**

Laden, O. bin, 2, 5, 11–12, 97, 142, 153, 158, 171, 174, 222–223n. 1
LaHaye, T., 51, 204n. 30
Laird, M., 93
Leo I, Pope, 66
Leo III, Pope, 66
Lerner, M., 187
Lessing, G., 73
Levitt, S., 4
Lewis, B., 122, 123
Lincoln, A., 85, 206n. 1
Lindsey, H., 22, 50–51
Locke, J., 72
Louis XIV, King, 72
Lustick, I., 44–45
Luther, M., 68

**M**

Madison, J., 81, 82
Magnes, J., 53
Maimonides, M., 116
Ma'mum, al-, 114
Mark, St., 64
Marty, M., 160, 223n. 5

Matt, W. M., 217*n*. 15
McBrien, R., 66, 67, 208*n*. 16
McCain, J., 75, 76, 167, 170, 210*n*. 2
McCloskey, P., 48
McCune, R. C., 209*n*. 26
McKinney, C., 48
McVeigh, T., 157
Meacham, J., 77
Mearsheimer, J., 49
Mendelssohn, M., 73
Menocal, M. R., 116
Mohler, A., 148
Montazeri, H. A., Grand Ayatollah,
   144–146, 221*n*. 10
Moore, R., 212*n*. 20
Mortenson, G., 131, 182–183,
   227*n*. 10
Moses, 18, 22, 29, 66, 86
Mossadeq, M., 2, 141
Mu'awiya, 110, 111
Mubarak, H., 53
Muhammad. *See In Subject Index*
Mullen, M., 182
Mussavi, M. H., 145

N

Nafisi, A., 146
Na'im, A. A. an-, 135, 216*n*. 10
Naphy, W., 208*n*. 22
Nasr, V., 140, 141, 220*n*. 2
Nathan (the prophet), 23–24
Netanyahu, B., 52–53, 201*n*. 14
Newton, I., 72
Nixon, R., 93
Noah, 27, 85, 203*n*. 29, 214*n*. 2
Noor, Queen, 170
North, G., 90, 91
Nuseibeh, S., 55, 205*n*. 35

O

Obama, B., 6, 48, 52–53, 96, 137, 148,
   154, 169, 194–195*n*. 7, 204*n*. 31
Olmert, E., 168

P

Pahlavi, M. R., Shah, 1, 2, 141, 221*n*. 10
Pape, R., 4, 129
Parsi, T., 222*n*. 13

Parsley, R., 167, 169–170, 171, 174, 175,
   225*n*. 21
Patel, E., 186–187
Paul, the Apostle, 60–63, 65, 74, 84, 94,
   165, 206–207*n*. 11
Paul VI, Pope, 68
Penn, W., 80
Percy, C., 48, 202–203*n*. 22
Peter, the Apostle, 61, 62, 65
Petraeus, D., 96
Phillips, K., 7, 89, 212–213*n*. 22
Pinsker, L., 30
Pontius Pilate, 60
Popper, A., 47, 162, 202*n*. 21
Prothero, S., 180
Ptolemy, 28

Q

Qazwini, H., 226*n*. 4
Qutb, S., 126, 129, 132

R

Rabboo, Y. A., 53
Rabin, Y., 33–36, 48, 163, 164,
   203*n*. 25
Rafsanjani, H., 145
Ramadan, T., 132–133, 134
Rashid, H. al-, 113–114
Rauf, F. A., Imam, 133–134, 176
Raymond of Agiles, 67
Reagan, R., 6, 59, 86, 221*n*. 12
Reed, R., 90
Relin, D., 182
Rice, C., 173–174
Robertson, P., 59, 89–92, 167, 171,
   174, 175
Roosevelt, T., 86
Rupp, G., 3
Rushdie, S., 101, 145, 151, 216*n*. 8
Rushdoony, R. J., 90, 91

S

Sachs, J., 12–13
Sadat, A., 59, 126
Sadr, M. al-, 152, 153
Said, E., 122
Saladin, 115, 209*n*. 31
Salah al-Din (Saladin), 115, 209*n*. 31

Samuel, 19, 20
Sanford, M., 94
Sarah, 17, 18
Saul, King, 19, 27, 196n. 6, 196n. 10
Savage, C., 213–214n. 30
Sayyid Ahmad Khan, 125–126, 132
Servetus, M., 70
Shah Muhammad Reza Pahlavi. *See*
    Pahlavi, M. R.
Shamir, Y., 5, 44, 163
Sharlet, J., 93, 94
Sharon, A., 34, 53, 163, 201n. 12
Shehadeh, R., 202n. 20
Sheptrut, H. ibn, 116
Shriver, D., 84
Simon, 28
Sistani, A., al-, Grand Ayatollah, 152, 186,
    222n. 18
Sizer, S., 49
Skelski, H., 198n. 20
Smith, W. C., 228n. 20
Solomon, King, 19, 20–21, 24, 66
Sorkin, D., 72–73
Stein, J., 139
Steinbrook, B. J., 94
Stillman, N. A., 198n. 17, 217n. 15,
    218n. 27

**T**

Takeyh, R., 141, 143
Taylor, C., 92
Truman, H., 141, 206n. 1
Turabi, H. al-, 11–12
Turner, H. R., 217n. 22
Tutu, D., 213n. 23

**U**

Umar ibn al-Khattab, 108–109, 110
Urban II, Pope, 67
Uriah, 23
Uthman ibn Affan, 109, 110

**V**

Viorst, M., 28, 197n. 17
Vishanoff, D., 218n. 24

**W**

Wallis, J., 189
Walsh, J., 3, 194n. 3
Walt, S., 49
Washington, G., 80, 81, 83, 86,
    211n. 13
Weizman, E., 35–36, 164,
    198–199n. 2
Wendel, F., 208–209n. 23
West, C., 187
Westmoreland, L., 212n. 20
White, D., 193n. 1
Williams, R., 79
Wilson, W., 86
Winthrop, J., 78, 86
Wright, L., 11–12

**Y**

Yates, K., Jr., 22
Yavin, H., 202n. 20
Yazid, 111, 118
Yoder, J. H., 61

# SUBJECT INDEX

## A

Abbasid dynasty, 112–115, 116
*Abington Township School District versus Schempp*, 76
Abortion, 76, 87, 89, 90, 165
*Abraham* (Feiler), 18
Abraham, Mosque of, 15–16
Abrahamic religions, 17–18; commonalities among, 11, 134; educational resources on, 180–183; flexible political approaches in, 10–11, 13–14; Islamic view of, 99; lethal extremism among, 56, 158, 174–175; overview of, 13–14; peace making in, 56–57, 178–192; prophets common to, 22–23; stereotypes among, 97; 21st-century paradigms for, 188–192. *See also* Christianity; Islam; Judaism
Abu Ghraib, 174
Acts, book of, 61–62, 206n. 8
*Adultery and Divorce in Calvin's Geneva* (McCune), 209n. 26
Afghanistan: demonstrations in, 97; Karzai government in, 137; mujahideen of, U.S. support for, 5, 142; Muslim militants in, 5; novels about, 182; Shi'ite Muslims in, 138; Soviet invasion of, 5, 142, 193n. 2; Taliban in, 5, 130–131, 142, 172; 2009 election in, 137, 138; U.S.-led war in, 137, 138, 166, 174, 182; women in, 130–131
African Americans: Christian racists and, 85; slavery and, 79, 83, 84–86, 211n. 17
Al-Aqsa mosque, 45, 67
Al-Azhar University, 115, 125, 126, 132
Alexandria, Egypt, 64
*Aliyah*, 40
Al-Khalil, 195n. 1
*All the Shah's Men* (Kinzer), 141

*All Things Considered*, 176
Al-Qaeda, 222–223n. 1; in Afghanistan, 6, 142, 148; bin Ladin and, 2, 5, 11–12, 97, 142, 153, 158, 171, 174, 222–223n. 1; in Iraq, 153–154; militant groups supported by, 172; militant worldview and, 171; in Pakistan, 148; terrorism of, 157–158, 171
Amalekites, 19
"Amazing Faiths," 184
ABC, 194n. 3
*American Facists* (Hedges), 6–7, 89, 166
American Friends Service Committee, 205n. 35
*American Gospel* (Meacham), 77
American Israel Public Affairs Committee (AIPAC), 49, 50
American Jewish Committee, 187, 228n. 19
American Jewish Congress, 205n. 37
*American Theocracy* (Phillips), 7, 89, 212–213n. 22
Americans for Peace Now, 187
Amish, 80, 190
Amman Message, 186
Amnesty International, 42
Amos, book of, 24
Anabaptists, 70
Anglicanism, 80, 81, 82, 210n. 5
Anglo-Iranian Oil Company, 141
Antichrist, 160
Anti-Semitism, 190. *See also* Jews: persecution of
Apartheid, 89
Apocalypse, 158, 159–160
Apostles, on relating to the state, 60–63
Arab East Jerusalem, 45
Arabs: Abraham and, 17; Israeli, 38–42
*Arc, The* (Rand Corporation), 204–205n. 33
Ark of the Covenant, 19, 196n. 7

Armageddon, 51, 160, 203n. 29
Armenian Orthodox Christians, 64, 65
Army of God, 165
Armyofgod.com, 224n. 12
Aryan Nations, 165
Ashura, 111
Assimilation, 29, 30, 31
Assyria, 21
Assyrian Christians, 65
Atlanta Olympics bombing, 157
Atlantic Monthly, 122, 146
Autoemancipation (Pinsker), 30
"Axis of Evil," 138
Ayyubids, 115

**B**

Baath Party, 92, 149–152, 153
Babylon, 21, 28, 29
Babylonian Talmud, 29
Bangladesh, 119, 131, 138
Baptists, 21, 58–59, 82, 85, 148, 169,
    206n. 2
"Being," 226n. 5
Beliefnet, 210n. 2
Bible, 13; Christian Coalition and, 90,
    91–92; Christian fundamentalists'
    interpretation of, 159–160, 165–166,
    167; Puritans and, 79; slavery in, 84–86,
    211n. 16, 211n. 17. See also Hebrew
    Bible; specific book headings
Blink (Gladwell), 4
Block of the Faithful (Gush Emunim),
    33–34, 37, 43, 44–45, 48, 161–165
Blood Brothers (Chacour), 200n. 11
Books, for interfaith education, 181–182
Born Again (Colson), 93
Brethren, 80
Britain: colonial rule of, 127; Iran
    oil and, 141
BBC, 16
British Mandate, 30–31
"Burn the Qur'an" event, 96–97
Bush (G. W.) administration, 92, 148,
    166, 171
Byzantine Empire, 64, 65, 112

**C**

Caliphs, 107, 108–117, 119
Calvin (Wendel), 208–209n. 23
Calvin and the Consolidation of the
    Genevan Reformation (Naphy), 208n. 22

Calvinism, 68–72, 78
Camp David peace process, 35, 36, 53, 59
Campus Crusade for Christ, 22
Can America Survive? (Hagee), 167,
    168–169
"Can You Tell a Sunni from a Shi'ite?"
    (Stein), 139
Canadian Broadcasting Network, 208n. 21
Cave of the Patriarchs, 15–16
Central Asian Institute, 182–183
CIA, 2, 141, 220–221n. 6
CIA World Factbook, 220n. 4
Chalcedon, Council of, 64, 207n. 14
China, 122
Christian America and the Kingdom of
    God (Hughes), 224n. 13
Christian America movement, 88–95, 166
Christian Coalition, 59, 89–93
Christian fundamentalists and extremists:
    American Puritan, 78–79; beliefs of,
    159–160; Christian America movement
    and, 88–95, 166; confronting, 174–177;
    dispensationalism and, 50–51, 159–160,
    163–164, 167–170, 203n. 29; fascist,
    166; Islamophobic of, 96–97, 120,
    133–134, 166–170, 175–177, 225–226n.
    24; Israel and, 47, 49–51, 160, 163–165,
    167–170; lethal approaches of, 70–71,
    74, 85, 86–87, 92, 165–170; Protestant
    Reformation and, 69–71; in U.S. politics,
    87, 88–95, 166–170, 175–177
Christian Identity movement, 165, 223n. 10
Christian militia groups, 165, 166
Christian religious right: Christian America
    movement and, 88–95, 166; dangers
    of, 88–89, 165; increased power of,
    5–7, 59, 88, 165–170, 213–214n. 30;
    organizations and proponents of, 89–95,
    165–170; in U.S. military, 166–167
Christian Zionism (Sizer), 49
Christianity: early church in, 60–63, 206–
    207n. 11, 206n. 8; the Enlightenment
    and, 72–73, 80, 82; historical lessons
    of, 74; history of religion and politics
    in, 58–74; in Holy Roman Empire,
    63–65; papal rise in, 65–68; Protestant
    Reformation in, 68–72; racism in, 85; in
    U.S. politics, 58–59, 73, 74, 75–95
Christians: in Iraq, 148; Islamic views and
    treatment of, 99, 111–112, 116–119;
    Middle Eastern, 64–65, 109, 118; peace
    making role of, 189–190; persecutions
    of, 62, 63, 64; religious illiteracy of, 180

*Christ's Churches Purely Reformed* (Benedict), 208*n*. 22

Churches for Middle East Peace (CMEP), 50, 203*n*. 27

Church-state separation: Christian history and, 58–74; contemporary Christians' views on, 59; issues of, 9–10; in United States, 75–95. *See also* Religion-politics interplay

Citizenship: in Israel, 38–42, 190; in religion-defined states, 38

Civil Rights movement, 85–86

Civil War, American, 85

*Clash of Civilizations and the Making of World Order, The* (Huntington), 122

Clash-of-civilizations hypothesis, 121–123, 191

Cocksure Christians, 165–170. *See also* Christian fundamentalists and extremists; Christian religious right

*Colbert Report, The,* 212*n*. 20

Cold War era, 88, 122

Colonialism, 121, 123–127, 138, 140, 141

*Commentary on the Psalms* (Calvin), 208*n*. 23

"Common Word Between Us and You, A," 185

Comparative religion, 196*n*. 10

"Comparative Religion–Whither and Why" (Smith), 228*n*. 20

Consistory, 69–70, 209*n*. 26

Constantinople, 64, 65

Coptic Orthodox Church, 64, 65

Coral Ridge Presbyterian Church, 75

Cordoba, 115–116, 134

II Corinthians, 207*n*. 11

Cornerstone Church, 167

Council of Chalcedon, 64, 207*n*. 14

Council of Foreign Relations, 222*n*. 18

Covenants, God's, 21, 27, 168

Creation Museum, 159

Crusades, 67–68

**D**

*Daily Show with Jon Stewart,* 139

Damascus, 65, 108, 110, 111–112

Danish cartoon crisis, 216*n*. 8

Day of Judgment, in Islam, 102

Declaration of Independence, 80, 81

Declaration of principles on Interim Self-Government Arrangements. *See* Oslo Accords

Deists, 73, 80, 209*n*. 30

Democracy: in early Islam, 109; in Iran, 140, 141, 142–147, 155–156; in Iraq, 147–149, 152–154, 155–156; Muslim attitudes toward, 128, 134; in Muslim countries, 9, 120–121, 137–156, 155–156, 173–174, 191; theocracy and, 9–10, 73, 143; U.S. support for, in Muslim countries, 173–174; variations of, 9–10

*Democracy in Iran* (Gheissari and Nasr), 140, 141

Dialogue programs, interfaith, 183–188, 227*nn*. 10–14, 228*nn*. 19–22

Dictatorships: Christian right's support for, 89, 92, 94–95; U.S. government support for, 142, 173

Dispensationalism, 50–51, 159–160, 163–164, 167–170, 203*n*. 29

*Diwan,* 108, 110

Dome of the Rock, 45, 112

Dominion theology, 89–92, 94

Double predestination, 70–71

Druze, 40, 200*n*. 10

*Dying to Win* (Pape), 4, 129

**E**

Eastern Orthodox, 65

Ecclesiastes, 20

Ecclesiastical Ordinances (Calvin), 69

Ecumenical organizations, 183–188

Edict of Milan, 64

Edmond, Oklahoma, anti-Muslim protest in, 176

Education, interfaith, 179–183, 191. *See also* Schools

Egypt: ancient Hebrews in, 17, 18, 21; Christianity in, 64–65; early Islam in, 109, 115; government of, 127; Israeli peace with, 35, 36, 59, 193*n*. 2; reformers in, 125–126; Sunni Muslims in, 138; women in, 130, 131

Electromagnetic pulse (EMP) explosion, 168–169

Elon Moreh, 43

Emory University School of Law, 135

*Encyclopedia of Jews in the Islamic World* (Stillman), 198*n*. 17, 218*n*. 27

*End of Days, The* (Gorenberg), 45–47

Enlightenment, the, 72–73, 80, 82

Ephesians 6:5-9, 84

Episcopal Church, 211*n*. 18

Evangelical Christians: dispensationalism and, 50–51, 160–161, 163–164, 167–170, 203n. 29; Israel and, 47, 49–51; progressive, 189; prophecy and, 21–22, 50–51; religious right and, 88–95, 89; in U.S. military, 166–167; U.S. movements of, 89; in U.S. politics, 58–59, 88–95, 166–170. See also Christian fundamentalists; Christian religious right

Evolution theory, 159, 212n. 19, 223n. 3

Exodus, 18, 22, 86, 211n. 16

Extremists: countering, peaceful approaches to, 178–192; fundamentalism and, 157–177; lethal power of, 12–13, 56, 157–159, 161, 174–175, 192; sacred text interpretation by, 106, 133, 165–166, 167. See also Christian fundamentalists; Christian religious right; Fundamentalism; Jewish extremists; Muslim extremists

Ezekiel, 197n. 14

**F**

Fall and Rise of the Islamic State, The (Feldman), 191

Family, The, 93–95, 214n. 33

Family, The (Sharlet), 93

Fascism, 166

Fate of Zionism, The (Hertzberg), 55–56

Fatimids, 115, 116

Fatwas, 117, 150–151

Fellowship, The, 93–95, 214n. 33

Female circumcision, 130, 219n. 12

Female infanticide, 102

Fiddler on the Roof, 30

First Amendment, 82, 88, 177

First Muslims, The (Afsaruddin), 217n. 16

First Zionist Congress, 30

Five Pillars of Islam, 101, 170

Foreign Affairs, 121–122

Foreign Policy, 132

Fort Hood tragedy, 224–225n. 14

Foundation for Middle East Peace, 199n. 3, 223n. 9

Franks, 66, 67

Freakonomics (Levitt and Dubner), 4

French colonial rule, 127

French Revolution, 73

Fresh Air, 147–148, 168, 181, 222n. 14, 225n. 19

Fundamentalism, 157–177; anti-, 190; commonalities in, 14, 159, 160–161;

confronting, 174–177, 186; countering, peaceful approaches to, 178–192; in cross-cultural context, 160; definition of, 159–161; lethal potential of contemporary, 157–159, 161, 174–175, 192; worldview of, 160–161, 169, 171. See also Christian fundamentalists; Christian religious right; Extremists; Jewish extremists; Muslim extremists

Fundamentalism Project, The (Marty and Appleby), 223n. 5

**G**

Gallup Organization, 128–130, 173, 219n. 7, 219n. 10

Gaza Strip: HAMAS in, 5, 48, 172; Israeli confiscation of, 43, 47; Jewish extremist settlers in, 33, 34, 43, 44–48; map of, 54; Occupied, 42–48; Palestinian refugee camps in, 40; population of, 199n. 3

Gelasius I, 66

"Generation Joshua," 214n. 31

Genesis, 27; 1:26-31, 90; 9:24, 85; 12, 17; 12:1-3, 15, 35; 15:5, 17; 16:10, 17; 21:12, 17; 21:13, 17; 21:18, 17; 21:20-21, 17; 22, 195n. 4; 25:9, 17; dominionism and, 90; evolution and, 159

Geneva, Calvin's, 69–72, 90

Geneva Accord, 53, 204n. 32

Geneva Consistory, 69–70, 209n. 26

Globalization, 9–10

Gnostic documents, 207n. 12

God: America and, 83, 86–87, 88, 92; American leaders and, 94; Christian Calvinist view of, 69–71; Christian deist view of, 80, 83; Christian Quaker view of, 80; injustice and, 63; Islamic view of, 99; Jewish relationship with, 20, 21, 24–25, 31–32

God in the White House (Balmer), 206n. 3

"God's plan": dispensationalism and, 50–51, 160–161, 163–164, 167–170, 203n. 29; fundamentalist extremism and, 14, 50–51, 158–159, 161, 167–170; Islamic views of, 105, 171; reconstructivism and, 89–93; U.S. Manifest Destiny and, 86–87

God's Politics (Wallis), 189

Good Morning America, 194n. 3

Grand Mosque occupation, 2, 142

Great Mosque, 17

Great Synagogue, 67

*Great Theft, The* (El Fadl), 134–135
Great Umayyad Mosque, 112
Greek Catholics, 65
Greek Orthodox, 118
Greek philosophy, 123
Green Line, 51–52
"Ground Zero Mosque" (Cordoba
    House), 96–97, 133–134, 176, 214*n*. 1,
    220*n*. 19
Gulf War of 1991, 142, 150–152
Gush Emunim, 33–34, 37, 43, 44–45, 48,
    161–165


**H**

Habitat for Humanity, 186
Hadith, 13, 100–101, 102, 107–108, 114,
    124, 215*n*. 7
Haiti, 92
Hajj, 117
Halabja, Iraq, 150
Ham, curse of, 84–85
HAMAS (Islamic Resistance Movement),
    5, 48, 55, 132, 172, 173–174
Hanbali school of Islamic law, 194*n*. 5
Haram ash-sharif, 45
Harvard University, 3, 79, 181
Hasmonean dynasty, 28
Hate speech, 175, 185
Hebrew Bible: Hebrew dynasties in,
    19–21; Jewish history in, 16–27;
    prophets in, 17–18, 21–26; religion-and
    politics interplay in, 27–28, 195*n*. 3.
    *See also specific book headings*
Hebrews, Epistle to the, 62
Heretics, Christian prosecution of, 68,
    70–71, 79
*Hidden Iran* (Takeyh), 141, 143
Hijra, 103
History: fundamentalists and, 14;
    importance of knowing, 13–14, 77–78;
    Jewish, 15–32; U.S., 76–87
*History of the Arab Peoples, A* (Hourani),
    218*n*. 25, 218*n*. 28
*History of the Jewish People, A* (Ben
    Sasson), 198*n*. 17
Hizbullah (Party of God), 5, 6, 13,
    163–164, 168, 172
Holocaust, 29, 31, 146, 200*n*. 9
Holy Roman Empire, 63–65, 66, 71
Homosexuality, 87, 89, 90, 95
*Honest Patriots* (Shriver), 84
Honor killings, 130, 219*n*. 12

Hope: approach of, 178–180; steps for,
    179–192
*How to Win a Cosmic War* (Aslan), 171
Hudaybiyya, Treaty of, 104
Human rights: education and, 182–183;
    in Iran, 146–147; in Israel, 40–42, 190,
    201*n*. 12, 201*n*.14; Muslim attitudes
    toward, 128, 130–131; Muslim
    proponents of, 132–136; promoting,
    191–192; in United States, 87, 91; U.S.
    role in promoting, 188–190. *See also*
    Social justice; Women
Human Rights Watch, 42
Hurricane Katrina, 169, 225*n*. 19


**I**

Iftar meals, 183, 186
Ignorance, 7–8, 139, 180; overcoming,
    180–183
Imams, 111, 115
India: independence of, 119; Islamic, 97,
    118–119, 124; secular state of, 135;
    Sunni Muslims in, 138
Indian Removal Act, 87
Indonesia, 97, 119, 120, 127, 131, 135,
    138, 187–188
Indulgences, 67–68, 69
*Inherit the Wind*, 223*n*. 3
Injustice, 63
Inquisition, 68, 70
Institute for Interfaith Dialogue (IID), 183
Institute for International Peace
    Studies, 132
*Institutes of Biblical Law, The*
    (Rushdoony), 90
*Institutes of the Christian Religion*
    (Calvin), 69, 70, 71, 90, 209*n*. 24
Interfaith: dialogue, 183–188, 227*nn*.
    10–14, 228*nn*. 19–22; education,
    179–183, 191
Interfaith Alliance, 183
Interfaith Youth Corp (IFYC), 186–187
International Christian Embassy, 163–164
International Quaker Working Party,
    205*n*. 35
Interventionist stance, 122
Intifada, Palestinian, 47–48
Iran: CIA-led coup in, 141; Constitutional
    Revolution of 1906 of, 140; democracy
    in, 140, 141, 142–147, 155–156;
    demographics of, 139, 147; ecumenical
    meetings in, 2, 3; government of, 127,

142–147; human rights in, 146–147; Iraq and, 2, 11, 118, 138, 141–142, 152; Islamic Republic of, 2, 3, 127, 142–147, 190–191; Israel and, 146; media coverage and stereotypic view of, 3–4, 138, 191, 193–194n. 3; nuclear politics in, 145, 168–169; political diversity within, 3–4, 137, 138, 146–147; pre-revolutionary, 140–141; revolution of, 1–3, 118, 140, 142; Safavid Dynasty of, 118, 124, 140; shahs of, 118, 140–141; Shi'ite Islam in, 118, 138, 146, 155; 2009 election and protests in, 3–4, 137, 138, 146–147, 155, 169; U.S. Christian extremists and, 168–169; U.S. embassy hostage crisis in, 1–2, 3, 4–5, 140, 193–194n. 3; women in, 130

Iran-Contra Affair, 146, 221–222n. 12

Iraq: Abbasid dynasty of, 112–115, 116; al-Qaeda in, 153–154; Baath party in, 149–152, 153; Christians in, 148; democracy in, 147–149, 152–154, 155–156; Hussein regime in, 2, 139, 141–142, 148, 149–152; Iran and, 2, 11, 118, 138, 141–142, 152; 1991 Gulf War and, 142, 150–152; political and religious conflict within, 148–149, 152–154; postwar government of, 147–149, 152–154; religious demographics of, 139; Robertson's plan for Syria and, 91–92; Safavids and Ottomans in, 118; Shi'ite Muslims in, 138, 139, 150, 152, 154, 155; Sunni Muslims in, 139, 148–149, 150; 2010 election in, 137; U.S.-led war and reconstruction in, 6, 138, 139, 147–149, 154, 166, 174; women in, 153

"Iraq: Grand Ayatolla Ali al-Sistani," 222n. 18

"Iraqi Constitution May Curb Women's Rights," 153

"Is America Islamophobic?", 95

Isaiah 10:21, 198n. 18

Islam: Christian extremists' hostility against, 168–170; culture and civilization of, 113–119, 122–123; diversity within, 97, 122, 131–132, 139, 154–156, 172–174; educational resources on, 181–183; Five pillars of, 101, 170; historical lessons of, 119; history of, 96–119, 218n. 25; leadership crisis in early, 107–110, 139; messengers in, 197n. 13; Muhammad's message and,

101–103; origins of, 98–101; progressive voices in, 132–136; prophets of, 22–23, 26, 98–99, 197n. 13; relationships with non-Muslims in early, 99, 104–107, 109, 111–112, 116–119; religion and politics in contemporary, 120–136; religion and politics in historical, 96–119; renewal and reform movements in, 123–128; scholarship in, 113–114, 123, 125, 126; spread of, 115–119

*Islam and the Secular State* (an-Na'im), 135, 216n. 10

*Islam: The Straight Path* (Esposito), 219n. 6

Islamic Center of America, 226n. 4

Islamic law. See Sharia

"Islamic Law" (Vishanoff), 218n. 24

Islamic Republic of Iran. See Iran

Islamic Resistance Movement (HAMAS), 5, 48, 55, 132, 172, 173–174

Islamic state(s): Abbasid, 113–115; characteristics of, 107, 119; contemporary debates about, 120–136, 137–156, 190–191; of early caliphs, 107–110; framework for understanding, 154–156; of Iran, 2, 3, 142–147, 190–191; militant proponents of, 172–174; in Muhammad's Medina, 103–110, 216n. 11; Ottoman, 30, 117–118, 124; progressive views on, 132–136, 174; rashidun ("Rightly Guided Caliphs") model of, 111, 119, 143; secular state versus, 135; of Sudan, 11–12; Umayyad, 111–113, 115–117

Israel, ancient: divided kingdoms of, 21; Hebrew dynasties of, 18–21, 28, 29; Jewish history and, 15–29; prophets of, 17–18, 21–26

Israel, modern: Arab citizens of, 38–42, 190; border map of, 39; citizenship in, 38–42, 190, 200n. 8; demographics of, 44; establishment of, 29–32, 37–38; future of, 51–57, 164–165; government structure of, 37–38, 200n. 7; human rights advocates in, 41–42, 201n. 12, 201n.14; Iran and, 146; Jewish extremists in, 161–165; key issues within, 36–38; Labor governments of, 43, 162; Likud governments of, 5, 43, 44, 162–163; military of, 40, 44, 47; Muslim anger against, 146, 155–156; Muslim militants and, 172; Occupied Territories of, 42–48, 190, 199n. 3;

religion and politics in, 33–57; security of, 36, 43, 44, 47–48, 52, 53, 163; systemic discrimination in, 40–42; ultra-Orthodox Jews and, 161–165; United States and, 48–51, 52–53, 55–56, 168, 202–203n. 22; U.S. Christian fundamentalists and, 47, 49–51, 160, 163–165, 167–170; war of 1948 of, 31, 40; war of 1967 of, 36, 43

*Israel Lobby and U.S. Foreign Policy, The* (Mearsheimer and Walt), 49

Israeli settlements: history and development of, 43, 162; Jewish extremists in, 15–16, 33–35, 37, 44–51, 56, 161–165; maps of, 46, 54; peace process and, 51–57, 162–163; population of, 199n. 3; U.S. policy and, 48–51, 52–53, 55–56

Israeli-Egyptian peace settlement, 35, 36, 59, 193n. 2

Israeli-Palestinian conflict: books on, 199–200n. 4; Christian fundamentalists and, 49–51, 163–165, 167–168; dynamics of, 43, 51–57, 163; "final status" issues in, 53; future of, 51–57; Israeli Arabs and, 38–42, 202n. 20, 202n. 21; Jewish extremist settlers and, 33–34, 44–52, 56, 162–163; Occupied Territories and, 42–48, 163, 190; one-state solution to, 53–56; peace efforts and peace makers in, 35–36, 48–49, 51–57, 120, 202–203n. 22, 203–205nn 27–37, 203n. 25; two-state solution to, 51–53; U.S. Jewish peace advocates and, 187; U.S. policy and, 48–51, 52–53, 55–56; volatility of, 36, 56–57

Istanbul, 117

*Ithna'ashari* school, 118

**J**

J Street, 187, 228n. 19
Jamestown, 79
"Jefferson Bible," 81
Jeremiah, 22, 25–26
Jerusalem: ancient establishment of, 19–20; Arab East, 45; Christian crusades to, 67–68; conquests of, 28–29; contemporary status of, 31; importance of, 178; Muslim conquests of, 108, 115; proposal to move U.S. embassy to, 49–50, 213n. 23

*Jerusalem Countdown* (Hagee), 167

*Jerusalem Post,* 181
Jerusalem Talmud, 29
Jesus: Herodian rule and, 29; hope for return of, 62, 159–160, 163; as Messiah, 20; pacifism of, 61, 67; on politics and religion, 59, 60–63; Qur'an on, 99

Jewish Council for Public Affairs, 50

Jewish extremists and militants, 5; of Israeli settlements, 15–16, 33–35, 37, 44–48, 51–52, 56, 161–165; lethal potential of, 161–165; peace process and, 33–34, 48–49, 56; types of contemporary, 161–165; U.S. policy and, 48–51; worldview of, 16, 45–47

Jewish scholars, in Diaspora, 29

Jewish state. *See* Israel, modern

Jewish Zealots, 60

Jews: Ahmadinejad on, 146; assimilation of, 29, 30, 31; Christian crusades and, 67; Christian inquisitions and, 68; definition of Jewish state and, 36–37, 51–57, 161, 200n. 8; Diaspora of, 29–30, 36–37; history of, 15–32, 197–198n. 17; interfaith dialogue with, 183, 187, 228n. 19; Islamic views and treatment of, 99, 104–107, 111–112, 116–119, 146; persecution of, 30, 67, 68, 190; right of return of, 40. *See also* Israel; Judaism; Zionist movement

*Jews of Arab Lands, The* (Stillman), 217n. 15, 218n. 27

Jihad: meaning of, 151; Saddam Hussein's, 150–152

John 1:8, 99

Jordan, 120

*Jordan Times,* 173

Judah, 21

Judaism: in exile, 29–30; history of, 15–32, 197–198n. 17; view of God in, 20, 21, 24–25, 27

Judea, modern, 42–48

*Judenstaat, Der* (Hertzl), 30

Judges, Hebrew, 21

**K**

Kaaba, 17, 102, 104, 142
Kach movement, 161
Karamah, 131, 219n. 14
Karbala, massacre at, 112
Kibbutz movement, 37, 200n. 6
*Kingdom Coming* (Goldberg), 6–7, 89
Kiryat Arba, 15, 16

*Kite Runner, The* (Hosseini), 182
Knesset, 34, 37, 44, 200*n*. 7
Ku Klux Klan, 165
Kurds, 127, 149, 150, 153
Kuwait, 142, 150–152

**L**

Lamentations, book of, 197*n*. 14
*Late Great Planet Earth, The* (Lindsey), 22, 50–51, 196*n*. 8
League of Nations, 31
Lebanon: Hizbullah in, 5, 6, 13, 163–164, 168, 172; Israeli invasion of, 5, 163–164, 168; Maronite Church in, 65, 207*n*. 15; religious diversity of, 207–208*n*.15; Shi'ite Muslims in, 138
"Left Behind" series, 51, 169, 204*n*. 30, 225*n*. 20
"Legal Reform" (al-Hibri), 219*n*. 14
Liberia, 92
*Life and Morals of Jesus of Nazareth, The* (Jefferson), 81
*Life of Muhammad, The* (Ibn Ishaq), 216*n*. 11
Likud governments, 5, 43, 44, 162–163
Literacy, religious, 180–183
*Lives of the Popes* (McBrien), 208*n*. 16
*Looming Tower, The* (Wright), 11–12
"Loving God and Neighbor Together," 185
Luke, 60; 19:41-42, 178

**M**

Maccabean Revolt, 28
Maccabees, 197*n*. 15
Manifest Destiny, 86–87, 95
Mar Elias school system, 41–42
Mark 6:4, 25
Maronite Church, 65, 207*n*. 15
Masada, 29
Massachusetts, colonial, 78–79, 210*n*. 5
Matthew, 20; 22:15-22, 60
*Mawla,* 107–108
*Mayflower,* 78
Mecca: Kaaba in, 17, 102, 104, 142; Muhammad in, 101–103; pilgrimage to, 117
Media coverage: of Iran, 3–4, 138, 191, 193–194*n*. 3; of Iraq, 138; of Muslims, 120, 172–173; negative slant of, 179; oversimplification and stereotyping in, 3, 7–9, 131, 172–173; presuppositions in, 8–9

Medina (Yathrib), 103–110, 216*n*. 9, 216*n*. 11
Mennonites, 80
Messengers, 197*n*. 13. *See also* Prophets
Messiah: Christian view of, 20; Jewish views of, 20; Orthodox Jews and, 36–37, 45, 161, 162
3 Micah 6:8, 26
Middle Eastern Christians, 64–65, 109, 118
Middle Tennessee University, 176
Milan, Edict of, 64
*Milestones* (Qutb), 126
Militants. *See* Christian fundamentalists; Christian religious right; Jewish extremists; Muslim extremists
Miracles, 98–99, 214–215*n*. 3
Mi'raj, 214–215*n*. 3
Moghul Empire, 118–119, 124
Monarchies: of ancient Israel, 18–21, 28, 29; Christian, 66–67, 71, 74
Mongol invasions, 115, 117, 123
Moral Majority, 6, 50, 59, 89
Mormons, 190
Mt. Herzl cemetery, 34
Mt. Sinai, 22
Mufti, 117, 151
Muhammad: death of, 107, 108, 139; governance approach of, 103–110; hadith of, 13, 100–101, 102, 107–108, 114, 124, 215*n*. 7; on human responsibility, 178; on jihad, 151; message of, 101–103; on religious renewal, 124; roles of, 22, 98–101; on scholarship, 123; successors to, 107–110; supernatural stories of, 214–215*n*. 3
*Muhammad at Medina* (Matt), 217*n*. 15
Mujahideen (freedom fighters), 5, 142
Murfreesboro, Tennessee, mosque protest in, 176
Muslim Brotherhood, 126, 132
Muslim countries: anger and frustration in, 155–156, 173–174; clash-of-civilizations hypothesis and, 121–123, 191; colonial legacy of, 121, 123–128, 138, 140, 141, 148, 155, 173; democracy in, 9, 120–121, 137–156, 155–156, 173–174, 191; framework for understanding, 154–156; Iran and Iraq case studies of, 137–156; Israel and, 146, 155–156; nation-state system and, 127, 136, 140–141; political diversity among, 120–121, 127–128,

136, 154–156, 172–174; superpower domination and, 123, 127–128, 138; women in, 130–131, 153, 182, 219n. 14. *See also* Islamic state(s)

Muslim extremists and militants: in Afghanistan, 5, 6, 142; anti-Christian, 97; complexity of, 154; inspirations for, 126, 129, 132; international terrorism and, 6, 142, 157–159, 171; in Iraq, 153–154; lethal potential of, 129, 157–159; moderate and progressive Muslims *versus*, 132–136, 185–186; Palestinian, 48; as percentage of global population, 129; Qur-an interpretation and, 105–106, 133, 135; stereotypes and, 97, 120, 131, 172–173, 177; types of contemporary, 171–174; worldview of, 171

Muslim University of Aligarh, 125

Muslims: Abraham and, 17–18; American phobia towards, 96–97, 133–134, 166–170, 175–177; attitude survey of, 128–132, 172–173; Christian crusades and, 67–68; conquests of, 108–109, 111; contemporary struggles among, 120–136; diversity among, 122, 132, 172–174; early split among, 107–110; interfaith dialogue with, 183–188, 227n. 10–14; learning about, 181–183; moderate and progressive, 132–136, 185–186; peaceful, 185–186; relationships of, with non-Muslims, 99, 104–107, 109, 111–112, 116–119; stereotyping of, 97, 120, 123, 131, 168, 172–173, 177; Umayyad and Abbasid dynasties of, 111–117; in United States, 174–176, 181, 190; U.S. founders and, 83. *See also* Islam; Shi'ite Muslims; Sunni Muslims

**N**

Nadir, 106

*Nathan the Wise* (Lessing), 73

National Council of Churches (NCC), 41, 50, 65, 130, 164, 227n. 11

National Council of Service, 41

National Front (Iran), 141

NPR (National Public Radio), 147, 168, 176, 181, 222n. 14

National Religious Party, 43

Nation-state system, 127, 136, 140–141

Native Americans, genocide and displacement of, 79, 83, 84, 85–87

Natural disasters, 169

Natural religion, 72–73, 80

*NBC Nightly News*, 224n. 11

*New Religious America, A* (Eck), 212n. 21

New Testament: on church-state relationship, 60–63, 74; on slavery, 84. *See also specific New Testament book headings*

*New York Times*, 139, 141, 153, 181, 185

*New Yorker*, 135

*Newsweek*, 58, 77

Nicaea, council of, 64

Nicene Creed, 64

Nigeria, 139

*No god but God* (Aslan), 171

Nobel Peace Prize, 42

Notre Dame University, 132

**O**

Obama administration, 52–53

Occasions of revelation, 99–100

Occupied Territories, 42–48, 162. *See also* Gaza Strip; West Bank

Oil revenues, 124–125, 135, 141, 148, 150, 155, 222n. 17

*Oklahoma!*, 87

Oklahoma, anti-shariah initiative in, 177

Oklahoma City, interfaith dialogue programs in, 184

Oklahoma City bombing, 157

Oklahoma State University, 22, 94

*Oklahoman*, 176

Old Testament. *See* Hebrew Bible; *specific book headings*

Online educational resources, 181

"Open table" events, 183, 184, 186

Ordination, 61–62, 196n. 10

Oriental Orthodox, 64–65, 118

Orthodox Christians, 64–65, 111–112

Orthodox Jews: Jewish state and, 36–37, 38; right-wing extremist, 33–34, 161–165; and Temple in Jerusalem, 45; ultra-, 161–165; in United States, 190

Oslo Accords, 33, 36, 48, 49, 55, 163, 203n. 25

Ottoman Empire, 30, 117–118, 124

*Outliers* (Gladwell), 4

Outreach, interfaith, 183–188

*Overthrow* (Kinzer), 221n. 6

Oxford University, 132

## P

Pacifism, Christian, 61, 67, 80
Pakistan, 97, 119, 120, 127, 131, 138;
    educational work in, 182–183
Palestine: British Mandate in, 30–31;
    HAMAS in, 5, 48, 55, 132, 172,
    173–174; Occupied, 42–48; partition
    plan for, 31, 51–52
Palestine: Peace Not Apartheid (Carter), 49
Palestinian Arab state, 51–57
Palestinian Authority, 53, 120
Palestinian Liberation Organization (PLO),
    48, 53, 55, 199n. 2
Palestinians: discrimination against, 40–42;
    harassment of, 44, 47, 52, 202n. 20,
    202n. 21; as Israeli citizens, 39–42,
    190; in Israeli Occupied Territories,
    16, 40, 42–48; militant, 172; refugee,
    40; resistance of, 47–48; right of return
    of, 40, 53. See also Israeli-Palestinian
    conflict
Papacy: history of, 65–68; Protestant
    Reformation and, 68–69
Parliamentary system, 37–38
Partition plan, 31, 51–52
Party of God (Hizbullah), 5, 6, 13,
    163–164, 168, 172
Passover Seders, 183
Pastoral Care (Gregory I), 208n. 16
Patrick Henry College, 92–93, 214n. 31
Pennies for Peace, 227n. 10
Pennsylvania, colonial, 79, 80
Pensions, early Islamic, 108, 110
Pentateuch. See Hebrew Bible
People of the Book, 99, 104–107, 109,
    111–112, 116, 146
Persia, Jerusalem ruled by, 28
Pew Forum on Religion and
    Public Life, 180
Pew Research, 6, 195n. 7
Philistines, 19
Pilgrims, American, 78–79
Playboy, 58–59, 206n. 1
Pledge of Allegiance, 88
Pluralism Project, The, 181, 212n. 21
Political action committees, pro-Israel,
    48–51
Political correctness, 224–225n. 14
Politics-religion interplay.
    See Religion-politics interplay
Popes: history of, 65–68; interfaith
    dialogue and, 184–185

Predestination, 70–71
Premillennial dispensationalism, 50–51,
    160–161, 163–164, 167–170, 203n. 29
Presbyterian Church (USA), 50
Presidential Prayer Breakfast, 93–94, 95,
    214n. 33
Priests, 196n. 10
Promised Land: establishment of Israel
    as, 30–32; in Hebrew Bible, 18; hope
    for return to, 29–30; Israeli extremist
    settlers and, 34, 35, 37, 162–163;
    Orthodox Jews and, 36–37, 161
Prophets: evangelical Protestant view of,
    21–22; of Hebrew Bible, 17–18, 21–26;
    of Islam, 22–23, 26, 98–99, 197n. 13;
    religious and political roles of, 22–26
Prophets, The (Heschel), 22, 196n. 9
Protestant Reformation, 68–72
Proverbs, book of, 20
Psalms, 20; 132:11-18, 20; 137, 197n. 14,
    211n. 17
Purim, 15
Puritans, 78–79

## Q

Quakers, 80, 205n.35
Qur'an, 13; 2:62, 216–217n. 13; 2:190-191,
    105; 2:256, 104, 227–228n. 15; 4:62,
    100; 5:4-48, 216n. 12; 5:32, 129; 5:69,
    216–217n. 13; 33:21, 100; 33:40, 99;
    37:102-113, 195n. 4; 80:1-12, 99–100;
    81:8-9, 102; 96:1-2, 98; Abraham
    stories in, 18, 195n. 4; on fighting and
    killing, 105–107, 117, 129, 227–228n.
    15; interpretation of, approaches
    to, 105–106, 133, 135, 160; Islamic
    governance and, 103; Muhammad in,
    98–100; on non-Muslims, 99, 104–106,
    109, 117, 216–217n. 13, 216n. 12;
    origins and significance of, 22, 98–99;
    prophets in, 98–99; recitation of, 215n.
    4; sharia and, 114
Quraysh, 106
Qurayza, 106

## R

Rabin assassination, 33–34, 48, 163
Racism, Christian, 85
Ramadan, 183, 186
Rand Corporation, 204–205n. 33

Rapture, the, 159–160
Rashidun ("Rightly Guided Caliphs"), 110, 119, 143
Rational approach, to religion, 72–73, 209*n*. 30
*Reading Lolita in Tehran* (Nafisi), 146
Reagan administration, 49–50, 89, 146, 213*n*. 23, 221–222*n*. 12
Reason, centrality of, 72–73, 80
"Reclaiming America for Christ" conferences, 75
Reconstructionism, 89–93
Reform Jews, 200*n*. 8
Regent University Law School, 92
*Religion, Politics, and Oil* (Kimball), 222*n*. 17
"Religion and Ethics News Weekly," 181
Religion-politics interplay: Biblical prophets and, 22–26; in Christian history, 58–74; confusion about contemporary, 8–10; contemporary lessons in, 12; contextual approaches to, 74, 133, 154–156; flexible approaches to, 10–11, 13–14, 74; fundamentalism and, 157–177; hope for peace making in, 178–192; in Iran and Iraq, 137–156; in Islam today, 120–136; in Islamic history, 96–119; in Israel, 33–57; in Jewish history, 15–32; in New Testament, 60–63, 74; overview of, 13–14; questions of, 7; in revolutionary Iran, 1–5; 21st-century paradigms for, 188–192; in United States, 74, 75–95, 188–190; in U.S. politics, 58–59, 75–95; volatility of contemporary, 5–8, 12–13, 14. *See also* Church-state separation
Religious education, interfaith, 183–188
*Religious Literacy* (Prothero), 180
Religious right. *See* Christian fundamentalists; Christian religious right; Jewish extremists; Muslim extremists
"Render unto Caesar" statement, 59, 60, 74, 79
Republican Party, 89
Revelation, occasions of, 99–100
Revolutionary War, 78
Rhode Island, colonial, 79
Right of return, 40, 53
*Roe versus Wade*, 76, 89
Roman Catholics: crusades of, 67–68; inquisitions of, 68, 70; interfaith dialogue and, 184–185; Middle

Eastern, 118; papal history and, 65–68; Protestant Reformation and, 68–69, 71; religious inclusivity and, 184–185; in U.S. politics, 58
Roman Empire, 28–29, 62–64
Romans 13:1-2,6-7, 61
Rome, papacy in, 65–68
"Roots of Muslim Rage, The" (Lewis), 122

**S**

Sacred people, in religions compared, 196*n*. 10
Sacred texts, interpretation of: by Christian fundamentalists, 159–160, 165–166, 167; contextual approach to, 133; selective or rigid approach to, 105–106, 133, 135, 151, 159, 160, 165–166, 195*n*. 3
Safavid Dynasty, 118, 124, 140
Sages, 196*n*. 10
Salafis, 125
Salem witch trials, 70–71, 78
Samaria, modern, 42–48
*Samed: Journal of a West Bank Palestinian* (Shehadeh), 202*n*. 20
I Samuel, 18–19; 8:5, 19; 8:6, 19; 8:11-17, 19; 15, 196*n*. 6, 217*n*. 14; 28:17-19, 19
II Samuel 11:26-12:7, 23
Satan, 51, 91, 92, 155, 160, 166
*Satanic Verses, The* (Rushdie), 101, 145, 151, 216*n*. 8
Saudi Arabia, 2, 124–125, 130, 131, 135, 139
SAVAK, 221*n*. 10
"Saving remnant," 30, 198*n*. 18
Saviors, 196*n*. 10
"Scandal Puts Spotlight on Christian Law School" (Savage), 213–214*n*. 30
*Schempp, Abington Township School District versus*, 76
Schools and education: contemporary Muslim, 125, 129, 130–131; in Pakistan, 182–183; religion in U.S., 75–76, 87, 210*n*. 3, 212*n*. 19
Science, rejection of, 159, 161, 212*n*. 19, 223*n*. 3, 223*n*. 4
*Science in Medieval Islam* (Turner), 217*n*. 22
Scopes trial, 159, 212*n*. 19, 223*n*. 3
Seal of the United States, 88

Secularists: and church-state separation, 9; Hussein regime and, 150, 152; Jewish, 37, 38, 42, 56

Separatism, 190

September 11 terrorist attacks, 2, 3; al-Qaeda and, 157–158, 171; anti-Muslim sentiment following, 96, 120, 166, 175–177, 220n. 19; decade following, 6, 120, 138, 166, 186, 192; impact of, 157–158, 157–159, 186; Muslim attitudes toward, 129

Settlements. *See* Israeli settlements

*700 Club, The*, 90, 91

Shamans, 196n. 10

Shariah, 100; adaptability of, 114–115; defined, 114; Hanbali, 194n. 5; history of, 114–115, 117; interpreters and interpretation of, 117, 119, 151; in Iraq, 153; Oklahoma law against, 177; Ottoman, 117; progressive interpretations of, 130, 134–135; in Sudan, 12; Taliban, 130–131; Wahhabi, 124, 134–135, 194n. 5; women and, 130

*Shia Revival, The* (Nasr), 220n. 2

Shi'ite Muslims, 124; contemporary demographics of, 138, 139; Fatimid, 115, 116; history and beliefs of, 107–108, 111, 112–113, 118, 139, 220n. 2, 221n. 8; in Iran and Iraq, 118, 138, 139, 146, 150, 152, 154, 155, 221n. 8; in Lebanon, 163–164; Safavid Dynasty of, 118; shariah of, 115; Sunni Muslims and, 139, 148–149, 150, 155

Short-term political pragmatism, 142, 164

*Silent No More* (Parsley), 169–170, 225n. 21

Six-Day War, 36, 43, 201–202n. 15

Slavery: in the Bible, 84–86, 211n. 16, 211n. 17; U.S., 79, 83, 84–86, 211n. 17

Social justice: in Christianity, 61; in Islam, 102, 125; in Jewish Zionist movement, 38, 55. *See also* Human rights

*Social Justice in Islam* (Qutb), 126

Sojourners, 189, 228n. 22

South Africa, 89, 213n. 23

Southern Baptist Convention, 85

Southern Baptist Theological Seminary, 25–26, 85, 148

Sovereign Citizen movement, 165, 224n. 11

Spain, Islamic, 111, 113, 115–116, 123

Spanish Inquisition, 68

"Speaking of Faith," 181, 226n. 5

Statute Establishing Religious Freedom in Virginia, 81–82

Sudan, 11–12

Sufis, 124

Sultans, 117

*Summa Theologiae* (Aquinas), 208n. 16

Sunnah, 100

Sunni Muslims: beliefs and history of, 107, 111, 114–115, 139; contemporary demographics of, 138–139; in Iraq, 139, 148–149, 150; shariah of, 114–115; Shi'ite Muslims and, 139, 148–149, 150, 155. *See also* Wahhabism

Sykes-Picot Agreement, 222n. 15

Syria, 91–92, 138, 149–150

Syrian Orthodox Christians, 64, 65

## T

Taj Mahal, 119

Taliban, 5, 6, 114, 130–131, 142, 172

Talmud, 29

Teaching Company, 181, 226n. 6

*Tehran Times*, 181

Temple, in Jerusalem: in ancient times, 19–20, 25, 28, 29; beliefs about rebuilding of, 45, 51

Ten Commandments, public posting of, 212n. 20

*Tennessean*, 176, 177

Tent of Meeting, 22

Terrorism: anti-Muslim sentiment and, 120, 166; examples of U.S., 157; extremism and, 157–159; militant Muslims and, 6, 142, 157–159, 171; Muslim attitudes toward, 129, 172–173, 175, 186; Muslim condemnation of, 120, 133; rise of, 4, 6, 8; suicidal, 4, 48, 120, 129, 157–158, 159; war on, 166, 171, 175

Theocracy: Christian America movement and, 90; democracy and, 9–10, 73, 143, 156; fundamentalist extremism and, 158–159

Theocratic republic, of Iran, 142–146

Theodicy, 63

Thessalonians, 62

*They Dare to Speak Out* (Findley), 203n. 22

Thirty Years' War, 71

*Thomas Jefferson* (Hitchens), 210–211n. 11

*Thousand and One Nights,* 113
*Thousand Splendid Suns, A* (Hosseini), 182
*Three Cups of Tea* (Mortenson and Relin), 131, 182
*Tikkun,* 187, 228*n.* 19
Tikrit, Iraq, 150
*Time,* 1, 96, 141, 148
I Timothy, 2:1-2, 61
*Tipping Point, The* (Gladwell), 4
Toleration, religious: in colonial America, 79, 80, 81–83, 211*n.* 13; the Enlightenment and, 73, 82; in Islam, 104–105, 116, 118, 133, 135; respect and, 83; Roman Catholic Church and, 184–185; in U.S. history, 73, 79, 80–83, 188; U.S. role in promoting, 188–190
Torah. *See* Hebrew Bible
Torture, Inquisitional, 68
"Trail of Tears," 87
*Treacherous Alliance* (Parsi), 222*n.* 13
Treaty of Hudaybiyya, 104
Tribulation, the, 160, 164
Turkey, 120, 131, 135
*Turning Tide, The* (Robertson), 90–91

**U**

Uganda, 94–95
*'Ulama,* 113
Ultra-orthodox Jews, 161–165
Umayyad dynasty, 111–113, 115–117
Ummah, 103, 105, 171, 179
Uniate churches, 118
Union of American Hebrew Congregations, 187, 228*n.* 19
Union Theological Seminary, 84
United Arab Emirates, 2005 conference in, 173–174
UN partition plan, 31, 51–52
UN Resolution 242, 36, 163, 202*n.* 15
UN Resolution 338, 163
United States: anti-Muslim sentiment in, 96–97, 120, 133–134, 166–170, 175–177, 190; attorney-firing scandal in, 92; Christian fundamentalism in, 165–170; Christian religious right in, 5–7, 59, 88–95, 166–170, 213–214*n.* 30; as Christian *versus* secular nation, 75–95; clash-of-civilizations hypothesis and, 121–123; colonial, 78–82; denominations of presidents of, 58–59; experimental approach of, 76–77, 80, 188–190; founding and founders of,

73, 75, 76–83, 86, 92, 95; God and, 83, 86–87, 88, 92, 94; Israel and, 48–51, 52–53, 55–56; Jewish immigration to, 30, 31; Muslim attitudes toward, 128, 129, 155, 173–174; Muslims in, 175–177, 181, 190; Native American genocide/ displacement in, 79, 83, 84, 85–87; 1988 presidential election, 89; official motto of, 88; religion-politics interplay in, 74, 75–95, 188–190; religious toleration in, 73, 79, 80–83, 188–190; short-term policies of, in Iraq, Afghanistan and Iran, 142; slavery in, 79, 83, 84–86; terrorism in, 157; 21st-century, 188–190; 2004 presidential election, 170; 2008 presidential election, 6, 170, 189
U.S. Catholic Conference of Bishops, 50
U.S. Congress: the Family and, 94–95; national motto approved by, 88; pro-Israel lobby and, 48–50, 202–203*n.* 22
U.S. Constitution, 75–76, 80–81, 82, 83, 188, 190, 210*n.* 2
U.S. Department of Justice, 92, 213–214*n.* 30
U.S. House Foreign Affairs Committee, 213*n.* 23
U.S. military, 166–167, 182
"U.S. Religious Knowledge Survey" (Pew), 180
U.S. State Department, human rights reports, 42
U.S. Supreme Court: on abortion, 76, 89; Christian Coalition and, 90; on church-state separation, 75–76
University of California, Los Angeles, 134
University of Oklahoma, 227*n.* 10
University of Virginia, 81
*Urim,* 19

**V**

Vandals, 64
Vatican archives, 208*n.* 21
Venezuela, 92
*Venture of Islam, The* (Hodgson), 218*n.* 25
Virginia, colonial, 79, 81–82
Visigoths, 64
Viziers, 114, 116, 117

**W**

*Wade, Roe versus,* 76, 89
Wahhabism, 5, 29, 124–125, 130, 134–135, 139, 194*n.* 5

War of 1948, 31, 40
War of 1967, 36, 43
*Wars of the Jews, The* (Josephus), 197*n*. 15
West Bank: "Apartheid Wall" in, 52;
    demographics of, 46; harassment of
    Palestinians in, 44, 47, 52, 202*n*. 20,
    202*n*. 21; Israeli confiscation of, 43,
    47; Jewish extremist settlers in, 15–16,
    33, 34–35, 44–48, 52, 56, 161–165,
    168; maps of, 46, 54; Occupied, 42–48,
    162; Palestinian refugee camps in, 40;
    population of, 199*n*. 3
Western civilization, 122–123
Western culture, Muslim attitudes toward,
    125, 126, 128, 130, 136
Western Europe: colonialism of, 121,
    123–128; Muslim attitudes toward, 128
*Western Muslims and the Future of Islam*
    (Ramadan), 133
Westphalia, 1648 Treaty of, 71
*What Every Muslim Should Know About
    the Shari'ah* (Rauf), 134
*What Went Wrong?* (Lewis), 123
*What's Right with Islam* (Rauf), 134
*When Religion Becomes Evil* (Kimball),
    12, 208*n*. 20, 219*n*. 12
*When the Rain Returns* (Bergen et al.),
    205*n*. 35
White House interns, 93
*Who Speaks for Islam?* (Gallup), 128–130,
    173, 219*n*. 7, 219*n*. 10

Witchcraft hysteria, 70–71, 78
Women: in Islam, 102, 104, 130; in
    Muslim countries, 130–131, 153,
    182, 219*n*. 14; religious leadership of,
    211–212*n*. 18; in United States, 86,
    211–212*n*. 18
World Harvest Church, 169
World Jewish Congress, 205*n*. 37
World Trade Center site, 96–97, 133–134,
    176. *See also* September 11 terrorist
    attacks
World War I, 30–31
World War II, 29, 31


**Y**

Yamit, Israel, 34
Yathrib. *See* Medina
*Yellow Wind, The* (Grossman),
    202*n*. 20


**Z**

Zamzam, 17
Zionist movement: Gush Emunim
    and, 162–165; history of, 29–32;
    one-state solution and, 53, 55–56;
    social justice ideals of, 38, 55; socialist
    ideals of, 37, 200*n*. 6; ultra-Orthodox
    Jews and, 161

# Beyond Forgiveness

## *Reflections on Atonement*

Phil Cousineau

---

Paper

ISBN: 978-0-470-90773-3

---

"If we harbor thoughts of violence or hatred, or seek revenge or retribution, we are contributing to the wounding of the world; if we transform those thoughts into forgiveness and compassion, and then make amends or restitution, we are contributing to the healing of the world. This timely, powerful, and compassionate book helps show us the way."
— **Deepak Chopra,** author of *The Book of Secrets* and *The Path to Love*

"Nothing will help us survive the present age more than breaking the tragic cycles of violence and revenge. To do so, we must honor our soul's desire for deeper forms of reconciliation, a process that Phil Cousineau reveals here as the ritual act of atonement. His book is a profoundly important contribution to the healing of the world."
— **Robert A. Johnson**, author of *Transformation, Inner Work,* and *Owning Your Own Shadow*

"*Beyond Forgiveness: Reflections on Atonement* is an inspiring, practical, and compelling book, relevant for our times. Cousineau provides a profound and provocative book that has us ponder where we might need to forgive ourselves and others and to look at atonement and what it ignites in the human spirit."
— **Angeles Arrien**, Ph.D., author of *The Second Half of Life*

**Beyond Forgiveness** shows how acts of atonement—making amends, providing restitution, restoring balance—can relieve us of the pain of the past and give us a hopeful future.

**Phil Cousineau** is an award-winning writer and filmmaker, editor and lecturer, cultural observer and TV host. He has published twenty-six nonfiction books, written fifteen documentary films, and is currently the host and co-writer of *Global Spirit* on Link TV. Learn more at www.beyondforgiveness.org

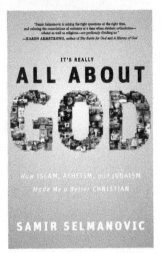

# It's Really All About God

## How Islam, Atheism, and Judaism Made Me a Better Christian

Samir Selmanovic

Paper

ISBN: 978-0-470-92341-2

"Samir Selmanovic is asking the right questions at the right time, and refusing the consolations of certainty at a time when strident orthodoxies—atheist as well as religious—are perilously dividing us."

—**Karen Armstrong**, author, *The Case for God*, *A History of God*, and *The Great Transformation*

"Why are thousands not saying what this man is saying? Such obvious truth must be made even more obvious, and this is exactly what Samir Selmanovic is doing for all of us and for the future of humanity. After you read this wise book, you will say, 'Of course!' and 'Thank God!'"

—**Fr. Richard Rohr**, O.F.M., Center for Action and Contemplation, Albuquerque, New Mexico

"We need a million more Samirs on the planet—people of conviction and humility who know that the vast mystery called God calls us not to the arrogance of 'ownership' but to the beloved community."

—**Parker J. Palmer**, author, *A Hidden Wholeness*, *Let Your Life Speak*, and *The Courage to Teach*

*It's Really All About God* is a very personal story and a thrilling exploration of a redeeming, dynamic, and radically different way of treasuring one's own religion while discovering God, goodness, and grace in others and in their traditions.

**SAMIR SELMANOVIC** (Ph.D) is a founder of Faith House Manhattan, an interfaith "community of communities" that brings together forward-looking Christians, Muslims, Jews, atheists, and others who seek to thrive interdependently. Samir is also the director of a Christian community called Citylights and serves on the Interfaith Relations Commission of the National Council of Churches and speaks nationally and internationally. He has been profiled in a number of local and national media, including the *New York Times*. Learn more about him at www.samirselmanovic.com.